T0302293

Credit Union Investment Management

Frank J. Fabozzi, CFA
Adjunct Professor of Finance
School of Management
Yale University
and
Editor
Journal of Portfolio Management

Mark B. Wickard
Senior Vice President — Investments
PaineWebber Credit Union Services Group

Published by Frank J. Fabozzi Associates

© 1997 By Frank J. Fabozzi Associates
New Hope, Pennsylvania

ISBN: 1-883249-13-9

FJF

To my wife, Donna,
and my son Francesco

MBW

To my wife, Regina,
and my children
Rachel, Amanda, and Mark, Jr.

Table of Contents

Preface

The goal of this book is to educate and enlighten those individuals in credit unions responsible for the investment process about the wide-range of investment products and the state-of-the-art techniques for evaluating investment alternatives and controlling portfolio risks. We debunk a good number of investment myths along the way.

Historically, too many credit unions have managed their investment portfolios with outdated techniques, policies, and philosophies. The truth is simply this: the vast majority of credit unions have evolved from managing their portfolios out of *fear* (keeping too much in overnight liquidity) to managing their portfolio by chasing an illusory "yield" offered by a host of "safe" government bond structures that were not recognized by the credit union to have an unacceptable risk/return profile. As this book will illustrate, "yield" is a potentially misleading measure and the concept of "safe" applies to more than simply credit risk.

The practices of credit unions over the past three decades has demonstrated the "follow the leader" mentality of investment management and a lack of understanding about the investment characteristics of so-called "risk-free" government and agency securities. This led to the over investment in Ginnie Mae passthrough securities in the 1970s because these securities are backed by the full faith and credit of the U.S. government and offered a higher "yield" relative to Treasury securities. Seeking safety, credit unions in the 1980s poured significant amounts into U.S. government bond funds without recognition of the multidimensional aspects of risk. Seeking yield enhancement as yields declined to historically low levels, credit unions in the 1990s jumped into derivative instruments (collateralized mortgage obligations (CMOs) and structured notes) failing to understand that the potential for yield enhancement comes only with the acceptance of additional risk in some form. While there were many types of CMO bonds that would have provided a more appropriate risk/return profile for a credit union, those selected were too often based on high promised "yields" but with significant interest rate risk exposure.

Not only has there been a lack of understanding of the risk characteristics of individual securities, but too often there has not been an understanding of the inherent risks of investment portfolio strategies relative to the liability side of the business. As a result, ill-conceived investment portfolio strategies were formulated.

Recognizing that managers of credit union portfolios need guidance in selecting investment alternatives and in structuring portfolios, the National Credit Union Administration has legislated investment guidelines. The two major sections are Part 703 (investing by natural person credit unions) and Part 704 (investing by corporate credit unions). At the time of this writing (late 1996), major legislative revisions have been proposed for Part 703 and Part 704 and are under consideration. The final adoption of these revisions is not scheduled until some time in 1997. (The initial target date for the revision was by mid-1996.) However, the investment principles, technology, and security characteristics set forth in this book are valid regardless of the revisions that are finally adopted. For readers who would like a summary as to how the final regulations affect the text in this book, complete the form that follows the Preface.

We hope that this book will give the credit union investment manager the skills to enhance investment returns and avoid securities and strategies that can have major adverse financial consequences to the institution.

We would like to thank Doug Henney, Cecily Hinkle, Steve Satkamp, Mark Sutton, Tom Naratil, and Marten Hoekstra of PaineWebber who provided support for this project. We would also like to thank the following members of the PaineWebber Credit Union Services Group for their assistance in various aspects of this project: Tobias Timm, Ed Dutcher, Greg Miller, Dan Peckham, Tom Lewis, Karen Hill, and Sue Sundeen. In particular, we would like to express a special thanks to Regina Wickard for helping coordinate the various phases of this project.

Frank J. Fabozzi
Mark B. Wickard

Update Form

If you are interested in obtaining updated information based on new regulations or changes to existing regulations which might change or modify a topic or section covered in this book, please copy this page, complete the information requested, and mail to the address indicated below:

REQUEST FOR UPDATES AND CHANGES TO
CREDIT UNION INVESTMENT MANAGEMENT, 1997 EDITION

Name: _____

Credit Union: _____

Position: _____

Address: _____

_____

_____

Phone: _____

Fax: _____

MAIL TO: PaineWebber Credit Union Services Group
            1500 Abbott Road
            Suite 200
            East Lansing, MI 48823
            ATTN: Regina Wickard

OR FAX TO: (517) 333-6800

Chapter 1

Introduction

The objectives of this chapter are to:

1. explain the investment management process;

2. explain the various regulatory provisions governing investment policies and permissible investments;

3. discuss the various types of risks faced by a credit union; and,

4. describe the key provisions of FAS 115.

This book is devoted to the management of the investment portfolio of credit unions. In this chapter, we provide an overview of the investment management process. This process involves five steps: (1) setting investment objectives, (2) establishing investment policies and practices, (3) selecting the portfolio strategy; (4) selecting the specific investments, and (5) monitoring and measuring performance and reporting to regulators. The discussion will also provide a roadmap for the chapters to follow. In this chapter we discuss these steps.

SETTING INVESTMENT OBJECTIVES

The first step in the investment management process is to set investment objectives. The investment objective will vary by type of financial institution. For credit unions, the investment objective is to earn a return on invested funds that is higher than the cost of acquiring those funds. This objective, simply stated, places a priority on managing all of the asset returns and all of the liability costs in a safe and profitable manner. The investment portfolio of a credit union represents the excess liquidity of the institution. Thus, it is vital not only from a profit standpoint, but from an asset-liability management (ALM) standpoint as well. Consequently, the proper execution of an ALM strategy fulfills a liquidity/funds availability role — an essential component of the investment process.

ESTABLISHING INVESTMENT POLICIES AND PRACTICES

The second step in the investment management process is establishing policy guidelines for meeting the investment objectives of the credit union. Setting policy is the responsibility of the Board through specific recommendations made by the asset/liability committee (ALCO) or investment committee.

Various sections of the Federal Credit Union Act set forth the securities, deposits, and other obligations in which a federal credit union may invest. The National Credit Union Administration's proposed amendments to 12 CFR Part 703 (*Investment and Deposit Activities*) interpret several provisions of the Act regarding permissible investments. We shall discuss these provisions in the chapters that follow when we describe the wide-range of investment vehicles.

Moreover, the proposed amendments to Part 703 specify that the board of directors must establish written investment policies that are consistent with the Act. The board is responsible for reviewing the investment policies at least once a year. Part 703 lists the minimum items that the investment policies should address. Some of the items that must be addressed are the purposes and objectives of the credit union's investment activities, the authorized investments by issuer and characteristics and concentration limits, the safekeeping of securities, the approved list of broker-dealers, trading policies, and procedures for risk management.

Risk Management

As just noted, the written investment policies and practices must address risk management. The risks cited in Part 703 are interest rate risk, credit risk, and liquidity risk. In addition, there are the following risks: yield curve risk, reinvestment risk, timing risk, volatility risk, exchange rate risk, and regulatory risk. Each of these risks is described below.

Interest Rate Risk The price of a typical fixed income security moves in the opposite direction of the change in interest rates: As interest rates rise (fall), the price of a fixed income security will fall (rise). This property is illustrated in Chapter 10. For a credit union that plans to hold a fixed income security to maturity and is capable of doing so, the change in its price prior to maturity is not of concern; however, for a credit union that may have to sell the fixed income security prior to the maturity date, an increase in interest rates will mean the realization of a capital loss. This risk is referred to as *interest rate risk*. As explained in Chapter 10, the actual magnitude of the price response for any security depends on various characteristics of the security such as coupon and maturity, and options embedded in the security. In the next chapter we will define what is meant by an embedded option.

To effectively manage interest rate risk it is necessary to quantify that risk. In Chapter 10, we explain how to quantify the interest rate risk of an individual security and a portfolio. The measure used is *duration*. This measure is the approximate percentage change in the price of a security or a portfolio for a 100 basis point change in yields. Thus, if a bond has a duration of 5, this means that its value will change by approximately 5% if interest rates change by 100 basis points.

When duration is used to measure the interest rate risk of a portfolio, an assumption is made about how yields change. Specifically, if a portfolio consists of securities with different maturities, it is assumed that the yield for each maturity changes by an equal number of basis points. This assumption is referred to as a *parallel shift assumption*. In Chapter 10 we look at how two portfolios with the same duration may have quite different risk exposures if the yield for each maturity does not change by the same number of basis points. This risk is referred to as *yield curve risk*.

A more accurate procedure for assessing the interest rate risk of a security or a portfolio is by calculating the potential total return from the position under different scenarios as to how interest rates can change. This approach can also be used to assess the yield curve risk of a portfolio. In Chapter 11 we show how the potential total return of a security or a portfolio can be calculated. The total return concept is emphasized in the revised Part 703.

Credit Risk *Credit risk* or *default risk* refers to the risk that the issuer of a security may default, i.e., will be unable to make timely principal and interest payments. Credit risk is gauged by quality ratings assigned by nationally recognized statistical rating organizations such as Moody's Investor Service, Standard & Poor's Corporation, Duff & Phelps, Fitch Investors Service, and Thomson Bankwatch. Part 703 requires that credit unions not rely solely on these ratings, but instead perform their own credit analysis unless the issuing entity is federally insured or fully guaranteed by the U.S. government or its agencies or enterprises. This requirement places an undue burden on credit unions. No other institutional investor is burdened by such a requirement.

Liquidity Risk For an individual security, liquidity risk involves the ease with which an issue can be sold at or near its value. The primary measure of liquidity is the size of the spread between the bid price and the offered price quoted by a dealer. The greater the dealer spread, the greater the liquidity risk. For an investor who plans to hold the bond until the maturity date and has the capacity to do so, liquidity risk is not a major concern. From the perspective of the overall position of a credit union, liquidity risk means the risk that the credit union will not have sufficient funds to meet immediate cash demands, either as a result of increased loan demand or deposit outflow.

The liquidity risk of a security is not necessarily reduced by the size of a given market. For example, while the markets for collateralized mortgage obligations and structured notes (two instruments we describe in later chapters) is large, because of the unique types of bonds created, the bid-ask spread at times can be large. This is particularly true for certain exotic products traded in these markets. This is due to the *structural risk* of the particular security.

Reinvestment Risk As explained in Chapter 9, the cash flows received from a security are usually (or, are assumed to be) reinvested. The additional income from such reinvestment, sometimes called "reinvestment income," depends upon the prevailing interest rate levels at the time of reinvestment, as well as on the reinvestment strategy. The variability in the returns from reinvestment from a given strategy due to changes in market rates is called *reinvestment risk*. The risk here is that the interest rate at which interim cash flows can be reinvested will fall.

Timing Risk Many securities contain an option that grants either the issuer or the investor the right to alter the cash flow of the security. Such an option is referred to as an *embedded option* — it is embedded within the security as opposed to being a stand alone option. A callable bond is the most common example of a bond with an embedded option. A callable bond allows the issuer to retire or "call" all or part of the issue before the stated maturity date. The issuer usually retains this right to have the flexibility to refinance the bond in the future if market interest rates decline below the coupon rate.

From the investor's perspective, there are three disadvantages of the call provision. First, the cash flow pattern of a callable bond is not known with certainty. Second, because the issuer will call the bonds when interest rates have dropped, the investor is exposed to reinvestment risk. That is, the investor will have to reinvest the proceeds received when the bond is called at relatively lower interest rates. Finally, the capital appreciation potential of a bond will be reduced. This last characteristic is explained in Chapter 10.

Timing risk also exists with mortgage-backed securities, investments that we describe in Chapters 5 and 6. For these securities, the cash flow depends on pre-payments of principal made by the homeowners in the pool of mortgages that serves as collateral for the security. The timing risk in this case is called *prepayment risk.*

Prepayment risk can only be assessed by looking at how changes in interest rates can affect prepayments. Before a mortgage-backed security can be purchased, it must pass certain tests that are explained in Chapter 7. Part 703 requires that the board of directors approve prepayment models that should be used for such tests.

Volatility Risk As will be explained in Chapter 8, the price of a bond with an embedded option depends on the level of interest rates and factors that influence the value of the embedded option. One of the factors is the expected volatility of interest rates. Specifically, the value of an option rises when expected interest rate volatility increases. In the case of a callable bond or mortgage-backed security, since the inves-tor has granted an option to the borrower, the price of the security falls because the investor has given away a more valuable option. The risks that a change in volatility will adversely affect the price of a security is called *volatility risk.*

Exchange Rate Risk A non-dollar-denominated bond (i.e. a bond whose pay-ments occur in a foreign currency) has unknown U.S. dollar cash flows. The dollar cash flows are dependent on the foreign-exchange rate at the time the payments are received. For example, suppose an investor purchases a bond whose payments are in Japanese yen. If the yen depreciates relative to the U.S. dollar, then fewer dollars will be received. The risk of this occurring is referred to as *exchange rate* or *cur-rency risk.* Part 703 prohibits credit unions from investing in non-dollar denomi-nated bonds. Consequently, a credit union will not be exposed to exchange rate risk.

Regulatory Risk Regulations that govern the permissible investments and invest-ment activities of a credit union are periodically revised. *Regulatory risk* is the risk that a change in regulations will require the disposal of securities or the alter-ation of a strategy that will impair the economic value of the institution.

The proposed revisions to Part 703 certainly bring this risk into consider-ation for many credit unions. However, the NCUA is attempting to mitigate the chilling effects of the proposed regulation by creating three levels of investment sophistication requiring three separate levels of evaluation, reporting, tracking, and monitoring.

Monitoring Risk Exposure

The manager of a credit union's investment portfolio is concerned with the risk exposure at the time of the implementation of an investment strategy. The risk exposure changes over time and consequently, it will be necessary to restructure a portfolio in order to control risk.

Monitoring risk exposure involves various activities. Part 703 sets forth these activities in terms of policy and reporting requirements. These requirements set forth: (1) tests that must be performed on mortgage-backed securities, (2) divestiture policies if a mortgage-backed security fails the required tests, (3) establishment of a trading policy, (4) reporting on trading activities, (5) independent evaluation of credit risk, (6) reporting the fair value of each investment, (7) evaluation of the impact on the portfolio of a 300 basis point change in yields, and (8) documentation of cash needs and how those needs were determined, and (9) establishment of a liquidity policy for meeting cash needs.

Whether a credit union must comply with these requirements depends on the types of investments in which the board of directors decides to invest. A credit union that elects to invest exclusively in certificates of deposit that are fully insured by the U.S. government and shares and deposits of corporate credit unions need not comply with the requirements.

If the amount invested in securities identified by the NCUA as having "greater potential risk" does not exceed the credit union's capital, then all the requirements of Part 703 must be followed with the exception of the evaluation of the impact of a 300 basis point parallel shift in yields on the portfolio. If the credit union's investment in these securities exceeds its capital, then all the requirements must be followed. Capital for this purpose is defined in Part 703 as "the total of all undivided earnings, regular reserves, other reserves (excluding the allowance for loan losses), net income, and accumulated unrealized gains (losses) on available-for-sale securities."

Accounting Requirements

Part 703 requires that credit unions follow Statement of Financial Accounting Standards No. 115, more popularly referred to as FAS 115, in preparing financial statements. We describe the key provisions of FAS 115 below.

Classification and Accounting Treatment for Assets With respect to the financial reporting of assets, there are three possible methods for reporting: (1) amortized cost or historical cost, (2) market value, or (3) the lower of cost or market value. Despite the fact that the real cash flow is the same regardless of the accounting treatment, there can be substantial differences in the financial statements using these three methods. In the *amortized cost method*, the value reported in the balance sheet reflects an adjustment to the acquisition cost for debt securities purchased at a discount or premium from their maturity value. This method is sometimes referred to as *book value accounting*. In the *market value accounting method*, the balance sheet reported value of an asset is its market value. When an asset is reported in the financial statements of an institution at its market value, it is said to be "marked to market." Finally, the *lower of cost or market method* requires comparison of market value to the amortized cost, with the lower of these two values reported in the balance sheet. The value reported cannot exceed the amortized cost.

Exhibit 1: Summary of Key Provisions of FAS 115

Account classification	Accounting method for assets	Will affect surplus?	Will affect reported earnings?
Held to maturity	Amortized cost	no	no
Available for sale	Market value	yes	no
Trading	Market value	yes	yes

FAS 115 specifies which of these three methods must be followed for assets. Specifically, the accounting treatment required for a security depends on how the security is classified. There are three classifications of investment accounts: (1) held to maturity, (2) available for sale, and (3) trading. The definition of each account is set forth in FAS 115 and we summarize each below.

The *held-to-maturity account* includes assets that the institution plans to hold until they mature. Obviously, the assets classified in this account cannot be common stock because they have no maturity. Similarly, an open end mutual fund has no maturity and should not be classified in this manner. For all assets in the held-to-maturity account, the amortized cost method must be used.

An asset is classified in the *available-for-sale account* if the institution does not have the ability to hold the asset to maturity or intends to sell it. A security that is acquired for the purpose of earning a short-term trading profit from market movements is classified in the *trading account*. For all assets in the available-for-sale and trading accounts, market value accounting is used. Thus, these two accounts more accurately reflect the economic condition of the assets held by the institution.

Exhibit 1 summarizes the accounting treatment of assets as set forth by FASB 115.

Treatment of Unrealized Gains and Losses When financial statements are prepared, the change in the value of assets must be accounted for. An unrealized gain or loss occurs when the asset's value has changed but the gain or loss is not realized since the asset is not sold. For example, if an asset has a market value of $100 at the beginning of an accounting period and is held in the portfolio at the end of the accounting period with a market value of $110, the unrealized gain is $10.

Any realized gain or loss affects the accounting surplus (capital). Specifically, a realized gain increases the surplus and a realized loss reduces the accounting surplus. In contrast to a realized gain or loss, any unrealized gain or loss may or may not affect the reported earnings.

Under FAS 115, the accounting treatment for any unrealized gain or loss depends on the account in which the asset is classified. Specifically, any unrealized gain or loss is ignored for assets in the held-to-maturity account. Thus, for assets in this account there is no affect on reported earnings or the accounting surplus. For the other two accounts, any unrealized gain or loss affects the accounting surplus as described above. However, there is a difference as to how reported earnings are affected. For assets classified in the available-for-sale account, unrealized gains or losses are not included in reported earnings; in contrast, for assets classified in the trading account, any gains or losses are included in reported earnings. These provisions are summarized in Exhibit 1.

SELECTING A PORTFOLIO STRATEGY

Selecting a portfolio strategy that is consistent with the objectives and policy guidelines of the credit union is the third step in the investment management process. The various types of strategies and their associated risks are explained in Chapter 12. A framework for assessing the potential impact of a strategy — the total return framework — is described in that chapter. It should be emphasized that the portfolio strategy should be chosen by management with the approval and continued oversight by the board.

SELECTING THE SPECIFIC INVESTMENTS

Once a portfolio strategy is specified, the next step is to select the specific investments to be included in the portfolio. This involves an evaluation of individual securities and their potential return performance.

Investment selection involves identifying mispriced bonds. The characteristics of a bond (that is, coupon, maturity, credit quality, and embedded options) must be carefully examined to determine fair value. A mispriced security provides the credit union with an opportunity to enhance return. A security whose market value is below the estimated fair value is cheap and should be purchased if it satisfies the investment objectives and is permitted by investment policy; a security whose market value is above the estimated fair value is rich and, if permitted, should be shorted. Since a credit union may not be permitted to short a security, such a security should be avoided.

The only way to determine whether a security is mispriced is by using a valuation model. The general principles of security valuation and the state-of-the art models are explained in Chapter 8. The assumptions that underlie these models and their critical role are explained in that chapter.

MONITORING AND MEASURING PERFORMANCE AND REPORTING TO REGULATORS

A credit union must be capable of measuring and monitoring performance. Some of the analysis that is derived in this step of the investment management process is used to prepare reports that the credit union must supply regulators. While we have listed these activities as the last of our five steps, in practice it is not the "last" step because investment management is an ongoing process.

Part 703 provides the framework for understanding how to measure and monitor performance. The purpose of this book is to understand the concepts set forth in Part 703. For example, Part 703 emphasizes management on a total return basis. Chapter 11 explains this framework. The proposed changes to Part 703 require and encourage credit unions to monitor and measure the potential changes in the value of a security given a substantial change in interest rates. Chapter 10 explains how to measure the sensitivity of an investment and portfolio to rate changes. Throughout this book, we highlight many of the key reporting requirements.

KEY POINTS

1. The investment management process involves five steps.

2. The first step in the investment management process is setting investment objectives.

3. The second step in the investment management process is establishing policy guidelines for meeting the investment objectives.

4. Part 703 specifies the regulations that must be followed in managing a credit union's investment portfolio.

5. The risks faced by a credit union are interest rate risk, yield curve risk, credit risk, liquidity risk, reinvestment risk, timing risk, volatility risk, and regulatory risk.

6. Part 703 sets forth policy and reporting requirements for monitoring of risk exposure.

7. The extent to which a credit union must comply with the investment policy and reporting requirements of Part 703 depends on the types of investments in which it invests and the amount invested in certain investments relative to the credit union's capital.

8. Financial reporting for credit unions is governed by FAS 115.

9. FAS 115 specifies how assets should be classified and how unrealized gains and losses should be treated.

10. The third step in the investment management process is selecting a portfolio strategy that is consistent with the objectives and policy guidelines of the credit union.

11. The fourth step in the investment management process is selecting the specific investments.

12. The fifth step in the investment management process is monitoring and measuring of the portfolio and reporting to regulators.

Chapter 2

Features of Investment Vehicles

The objectives of this chapter are to:

1. explain the features of fixed income instruments;

2. explain the coupon formula for a floating-rate instrument and restrictions on the coupon rate (caps and floors);

3. describe the various provisions for repayment of principal;

4. describe what a range note and step-up note are; and,

5. explain what an embedded option is and the various types of embedded options.

Part 703 requires that credit unions be familiar with the characteristics of the investments in which they invest. An investment characteristic is defined in Part 703 as "a feature of an investment such as its maturity, index, cap, floor, coupon formula, index, call provision, or average life." Below we describe the various features of investments. We limit our discussion to fixed income instruments. A fixed income instrument is an investment vehicle in which the interest payments are fixed by contract. The significance of the features of fixed income instruments will be discussed in more detail in later chapters.

MATURITY

The *term to maturity* of an investment is the number of years over which the issuer has promised to meet the conditions of the obligation. The *maturity* refers to the date that the debt will cease to exist, at which time the issuer will repay any debt outstanding. The maturity date is always identified when describing an instrument. For example, a description of an instrument might state "due 12/1/2000."

The practice in the financial market, however, is to refer to the "term to maturity" as simply its "maturity" or "term." As we explain below, there may be provisions that allow either the issuer or bondholder to alter the term to maturity.

There are three reasons why the term to maturity of a fixed income instrument is important. The most obvious is that it indicates the time period over which the investor can expect to receive interest and the number of years before the principal will be paid in full. The second reason is that the yield on a fixed income instrument depends on it. This will be explained in Chapter 8. Finally, the price of a fixed income instrument will fluctuate over its life as yields in the market change. The price volatility is dependent on its maturity. More specifically, with all other factors constant, the longer the maturity, the greater the price volatility resulting from a change in market yields. This will be explained in Chapter 10.

PAR VALUE

The *par value* of a fixed income instrument is the amount that the issuer agrees to repay at the maturity date. This amount is also referred to as the *principal, face value, redemption value,* or *maturity value.* Fixed income instruments can have any par value. Because fixed income instruments can have a different par value, the practice is to quote the price of a bond as a percentage of its par value. A value of 100 means 100% of par value. So, for example, if a fixed income instrument has a par value of $1,000 and is selling for $900, this instrument would be said to be selling at a price of 90. If a fixed income instrument with a par value of $5,000 is selling for $5,500, it is said to be selling for a price of 110. The reason why a fixed income instrument sells above or below its par value will be explained in Chapter 9.

REPAYMENT OF PRINCIPAL

The issuer of a fixed income instrument agrees to repay the principal by the stated maturity date. The issuer can agree to pay the entire amount borrowed at the maturity date. That is, the issuer is not required to make any principal repayments prior to the maturity date. Such instruments are said to have a *bullet maturity.*

In contrast, the issuer may agree to make periodic principal repayments prior to the maturity date. A fixed income instrument with this characteristic is said to be an *amortizing instrument.* The definitions' section of the proposed changes to Part 703 defines an amortizing security as "a security where the principal is reduced by contractual payments." The schedule of principal repayments may be such that most of the initial amount borrowed is repaid by the maturity date. The payment that the borrower must make at the maturity date to repay the remaining balance is called a *balloon payment.*

An amortizing feature is common for a loan agreement. For example, as explained in Chapter 4, mortgage loans have monthly scheduled principal repayments. For such loans, the monthly mortgage payments are structured so that when the last monthly mortgage payment is made, there is no balloon payment necessary. That is, the loan is said to be *fully amortized.* Automobile loans are another example of an amortizing instrument with no balloon payment required.

Loans used as collateral for the creation of a security are said to be securitized. Mortgage-backed securities are securities that use mortgage loans as collateral. Asset-backed securities are securities that use other types of loans as collateral. Because the underlying collateral is a loan with an amortizing feature, the resulting securities have an amortizing feature.

Another example of an amortizing feature is a bond that has a sinking fund provision. This provision requires that the issuer retire a specified portion of an issue each year. This kind of provision for repayment of debt may be designed to liquidate all of an issue by the maturity date, or it may be arranged to pay only a part of the total by the end of the term (i.e., a balloon payment is required).

Sinking fund provisions are generally rare in federal credit union eligible securities. However, a credit union may find such a provision in a government agency structured note, or possibly, a taxable municipal bond. (Both of these instruments are discussed in Chapter 4.) Sinking fund provisions are more common in long-term (10-year maturities or longer) corporate bonds and therefore could affect state chartered credit unions.

In the case of a bond, generally the issuer may satisfy the sinking fund requirement by either (1) making a cash payment of the par amount of the issue to be retired to the trustee, who then calls the bonds for redemption using a lottery, or (2) delivering to the trustee bonds purchased in the open market that have a par amount equal to the amount that must be retired. If the bonds are retired using the first method, interest payments stop at the redemption date.

Usually, the periodic payments required for sinking fund purposes will be the same for each period. A few indentures might permit variable periodic payments, where payments change according to certain prescribed conditions set forth in the indenture.

Usually, the sinking fund call price is the par value if the bonds were originally sold at par. When issued at a price in excess of par, the call price generally starts at the issuance price and scales down to par as the issue approaches maturity.

There is a difference between the amortizing feature for a bond with a sinking fund feature, and a mortgage-backed and an asset-backed security. The owner of a mortgage-backed security and an asset-backed security knows that assuming no default that there will be principal repayments. In contrast, the owner of a bond with a sinking fund provision is not assured that his or her particular holding will be called to satisfy the sinking fund requirement.

COUPON RATE

The *coupon rate*, also called the *nominal rate*, is the interest rate that the issuer agrees to pay each year. The annual amount of the interest payment made to owners during the term of the fixed income instrument is called the *coupon*. The coupon is determined by multiplying the coupon rate by the par value. For example, a fixed income instrument with an 8% coupon rate and a par value of $1,000 will pay annual interest of $80.

When describing a bond, the coupon rate is indicated along with the maturity date. For example, the expression "6s of 12/1/2000" means a bond with a 6% coupon rate maturing on 12/1/2000.

In addition to indicating the interest payments that the investor should expect to receive over the term of the bond, the coupon rate also indicates the degree to which the bond's price will be affected by changes in interest rates. As illustrated in Chapter 10, all other factors constant, the higher the coupon rate, the less the price will change in response to a change in interest rates. Consequently, the coupon rate and the term to maturity have opposite effects on a bond's price volatility.

Zero-Coupon Instruments

Not all fixed income instruments make periodic coupon payments. Instruments that are not contracted to make periodic coupon payments are called *zero-coupon instruments*. The holder of a zero-coupon instrument realizes interest by buying the instrument below its par value. Interest then is paid at the maturity date, with the interest being the difference between the par value and the price paid for the instrument. So, for example, if an investor purchases a zero-coupon instrument at a price of 70, the interest is 30. This is the difference between the par value of 100 and the price paid of 70.

Accrued Coupon Instrument

There is another type of instrument that does not pay interest until the maturity date. This type of instrument has contractual coupon payments but those payments are accrued and distributed along with the maturity value at the maturity date. For lack of a better term, these instruments can be called *accrued coupon instruments*. There are certificates of deposit with a maturity greater than one year and municipal bonds that have this characteristic.

Floating-Rate Instruments

The coupon rate on a fixed income instrument need not be fixed over its life. *Floating-rate instruments* or *variable-rate instruments* have coupon payments that reset periodically according to some formula, called the *coupon formula*. The formula specifies a *reference rate*. The typical coupon formula is:

Reference rate + Index spread

The *index spread*, often referred to as simply spread, is the additional amount that the issuer agrees to pay above the reference rate. For example, suppose that the reference rate is the 3-month Treasury bill rate and that the index spread is 100 basis points. Then the coupon formula is:

3-month Treasury bill rate + 100 basis points

So, if 3-month Treasury bill rate on the coupon reset date is 5%, the coupon rate is reset for that period at 6% (5% plus 100 basis points).

The index spread need not be a positive value. The index spread could be subtracted from the reference rate. For example, the reference rate could be the yield on a 5-year Treasury security and the coupon rate could reset every six months based on the following coupon formula:

5-year Treasury yield − 50 basis points

So, if the 5-year Treasury yield is 7% on the coupon reset date, the coupon rate is 6.5% (7% minus 50 basis points).

The reference rate for most floating-rate instruments is an interest rate or an interest rate index. There are floating-rate instruments where the reference rate is some financial index such as the return on the Standard & Poor's 500 or a non-financial index, such as the price of a commodity. Part 703 limits credit union investments to floating-rate instruments whose rate is tied to domestic interest rates only. The exception is the U.S. dollar denominated London interbank offered rate (LIBOR). Consequently, credit unions cannot invest in floating-rate instruments whose coupon rate is tied to an equity index, commodity prices, foreign interest rates, and foreign currency movements.

Caps and Floors A floating-rate instrument may have a restriction on the maximum coupon rate that will be paid at a reset date. The maximum coupon rate is called a *cap*. For example, suppose for our hypothetical floating-rate instrument whose coupon formula is the 3-month Treasury bill rate plus 100 basis points, there is a cap of 9%. If the 3-month Treasury bill rate is 8.5% at a coupon reset date, then the coupon formula would specify a coupon rate of 9.5%. However, the cap restricts the coupon rate to 9%. Thus, for our hypothetical floating-rate instrument, once the 3-month Treasury bill rate exceeds 8%, the coupon rate is capped out at 9%.

Because a cap restricts the coupon rate from increasing, a cap is an unattractive feature for the investor. In contrast, there could be a minimum coupon rate specified for a floating-rate instrument. The minimum coupon rate is called a *floor*. If the coupon formula produces a coupon rate that is below the floor, the floor is paid instead. Thus, a floor is an attractive feature for the investor.

Inverse Floaters Typically, the coupon formula on floating-rate instruments is such that the coupon rate increases when the reference rate increases, and decreases as the reference rate decreases. There are instruments whose coupon rate moves in the opposite direction from the change in the reference rate. Such issues are called *inverse floaters* or *reverse floaters*. A general formula for an inverse floater is:

$$K - L \times (\text{Reference rate})$$

For example, suppose that for a particular inverse floater K is 12% and L is 1. Then the coupon reset formula would be:

$$12\% - \text{Reference rate}$$

Suppose that the reference rate is 1-month LIBOR, then the coupon reset formula would be

$$12\% - 1\text{-month LIBOR}$$

If in some month 1-month LIBOR at the coupon reset date is 5%, the coupon rate for the period is 7%. If in the next month 1-month LIBOR is 4.5%, the coupon rate increases to 7.5%.

Notice that if 1-month LIBOR exceeds 12%, then the coupon reset formula would produce a negative coupon rate. To prevent this, there is a floor imposed on the coupon rate. Typically, the floor is zero. There is a cap on the floater. This occurs if 1-month LIBOR is zero. In that unlikely event, the maximum coupon rate is 12% for our hypothetical inverse floater. When the floor is set at zero, K is the cap for the inverse floater.

Suppose instead that the coupon reset formula for an inverse floater whose reference rate is 1-month LIBOR is as follows:

28% − 3 (1-month LIBOR)

If 1-month LIBOR at a reset date is 5%, then the coupon rate for that month is 13%. If in the next month 1-month LIBOR declines to 4%, the coupon rate is 16%. Thus, a decline in 1-month LIBOR of 100 basis points, increases the coupon rate by 300 basis points. This is because the value for L in the inverse's coupon formula is 3. Thus, for each one basis point change in 1-month LIBOR the coupon rate is changed by 3 basis points.

It should be noted that under proposed Part 703, there are monthly reporting requirements on all inverse floaters as enumerated in Part 703.3(b)(4). Furthermore, inverse floaters are mentioned by name in Part 703.3(b)(4)(ii)(c)(4) as being held to a heightened standard of reporting and disclosure.

Range Notes A *range note* is a floating-rate instrument whose coupon rate is equal to the reference rate as long as the reference rate is within a certain range at the reset date. If the reference rate is outside of the range, the coupon rate is zero for that period.

For example, a 3-year range note might specify that the reference rate is the 1-year Treasury bill rate and that the coupon rate resets every year. The coupon rate for the year will be the 1-year Treasury bill rate as long as the 1-year Treasury bill rate at the coupon reset date falls within the range as specified below:

	Year 1	Year 2	Year 3
Lower limit of range	4.5%	5.25%	6.00%
Upper limit of range	5.5%	6.75%	6.75%

If the 1-year Treasury bill rate is outside of the range, the coupon rate is zero. For example, if in Year 1 the 1-year Treasury bill rate is 5% at the coupon reset date, the coupon rate for the year is 5%. However, if the 1-year Treasury bill rate is 6%, the coupon rate for the year is zero since the 1-year Treasury bill rate is greater than the upper limit for Year 1 of 5.5%.

As in the case of inverse floaters, a range note is a derivative and requires deeper analysis. As such, only credit unions with managers that have a high level of investment sophistication, along with the requisite analytical tools, should invest in range notes or inverse floaters.

Step-Up Notes

There are instruments that have a coupon rate that increases over time. These instruments are called *step-up notes* because the coupon rate "steps up" over time. For example, a 5-year step-up note might have a coupon rate that is 5% for the first two years and 6% for the last three years. Or, the step-up note could call for a 5% coupon rate for the first two years, 5.5% for the third and fourth years, and 6% for the fifth year. When there is only one change (or step up), as in our first example, the issue is referred to as a *single step-up note*. When there is more than one increase, as in our second example, the issue is referred to as a *multiple step-up note*.

An example of an actual multiple step-up note is a 5-year issue (at issuance in May 1994) of Sallie Mae. The coupon schedule is as follows:

6.05% from 5/3/94 to 5/2/94
6.50% from 5/3/95 to 5/2/96
7.00% from 5/3/96 to 5/2/97
7.75% from 5/3/97 to 5/2/98
8.50% from 5/3/98 to 5/2/99

There is usually a distinct advantage to the issuer of step-up bonds because the right to call the bonds upon short notice (30 days or less) is usually retained. As is discussed below when we cover embedded options and in Chapter 9, the portfolio manager of a credit union must be able to quantitatively discern the value of any call feature. This is true whether a step-up bond or any bond with a call feature is being considered.

Deferred Coupon Bonds

There are issues whose coupon payment is deferred for a specified number of years. That is, there is no coupon payment for the deferred period and then a lump sum payment at some specified date and coupon payments until maturity.

EMBEDDED OPTIONS

An important aspect of an instrument is if it includes any embedded options. Part 703 defines an embedded option as follows:

> *Embedded option* means a characteristic of an investment which gives the issuer or the holder of the investment the right to change features such as rate and principal payment schedule. Embedded options include, but are not limited to, caps, floors, calls, and prepayment provisions.

As stated in Part 703, the reason why embedded options are important is because they "can result in the principal and/or interest cash flows of an investment varying in response to changes in interest rates."

An embedded option can result in an alteration of the coupon rate or the principal repayment. In addition, an embedded option can benefit the issuer or the investor. We have covered in this chapter and Chapter 1 all of the most common embedded options. Below we discuss these options further. Exhibit 1 provides a summary of embedded options with respect to what it alters (coupon rate or principal repayment) and the beneficiary of the option (issuer or investor).

Exhibit 1: Embedded Option Summary

Alters coupon rate	Benefits
cap in a floater	issuer
floor in a floater	investor

Alters principal repayment schedule	Benefits
call provision	issuer
accelerated sinking fund provision	issuer
prepayment provision	issuer
put provision	investor

Embedded Options that Alter Interest Payments

The most common examples of embedded options that affect the coupon rate are caps and floors embedded within floating-rate instruments. To understand why a cap is an embedded option, consider what happens if the coupon formula provides a coupon rate above the cap. In this case, the instrument holder effectively agrees to compensate the issuer by accepting a lower coupon rate. Thus, a cap is an option granted by the investor to the issuer. In contrast, a floor is effectively an option granted by the issuer to the investor since the issuer is willing to compensate the investor if interest rates go below the floor.

Embedded Options that Alter
The Principal Repayment Schedule

There are embedded options that may be included in an instrument that allow either the issuer or the investor to alter the principal repayment schedule. Call and prepayment provisions are examples where the issuer has the right. A put provision is an example of an embedded option granted to the owner of the instrument. We describe call and put provisions below.

Call Provision A provision that gives the issuer an option to pay off all or part of the amount borrowed prior to the stated maturity date is referred to as a call provision. An issuer generally wants the right to retire a bond issue prior to the stated maturity date because it recognizes that at some time in the future the general level of interest rates may fall sufficiently below the issue's coupon rate so that redeeming the issue and replacing it with another issue with a lower coupon rate would be economically beneficial. For the reasons explained in the previous chapter, this right is a disadvantage to the owner of the financial instrument.

In the government agency bond market, there has been a dramatically increasing issuance of callable bonds. A credit union that purchases a callable bond must be prepared to use a more sophisticated analysis to assess its investment merits beyond the traditional yield calculations. The valuation of callable bonds is covered in Chapter 8.

The price at which the issuer must pay to retire the issue is referred to as the *call price*. Typically, there is not one call price but a *call schedule* which sets forth a call price based on when the issuer can exercise the call option.

When a fixed income instrument is issued, typically the issuer may not call it for a number of years. That is, the instrument is said to have a *deferred call*. The date at which the instrument may first be called is referred to as the *first call date*.

The call schedule may be such that the call price at the first call date is a premium over the par value and scaled down to the par value over time. The date at which the instrument is first callable at par value is referred to as the *first par call date*. Typically, for the government agency bonds purchased by credit unions, the call price is always par. In such cases, the first call date is the same as the first par call date.

If a fixed income instrument does not have any protection against early call, then it is said to be a *currently callable issue*. Most newly issued bonds even if currently callable, usually have some restrictions against certain types of early redemption. The most common restriction is that prohibiting the *refunding* of the issue for a certain number of years. Bonds that are noncallable for the issue's life are more common than bonds which are nonrefundable for life but otherwise callable.

Many investors are confused by the term noncallable and nonrefundable. Call protection is much more absolute than refunding protection. While there may be certain exceptions to absolute or complete call protection, it still provides greater assurance against premature and unwanted redemption than does refunding protection. Refunding prohibition merely prevents redemption only from certain sources, namely the proceeds of other debt issues sold at a lower cost of money. The bondholder is only protected if interest rates decline, and the borrower can obtain lower-cost money to pay off the debt.

Another form of embedded option that acts just like a call provision is one that is included as part of the sinking fund provision. Many indentures include a provision that grants the issuer the option to retire more than the amount stipulated for sinking fund retirement. This is referred to as an *accelerated sinking fund provision*. It is an embedded option because if an issuer is restricted from calling or refunding an issue, it can to a certain extent circumvent this restriction by calling in the maximum amount permissible under the sinking fund provision.

Prepayment Provision Mortgage and consumer loans commonly permit the borrower to pay off all or part of the outstanding balance prior to the scheduled principal retirement date. This provision is called a *prepayment provision*. This feature carries over to instruments created from pooling loans. We will discuss this embedded option further in Chapters 5 and 6 when we cover mortgage-backed securities. Basically, a prepayment provision is nothing more than a call provision for mortgage- and asset-backed securities.

Put Provision A *put provision* included in a fixed income instrument grants the owner the right to sell the instrument back to the issuer at a specified price on designated dates. The specified price is called the *put price*. Unlike a call provision and prepayment provision which is a right granted to the issuer, a put option is a right granted to the instrument's owner.

KEY POINTS

1. The term to maturity of a bond is the number of years over which the issuer has promised to meet the conditions of the obligation.

2. The maturity of a bond affects its yield and its price volatility.

3. The par value (principal, face value, redemption value, or maturity value) is the amount that the issuer agrees to repay the bondholder at the maturity date.

4. Bond prices are quoted as a percentage of par value, with par being equal to 100.

5. An amortizing instrument is one in which the issuer agrees to make periodic principal repayments prior to the maturity date.

6. Mortgage loans and many consumer loans are amortizing instruments.

7. A mortgage-backed security and an asset-backed security are examples of amortizing instruments.

8. The interest rate that the issuer agrees to pay each year is called the coupon rate.

9. The coupon is the annual amount of the interest payment and is found by multiplying the par value by the coupon rate.

11. The coupon rate affects the price volatility of an issue.

12. Zero-coupon instruments are issues that are not contracted to make periodic coupon payments with the bondholder realizing interest at the maturity date equal to the difference between the maturity value and the price paid for the bond.

13. A floating-rate instrument is an issue whose coupon rate resets periodically based on a predetermined coupon formula.

14. The typical coupon formula for a floating-rate instrument is some reference rate plus an index spread.

15. A floating-rate instrument may have a cap which sets the maximum coupon rate that will be paid at a reset date.

16. A floor for a floating-rate instrument is the minimum coupon rate that must be paid at a reset date.

17. A cap is an embedded option that is a disadvantage to the investor while a floor is an embedded option that is an advantage to the investor.

18. Credit unions are not permitted to invest in floating-rate instruments whose reference rate is an equity index, non-U.S. interest rate index (except LIBOR), commodity price, or foreign exchange.

19. An inverse floater is a floating-rate instrument whose coupon rate moves in the opposite direction from the change in the reference rate.

20. A range note is a floating-rate instrument whose coupon rate is equal to the reference rate as long as the reference rate is within a certain range at the reset date, but will be zero otherwise.

21. A step-up note is an instrument whose coupon rate increases over time.

22. Embedded options are options granted to either the issuer or investor that allow for the alteration of the interest payment and/or the principal repayment schedule.

23. Caps and floors are embedded options that can alter the interest payments of a floating-rate instrument.

24. A call provision and a prepayment provision are embedded options that grant the issuer the right to alter the principal repayment schedule.

25. For a callable instrument, the call schedule specifies when the issuer can call the issue and the call price at each call date.

26. A deferred call means that the issuer may not call the issue for a number of years.

27. A currently callable instrument is an issue that does not have any protection against early call.

28. Most newly issued instruments even if currently callable, usually have some restrictions against refunding.

29. Call protection is much more absolute than refunding protection.

30. An accelerated sinking fund provision allows the issuer to retire more than the amount stipulated for sinking fund retirement.

31. A put provision is an embedded option that allows the investor to alter the principal repayment schedule.

32. A putable bond is one in which the bondholder has the right to sell the issue back to the issuer at a specified price on designated dates.

Chapter 3

Money Market Instruments

The objectives of this chapter are to:

1. describe what is meant by a money market instrument;

2. explain the different types of certificates of deposit and the limitations imposed on credit unions;

3. explain what Treasury bills are and how their yields are quoted;

4. explain what a repurchase agreement is, its credit risk, and ways to reduce credit risk;

5. explain what federal funds are;

6. explain and illustrate what a bankers acceptance is; and,

7. describe what commercial paper is, the credit risk associated with this instrument, and the limitations of investing in this instrument by credit unions.

Now that we know the investment management process and features of investments, we turn in this chapter to the investment vehicles in which a federal or state chartered federally insured credit union may invest. We can classify these investment alternatives into the following three general categories: (1) money market instruments, (2) non-mortgage-related instruments that are non-money market products, and (3) mortgage-related products. Our focus in this chapter is on money market instruments. In Chapters 5 and 6 we take a close look at mortgage-related products.

MONEY MARKET INSTRUMENTS

The money market is defined as the market for instruments maturing in one year or less. The instruments traded in this market include certificates of deposit, Treasury bills, federal agency discount paper, repurchase agreements, commercial paper, bankers acceptances, and federal funds.

Yields on money instruments are quoted in different ways. Some are quoted on a discount basis and others on an interest-bearing basis. Some base interest on a 360-day year while others use a 365-day year. We will discuss how each money market instrument is treated.

CERTIFICATES OF DEPOSIT

A certificates of deposit (CD) is evidence of a deposit at a bank or savings and loan association. There are three types of issuers of CDs. There are those issued by domestic depository institutions. These CDs are covered by the Federal Deposit Insurance Corporation (FDIC) for up to $100,000 in a given institution. There are CDs that are denominated in U.S. dollars but are issued outside of the United States. These CDs are called *Eurodollar CDs* or *Euro CDs*. A third type of CD is the Yankee CD. This is a CD denominated in U.S. dollars and issued by foreign bank with branches in the United States. For Yankee CDs, NCUA regulations require that the foreign branch be insured and regulated by the FDIC. This additional requirement applies only to the U.S. branch and not the CD itself or the parent bank overseas.

A credit union is permitted to invest in CDs. Any amount invested in a given institution that is not covered by federal deposit insurance exposes the credit union to credit risk. Part 703 requires that a credit union undertake credit analysis to assess this exposure. For CDs issued by federally insured domestic banks, the exposure is any amount invested above $100,000, the amount covered by deposit insurance.

At one time CDs were a fairly simple instrument. Specifically, there was a stated maturity date and a fixed rate. Today, we find more complex CD structures. There are not only simple floating-rate CDs in which the reference rate is an interest rate, but also those linked to non-interest rate indexes. Part 703 prohibits investment in such CDs by credit unions. A floating-rate CD may have a cap or floor.

There are step-up callable CDs. In the previous chapter we explained what a step-up coupon feature for a floating-rate instrument is and what a call feature is. A step-up callable CD is therefore one in which there is an embedded option.

Yields on domestic CDs are quoted on an interest-bearing basis. For CDs with a maturity of one year or less, interest is paid at maturity. For purposes of calculating interest, a year is treated as having 360 days. For CDs with maturities greater than one year, interest is normally paid semiannually, with a year taken to have 360 days. As in the case of domestic CDs, interest on Euro CDs with maturities of one year or less is paid at maturity. For Euro CDs with a maturity of more than one year (i.e., term Euro CDs), interest is paid annually rather than semiannually as in the case of domestic term CDs.

TREASURY BILLS

Treasury securities are obligations of the U.S. government. Consequently, they are perceived as having no credit risk. There are two categories of U.S. Treasury securities — discount and coupon securities. Current Treasury practice is to issue all securities with maturities of less than two years as discount securities. These securities are called Treasury bills. No periodic interest is paid. Instead, the investor realizes interest as the difference between the face value (maturity value) and the price paid. All securities with maturities of two years or longer are issued as coupon securities. Here we focus on Treasury bills. In Chapter 4 we will discuss Treasury coupon securities.

Treasury bills are issued on an auction basis according to regular cycles for securities of specific maturities. Three-month and 6-month Treasury bills are auctioned every Monday. The 1-year (52-week bill) Treasury bills are auctioned in the third week of every month.

The convention for quoting bids and offers is different for Treasury bills and Treasury coupon securities. Unlike coupon securities that pay semiannual interest, Treasury bill values are quoted on a *bank discount basis*, not on a price basis. The yield on a bank discount basis is computed as follows:

$$Y_d = \frac{D}{F} \times \frac{360}{t}$$

where

Y_d = annualized yield on a bank discount basis (expressed as a decimal)
D = dollar discount, which is equal to the difference between the face value and the price
F = face value
t = number of days remaining to maturity

As an example, a Treasury bill with 100 days to maturity, a face value of $100,000, and selling for $98,403 would be quoted at 5.75% on a bank discount basis:

$$D = \$100,000 - \$98,403 = \$1,597$$

Therefore, the yield on a bank discount basis is:

$$Y_d = \frac{\$1,597}{\$100,000} \times \frac{360}{100} = 5.75\%$$

Given the yield on a bank discount basis, the price of a Treasury bill is found by first solving the formula for Y_d for the dollar discount (D), as follows:

$$D = Y_d \times F \times t/360$$

The price is then:

$$\text{Price} = F - D$$

For the 100-day Treasury bill with a face value of $100,000, if the yield on a bank discount basis is quoted as 5.75%, D is equal to:

$$D = 0.0575 \times \$100,000 \times 100/360 = \$1,597$$

Therefore:

$$\text{Price} = \$100,000 - \$1,597 = \$98,403$$

The quoted yield on a bank discount basis is not a meaningful measure of the return from holding a Treasury bill for two reasons. First, the measure is based on a face value investment rather than on the actual dollar amount invested. Second, the yield is annualized according to a 360-day rather than 365-day year, making it difficult to compare Treasury bill yields with Treasury notes and bonds, which pay interest on a 365-day basis. Despite its shortcomings as a measure of return, this is the method the market has adopted to quote Treasury bills. Many dealer quote sheets and some reporting services provide two other yield measures that attempt to make the quoted yield comparable to that for a coupon bond and other money market instruments.

The measure that seeks to make the Treasury bill quote comparable to Treasury notes and bonds is called the *bond equivalent yield*, which we will explain in Chapter 8. The *CD equivalent yield* (also called the *money market equivalent yield*) makes the quoted yield on a Treasury bill more comparable to yield quotations on other money market instruments that pay interest on a 360-day basis. It does this by taking into consideration the price of the Treasury bill rather than its face value. The formula for the CD equivalent yield is:

$$\text{CD equivalent yield} = \frac{360Y_d}{360 - t(Y_d)}$$

As an illustration, consider once again the hypothetical 100-day Treasury bill with a face value of $100,000, selling for $98,403, and offering a yield on a bank discount basis of 5.75%. The CD equivalent yield is:

$$= \frac{360(0.0575)}{360 - 100(0.0575)} = 5.84\%$$

REPURCHASE AGREEMENTS

A *repurchase agreement* (or simply *repo*) is the sale of a security with a commitment by the seller to buy the security back from the purchaser at a specified price at a designated future date. Basically, a repurchase agreement is a collateralized loan, where the collateral is a security. Credit unions are permitted to invest in repos so long as the collateral conforms to regulations set forth by the National Credit Union Administration.

The agreement is best explained with an illustration. Suppose a government securities dealer has purchased $10 million of a particular Treasury security. Where does the dealer obtain the funds to finance that position? Of course, the dealer can finance the position with its own funds or by borrowing from a bank. Typically, however, the dealer uses the repurchase agreement or "repo" market to obtain financing. In the repo market the dealer can use the $10 million of the Treasury security as collateral for a loan. The term of the loan and the interest rate that the dealer agrees to pay (called the "repo rate") are specified. When the term of the loan is one day, it is called an *overnight repo*; a loan for more than one day is called a *term repo*.

The transaction is referred to as a repurchase agreement because it calls for the sale of the security and its repurchase at a future date. Both the sale price and the purchase price are specified in the agreement. The difference between the purchase (repurchase) price and the sale price is the dollar interest cost of the loan.

Let's go back to the dealer who needs to finance $10 million of a Treasury security that it purchased and plans to hold overnight. Suppose that a customer of the dealer has excess funds of $10 million. (The customer might be a municipality with tax receipts that it has just collected, and no immediate need to disburse the funds or even a large credit union with excess overnight liquidity who just received a large influx of deposited member money.) The dealer would agree to deliver ("sell") $10 million of the Treasury security to the customer for an amount determined by the repo rate and buy ("repurchase") the same Treasury security from the customer for $10 million the next day. Suppose that the overnight repo rate is 6.5%. Then, as will be explained below, the dealer would agree to deliver the Treasury securities for $9,998,194 and repurchase the same securities for $10 million the next day. The $1,806 difference between the "sale" price of $9,998,194 and the repurchase price of $10 million is the dollar interest on the financing.

If the customer used securities as collateral to obtain funds from a dealer, the transaction would be called a *reverse repo*. In this case, the customer is not investing but rather borrowing funds. That is, the dealer is a funding source rather than an outlet for a short-term investment.

The following formula is used to calculate the dollar interest on a repo transaction:

Dollar interest = Dollar principal × Repo rate × Repo term/360

Notice that the interest is computed on a 360-day basis. In our example, at a repo rate of 6.5% and a repo term of one day (overnight), the dollar interest is $1,806 as we show below:

= $10,000,000 × 0.065 × 1/360 = $1,806

The advantage to the dealer of using the repo market for borrowing on a short-term basis is that the rate is less than the cost of bank financing. From the customer's perspective, the repo market offers an attractive yield on a short-term secured transaction that is highly liquid.

There is a good deal of Wall Street jargon describing repo transactions. To understand it, remember that one party is lending money and accepting security as collateral for the loan; the other party is borrowing money and giving collateral to borrow money. When someone lends securities in order to receive cash (i.e., borrow money), that party is said to be "reversing out" securities. A party that lends money with the security as collateral is said to be "reversing in" securities. The expressions "to repo securities" and "to do repo" are also used. The former means that someone is going to finance securities using the security as collateral; the latter means that the party is going to invest in a repo. Finally, the expressions "selling collateral" and "buying collateral" are used to describe a party financing a security with a repo on the one hand, and lending on the basis of collateral, on the other.

The collateral in a repo is not limited to government securities. Money market instruments, federal agency securities, and mortgage-backed securities are also used. However, a credit union is only permitted to accept collateral that meet regulatory specifications. That is, all accepted collateral must be a legal investment for the credit union that funds the transaction.

Credit Risks
Despite the fact that there may be high-quality collateral underlying a repo transaction, both parties to the transaction are exposed to credit risk. The failure of a few small government securities dealer firms involving repo transactions in the 1980s has made market participants more cautious about the creditworthiness of the counterparty to a repo.

Why does credit risk occur in a repo transaction? Consider our initial example where the dealer used $10 million of government securities as collateral to borrow. If the dealer cannot repurchase the government securities, the customer may keep the collateral; if interest rates on government securities have increased subsequent to the repo transaction, however, the market value of the government securities will decline, and the customer will own securities with a market value less than the amount it loaned to the dealer. If the market value of the security rises instead, the dealer firm will be concerned with the return of the collateral, which then has a market value higher than the loan.

Repos are now more carefully structured to reduce credit risk exposure. The amount loaned is less than the market value of the security used as collateral, which provides the lender with some cushion should the market value of the security decline. The amount by which the market value of the security used as collateral exceeds the value of the loan is called "margin." Margin is also referred to as the "haircut." The amount of margin depends on the characteristics of the collateral.

Another practice to limit credit risk is to mark the collateral to market on a regular basis. (Marking a position to market means recording the value of a position at its market value.) When market value changes by a certain percentage, the repo position is adjusted accordingly. Suppose that a dealer firm has borrowed $20 million using collateral with a market value of $20.4 million. The margin is 2%. Suppose further that the market value of the collateral drops to $20.1 million. A repo agreement can specify either (1) a margin call, or (2) repricing of the repo. In the case of a margin call, the dealer firm is required to put up additional collateral with a market value of $300,000 in order to bring the margin up to $400,000. If repricing is agreed upon, the principal amount of the repo will be changed from $20 million to $19.7 million (the market value of $20.1 million divided by 1.02). The dealer would then send the customer $300,000.

One concern in structuring a repo is the safekeeping of the collateral. The most obvious procedure is for the borrower to deliver the collateral to the lender. At the end of the repo term, the lender returns the collateral to the borrower in exchange for the principal and interest payment. This procedure may be too costly, though, particularly for short-term repos, because of the costs associated with delivering the collateral. The cost of delivery would be factored into the transaction by a lower repo rate offered by the borrower. The risk of the lender not taking possession of the collateral is that the borrower may sell the security or use the same security as collateral for a repo with another party.

As an alternative to delivering the collateral, the lender may agree to allow the borrower to hold the security in a segregated customer account. Of course, the lender still faces the risk that the borrower uses the collateral fraudulently by offering it as collateral for another repo transaction.

There is only one legal and acceptable method of collateral delivery for a credit union according to the NCUA guidelines — a "tri-party repo." This method requires the borrower to deliver the collateral to the lender's custodial account at the borrower's clearing bank. The custodian then has possession of the collateral that it holds on behalf of the lender. This practice reduces the cost of delivery because it is merely a transfer within the borrower's clearing bank. If, for example, a dealer enters into an overnight repo with Customer A, the next day the collateral is transferred back to the dealer. The dealer can then enter into a repo with Customer B for, say, five days without having to redeliver the collateral. The clearing bank simply establishes a custodian account for Customer B and holds the collateral in that account.

Determinants of the Repo Rate

There is no one repo rate; rates vary from transaction to transaction depending on the following factors: quality of collateral, term of the repo, delivery requirement, and availability of collateral.

The higher the credit quality and liquidity of the collateral, the lower the repo rate. The effect of the term of the repo on the rate depends on the shape of the yield curve (discussed in the next chapter). As noted earlier, if delivery of the collateral to the lender is required, the repo rate will be lower. If the collateral can be deposited with the bank of the borrower, a higher repo rate is paid. The more difficult it is to obtain the collateral, the lower the repo rate. To understand why this is so, remember that the borrower (or equivalently the seller of the collateral) has a security that is a *hot* or *special issue*. The party that needs the collateral will be willing to lend funds at a lower repo rate in order to obtain the collateral.

BANKERS ACCEPTANCES

Simply put, a *bankers acceptance* is a vehicle created to facilitate commercial trade transactions. They are called bankers acceptances because a bank accepts the responsibility to repay a loan to the holder of the vehicle created in a commercial transaction. Bankers acceptances are sold on a discounted basis just as Treasury bills and commercial paper. Credit unions are permitted to invest in bankers acceptances.

The best way to explain the creation of a bankers acceptance is by an illustration. The following entities will be involved in our transaction:

- Guagliardo Italian Car Imports Corporation of America ("Car Imports"), a firm in Pennsylvania that sells automobiles
- Excellent Italian Autos ("EIA"), a manufacturer of automobiles in Italy
- Main Bank of Pennsylvania ("Main Bank"), a commercial bank in Pennsylvania, U.S.A.
- Milan National Bank ("Milan Bank"), a bank in Italy
- High Caliber Money Market Fund, a mutual fund in the United States that invests in money market instruments

The following commercial transaction is being considered by Car Imports and EIA. Car Imports wants to import 15 cars manufactured by EIA. EIA is concerned with the ability of Car Imports to make payment on the 15 cars when they are received.

Acceptance financing is suggested as a means for facilitating this commercial transaction. Car Imports offers $300,000 for the 15 cars. The terms of the sale stipulate that the payment is to be made to EIA 60 days after it ships the 15 cars to Car Imports. EIA determines whether it is willing to accept the $300,000. In considering the offering price, EIA will calculate the present value of the $300,000 since it will not be receiving the payment until 60 days after shipment. Suppose that EIA agrees to these terms.

Car Imports arranges with its bank, Main Bank, to issue a letter of credit. The letter of credit indicates that 60 days after shipment Main Bank will make good on the payment of $300,000 that Car Imports must make to EIA. The agreement to pay $300,000 60 days after shipment is called a time draft. The letter of credit will be sent by Main Bank to EIA's bank, Milan Bank. Upon receipt of the letter of credit, Milan Bank will notify EIA who will then ship the 15 cars. After the cars are shipped, EIA presents the shipping documents to Milan Bank and receives the present value of $300,000. EIA is now out of the picture.

Milan Bank presents the time draft and the shipping documents to Main Bank. The latter will then stamp "accepted" on the time draft. By doing so, Main Bank has created a bankers acceptance. This means that Main Bank agrees to pay the holder of the bankers acceptance $300,000 at the maturity date. Car Imports will receive the shipping documents so that it can procure the 15 cars once it signs a note or some other type of financing arrangement with Main Bank.

At this point, the holder of the bankers acceptance is Milan Bank. It has two choices. It can retain the bankers acceptance as an investment in its loan portfolio or it can request that Main Bank make a payment of the present value of $300,000. Let's assume that Milan Bank requests payment of the present value of $300,000.

Now the holder of the bankers acceptance is Main Bank. It has two choices: retain the bankers acceptance as an investment as part of its loan portfolio or sell it to an investor. Suppose that Main Bank chooses the latter and that High Caliber Money Market Fund is seeking a high quality investment with the same maturity as that of the bankers acceptance. Main Bank sells the bankers acceptance to the money market fund at the present value of $300,000. Rather than sell a bankers acceptances directly to an investor such as High Caliber Money Market Fund, Main Bank could have sold it to a dealer. The dealer would then find an investor such as a money market fund to resell the bankers acceptance. In either case, at the maturity date, the money market fund presents the bankers acceptance to Main Bank, receiving $300,000.

Investing in bankers acceptances exposes a credit union to credit risk. This is the risk that the accepting bank will not be able to pay the principal due at the maturity date. To properly assess this risk, a credit union should check the credit rating of the bank issuing the bankers acceptance. (In the next chapter we discuss such ratings.) Usually, only the largest and most creditworthy banks issue bankers acceptances. It is common for the U.S. Central Credit Union or corporate credit unions to be large investors in bankers acceptances.

FEDERAL FUNDS

Depository institutions are required to maintain reserves. The reserves are deposits at their district Federal Reserve Bank and are called *federal funds*. No interest is earned on federal funds. Consequently, a depository institution that maintains federal funds in excess of the amount required incurs an opportunity cost — the loss of interest income that could be earned on the excess reserves. At the same time, there are depository institutions whose federal funds are less than the amount required.

One way for a depository institution that has less than the required reserves to obtain funds in order to bring reserves to the required level is by entering into a repo with a nonbank customer. An alternative is for the bank to borrow federal funds from a depository institution that has excess reserves. The market in which federal funds are bought (borrowed) by banks that need these funds and sold (lent) by depository institutions that have excess federal funds is called the *federal funds market*. The interest rate which is determined by the supply and demand for federal funds is called the *federal funds rate*.

The federal funds rate and the repo rate are tied together since both are a means for a bank to borrow. The federal funds rate is usually, but not always, higher because the lending of federal funds is done on an unsecured basis, unlike a repo in which the lender has a security as collateral. The spread between the two rates varies depending on market conditions; typically the spread ranges from 5 to 25 basis points.

While the term of most federal funds transactions is overnight, there are longer-term transactions that range from one week to six months. Trading typically takes place directly between the buyer and seller — usually between a large bank and one of its correspondent banks. However, there are federal funds transactions that require the use of a broker.

Federal credit unions may sell funds to Section 107(8) institutions and credit unions at the prevailing market rate for federal funds transactions.[1] It is most common for a credit union to be an investor in fed funds (i.e., act as a lender) to obtain a higher yield than what may otherwise be available on an overnight basis from their corporate credit union.

COMMERCIAL PAPER

Commercial paper is a short-term unsecured promissory note issued in the open market that represents the obligation of the issuing entity. Corporate issuers of commercial paper can be divided into financial companies and nonfinancial com-

---

[1] Section 108(8) refers to that portion of the Federal Credit Union Act which defines permissible areas of investment in banks, S&Ls, and corporate credit unions by an investing federal credit union.

panies. There are three types of financial companies: captive finance companies, bank-related finance companies, and independent finance companies. The maturity of commercial paper is typically less than 270 days and the most common maturity range is 30 to 50 days or less.

Federal credit unions are not permitted to invest in commercial paper. State chartered federally insured credit unions are permitted if the state authorizes state chartered depository institutions to do so.

The four commercial rating companies — Moody's, Standard & Poor's, Duff and Phelps Credit Rating Co., and Fitch Investors Service — assign ratings to commercial paper. These ratings are shown in Exhibit 1.

Despite the fact that the commercial paper market is larger than other money market instruments, secondary trading activity is much smaller. Typically, an investor in commercial paper is an entity that plans to hold it until maturity. This is understandable since an investor can purchase commercial paper with the specific maturity desired. Should an investor's economic circumstances change such that there is a need to sell the paper, it can be sold back to the dealer or, in the case of directly placed paper, the issuer will repurchase it.

Commercial paper is typically a discount instrument but can be issued as an interest-bearing instrument. That is, it is sold at a price less than its maturity value. The difference between the maturity value and the price paid is the interest earned by the investor. For commercial paper, a year is treated as having 360 days. Commercial paper is quoted on a discount basis, as is Treasury bills.

The yield offered on commercial paper tracks that of other money market instruments. The commercial paper rate is higher than that on Treasury bills for three reasons. First, the investor in commercial paper is exposed to credit risk. Second, interest earned from investing in Treasury bills is exempt from state and local income taxes. As a result, commercial paper has to offer a higher yield to offset this tax-advantage of Treasury bills. Finally, the liquidity of commercial paper is less than that of Treasury bills. However, the liquidity premium demanded is probably small since, as stated earlier, investors typically follow a buy-and-hold strategy with commercial paper and so are less concerned with liquidity. The rate on commercial paper is higher by a few basis points than that on certificates of deposit, which we discussed earlier in this chapter. The yield advantage of commercial paper is explained as being due to the higher liquidity of certificates of deposit.

Exhibit 1: Commercial Paper Ratings

	Moody's	S&P	Duff & Phelps	Fitch
Prime-1	(P-1)	A-1/A-1+	Duff-1 (D-1)	F-1
Prime-2	(P-2)	A-2	Duff-2 (D-2)	F-2
Prime-3	(P-3)	A-3	Duff-3 (D-3)	F-3
Prime-4	(P-4)			

Note: The ranking is from highest to lowest credit rating assigned.

KEY POINTS

1. A certificates of deposit (CD) is evidence of a deposit at a bank or savings and loan association.

2. There are domestic CDs, Eurodollar CDs, and Yankee CDs.

3. A credit union is permitted to invest in CDs but must perform credit analysis to the extent that the amount invested exceeds the amount covered by federal deposit insurance.

4. CD structures range from simple plain-vanilla structures to complex structures with embedded options.

5. Treasury securities are obligations of the U.S. government and therefore they are perceived as having no credit risk.

6. A Treasury bill is a zero-coupon Treasury security which has a maturity of one year or less.

7. A repurchase agreement is the sale of a security with a commitment by the seller to buy the security back from the purchaser at a specified price at a designated future date.

8. Credit unions are permitted to invest in repos so long as the collateral conforms to regulations set forth by the National Credit Union Administration.

9. A repurchase agreement for a credit union must be structured as a tri-party repo to reduce credit risk exposure.

10. Repo rates vary from transaction to transaction depending on the quality of collateral, term of the repo, delivery requirement, and availability of collateral.

11. A bankers acceptance is a vehicle created to facilitate commercial trade transactions.

12. Credit unions are permitted to invest in bankers acceptances.

13. The sale of funds in the federal funds market represents a short-term investment by a credit union.

14. Commercial paper is a short-term unsecured promissory note issued in the open market that represents the obligation of the issuing entity.

15. Federal credit unions are not permitted to invest in commercial paper while state chartered federally insured credit unions are permitted if the state authorizes state chartered depository institutions to do so.

Chapter 4

Bonds and Other Non-Mortgage-Related Products

The objectives of this chapter are to:

1. describe the rating systems that are used by the nationally recognized statistical rating organizations to assign credit ratings to investments with credit risk;

2. describe the different types of Treasury coupon securities and how they are quoted;

3. explain what a Treasury STRIP is and how it is created;

4. explain what a municipal security is and the different types of structures;

5. explain bank obligations: non-negotiable CDs, negotiable bank CDs, deposit notes, and bank notes.

6. describe what a corporate bond is;

7. explain what a medium-term note and a structured note are;

8. explain the different types of asset-backed securities;

9. describe what corporate credit unions are and the investment vehicles that they offer; and,

10. explain what an investment company is.

In this chapter we turn our attention to non-mortgage-related products with longer maturities than one year. Specifically, we will look at Treasury coupon securities and zero-coupon instruments, federal agency securities, taxable municipal securities, bank-related term investments (CDs, deposit notes, and bank notes), corporate bonds, medium-term notes, asset-backed securities, corporate credit union shares, and investment company shares. We postpone an explanation of yield measures for these instruments until Chapter 8.

CREDIT RATINGS

All the investment vehicles described in this chapter with the exception of Treasury coupon securities and stripped Treasury securities expose an investor to credit risk. Some large institutional investors and most investment banking firms have their own credit analysis departments. Few individual investors and institutional bond investors, though, do their own analysis. Instead, they rely primarily on commercial rating companies that perform credit analysis and issue their conclusions in the form of ratings.

The four commercial rating companies are (in alphabetical order) (1) Duff & Phelps Credit Rating Co., (2) Fitch Investors Service, (3) Moody's Investors Service, and (4) Standard & Poor's Corporation. We described the rating system for commercial paper in the previous chapter. Each of these organizations is referred to as a nationally recognized statistical rating organization (NRSRO). The rating systems they employ for the securities that we will describe in this chapter are shown in Exhibit 1.

The four NRSROs rate a wide range of bond products. There are two NRSROs which rate banks only: Thomson BankWatch and IBCA Ltd. The former rates domestic and international banks (as well as some securities firms and insurance companies), while the latter primarily rates international banks. Exhibit 2 shows the ratings assigned by Thomson BankWatch.

In all rating systems the term *high grade* means low credit risk, or conversely, high probability of future payments. The highest-grade bonds are designated by Moody's by the letters Aaa, and by the others as AAA. The next highest grade is Aa (Moody's) or AA; for the third grade all rating agencies use A. The next three grades are Baa (Moody's) or BBB, Ba (Moody's) or BB, and B, respectively. There are also C grades. All rating agencies except Moody's uses plus or minus signs to provide a narrower credit quality breakdown within each rating category. Moody's uses 1, 2, or 3 for the same purpose. Bonds rated triple A (AAA or Aaa) are said to be *prime*; double A (AA or Aa) are of *high quality*; single A issues are called *upper medium grade*, and triple B (BBB or Baa) are *medium grade*. Lower-rated bonds are said to have speculative elements or be distinctly speculative.

Bond issues that are assigned a rating in the top four categories are referred to as *investment grade bonds*. Issues that carry a rating below the top four categories are referred to as *non-investment grade bonds* or more popularly as junk bonds or high yield bonds. Thus, the bond market can be divided into two sectors: the investment grade sector and non-investment grade sector.

Exhibit 1: Summary of Bond Rating Systems and Symbols

D&P	Fitch	Moody's	S&P	Summary Description
Investment Grade — High-Creditworthiness				
AAA	AAA	Aaa	AAA	Gilt edge, prime, maximum safety
AA+	AA+	Aa1	AA+	
AA	AA	Aa2	AA	High-grade, high credit quality
AA-	AA-	Aa3	AA-	
A+	A+	A1	A+	
A	A	A2	A	Upper-medium grade
A-	A-	A3	A-	
BBB+	BBB+	Baa1	BBB+	
BBB	BBB	Baa2	BBB	Lower-medium grade
BBB-	BBB-	Baa3	BBB-	
Speculative — Lower Creditworthiness				
BB+	BB+	Ba1	BB+	
BB	BB	Ba2	BB	Low grade, speculative
BB-	BB-	Ba3	BB-	
B+	B+	B1	B+	
B	B	B2	B	Highly speculative
B-	B-	B3	B-	
Predominantly Speculative, Substantial Risk or in Default				
	CCC+		CCC+	
CCC	CCC	Caa	CCC	Substantial risk, in poor standing
	CC	Ca	CC	May be in default, very speculative
	C	C	C	Extremely speculative
			CI	Income bonds — no interest being paid
	DDD			
DD	DD			Default
	D		D	

Exhibit 2: Summary of Bank Ratings by Thomson BankWatch

Rating	Description
A	Company possesses an exceptionally strong balance sheet and earnings record, translating into an excellent reputation and unquestioned access to its natural money markets. If weakness or vulnerability exists in any aspect of the company's business, it is entirely mitigated by the strengths of the organization.
A/B	Company is financially very solid with a favorable track record and no readily apparent weakness. Its overall risk profile, while low, is not quite as favorable as for companies in the highest rating category.
B	A strong company with a solid financial reporting and well received by its natural money markets. Some minor weaknesses may exist, but any deviation from the company's historical performance levels should be both limited and short-lived. The likelihood of a problem developing is small, yet slightly greater than for a higher-rated company.
B/C	Company is clearly viewed as a good credit. While some shortcomings are apparent, they are not serious and/or are quite manageable in the short-term.
C	Company is inherently a sound credit with no serious deficiencies, but financials reveal at least one fundamental area of concern that prevents a higher rating. Company may recently have experienced a period of difficulty, but those pressures should not be long-term in nature. The company's ability to absorb a surprise, however, is less than that for organizations with better operating records.
C/D	While still considered an acceptable credit, the company has some meaningful deficiencies. Its ability to deal with further deterioration is less than that for better-rated companies.
D	Company's financials suggest obvious weaknesses, most likely created by asset quality considerations and/or a poor structured balance sheet. A meaningful level of uncertainty and vulnerability exists going forward. The ability to address further unexpected problems must be questioned.
D/E	Company has areas of major weakness which may include funding/liquidity difficulties. A high degree of uncertainty exists as to the company's ability to absorb incremental problems.
E	Very serious problems exist for the company, creating doubt as to its continued viability without some form of outside assistance — regulatory or otherwise.

Thomson BankWatch uses a straightforward scale of "A" through "E," with "A" being the best and "E" being the worst. Narrower quality breakdowns are denoted as follows: A/B, B/C, C/D, and D/E. The cutoff for a minimum investment grade rating for Thomson BankWatch is C/D. This is roughly the equivalent to Baa3 in the Moody's rating system and BBB– in the rating system used by S&P, Fitch, and Duff & Phelps.

Two points are worth noting. First, the investment grade ratings between rating companies do not directly correspond with one another. Second, the minimum acceptable rating by the NCUA does not correspond to a rating of minimum investment grade by any of the rating companies. Presumably, this was to allow precautionary room for a credit rating downgrade and still allow the credit union the opportunity to divest itself of the security while the security was still considered to be investment grade. The investment divestiture paragraph of Part 703 does include a reference to a bank obligation being lowered below the minimum (B/C) standard of the NCUA. A sub-standard rating requires the investment to be subjected to the reporting requirements under Part 703.7, possibly resulting in a mandatory sale if the credit union does not have a plan of action.

U.S. TREASURY COUPON SECURITIES

Treasury securities issued by the U.S. Department of the Treasury that have maturities of two years or longer are issued as coupon securities. At issuance *Treasury notes* have a maturity between 2 and 10 years, and *Treasury bonds* have a maturity at issuance greater than 10 years. Although Treasury notes are not callable, there are outstanding Treasury bond issues that are callable within five years of maturity. Treasury bonds issued since February 1985 are not callable.

Primary and Secondary Markets

The Treasury regularly issues coupon securities with maturities of 2, 3, 5, 10, and 30 years. Two- and 5-year notes are auctioned each month. At the beginning of the second month of each calendar quarter (February, May, August, and November), the Treasury conducts its regular refunding operations. At this time, it auctions 3-year, 10-year, and 30-year Treasury securities.

The secondary market for Treasury securities is an over-the-counter market where a group of U.S. government securities dealers provide continuous bids and offers on specific outstanding Treasuries. This secondary market is the most liquid financial market in the world. In the secondary market, the most recently auctioned Treasury issues for each maturity are referred to as "on-the-run" or "current-coupon" issues. They are also referred to as the *benchmark issues* or *bellwether issues*. Issues auctioned prior to the current coupon issues typically are referred to as "off-the-run" issues; they are not as liquid as on-the-run issues. That is, the bid-ask spread is larger for off-the-run issues than for on-the-run issues because they are not as liquid.

Price Quotes and Accrued Interest

Treasury coupon securities are quoted on a dollar price basis in price units of $\frac{1}{32}$ of 1% of par (par is taken to be $100). For example, a quote of 92-14 refers to a price of 92 and $\frac{14}{32}$. On the basis of $100,000 par value, a change in price of 1% equates to $1,000, and $\frac{1}{32}$ equates to $31.25. A plus sign following the number of 32nds means that a 64th is added to the price. For example, 92-14+ refers to a price of 92 and $\frac{29}{64}$ or 92.453125% of par value.

When an investor purchases a Treasury coupon bond between coupon payments, the investor must compensate the seller of the bond for the coupon interest earned from the time of the last coupon payment to the settlement date of the bond. This amount is called *accrued interest*, computed as follows:

$$\frac{C}{2} \times \frac{\text{Number of days from last coupon payment to settlement date}}{\text{Number of days in coupon period}}$$

Market conventions determine the number of days in a coupon period and the number of days from the last coupon payment to the settlement date. For a Treasury coupon security, both are equal to the actual number of days. (This is referred to as "actual over actual" basis.)[1] The accrued interest for a Treasury coupon security is therefore determined as follows:

$$\frac{C}{2} \times \frac{\text{Actual number of days from last coupon payment to settlement date}}{\text{Actual number of days in coupon period}}$$

The total proceeds that the buyer of the bond pays the seller is equal to the price agreed upon by the buyer and the seller plus accrued interest.

When-Issued Market

Treasury securities are traded prior to the time they are issued by the Treasury. This component of the Treasury secondary market is called the "when-issued market," or "wi market." When-issued trading for both Treasury bills and Treasury coupon issues extends from the day the auction is announced until the issue day. Part 703 prohibits credit unions from trading in when issued securities.

STRIPPED TREASURY SECURITIES

The U.S. Treasury does not issue zero-coupon notes or bonds. However, government dealers have created such instruments, called STRIPS. This is done by dealers by separating each coupon payment and principal and selling each cash flow as a zero-coupon instrument. This process is called "coupon stripping."

---

[1] For corporate and municipal bonds, the day count convention is "30/360" which means a year is treated as having 360 days and a month as having 30 days. Therefore, the number of days in a coupon period is 180.

Exhibit 3: Creating Stripped Treasury Securities

Dealer purchases $500 million par of a 6% 10-year Treasury Issue

Security

| Maturity value: $500 million |
| Coupon: 6%, semiannual |
| Maturity: 10 years |

↓

Cash flow

| Coupon: $15 million Receipt in: 6 months | Coupon: $15 million Receipt in: 1 year | Coupon: $15 million Receipt in: 1.5 years | ..... | Coupon: $15 million Receipt in: 10 years | Maturity value: $500 million Receipt in: 10 years |

↓ ↓ ↓ ↓ ↓

Zero-coupon Treasury securities created

| Maturity value: $15 million Maturity: 6 months | Maturity value: $15 million Maturity: 1 year | Maturity value: $15 million Maturity: 1.5 years | ..... | Maturity value: $15 million Maturity: 10 years | Maturity value: $500 million Maturity: 10 years |

To illustrate the process, suppose $500 million of a Treasury issue with a 10-year maturity and a coupon rate of 6% is purchased to create zero-coupon Treasury securities. The cash flow from this Treasury issue is 20 semiannual payments of $15 million each ($500 million times 6% divided by 2) and the repayment of principal (corpus) of $500 million 10 years from now. As there are 21 different payments to be made by the Treasury, a receipt representing a single payment claim on each payment is issued, which is effectively a zero-coupon security. The maturity value for a receipt on a particular payment, whether coupon or corpus, depends on the amount of the payment to be made by the Treasury on the underlying Treasury issue. In our example, 20 coupon receipts each have a maturity value of $15 million, and one receipt, the corpus, has a maturity value of $500 million. The maturity dates for the receipts coincide with the corresponding payment dates by the Treasury. This is depicted in Exhibit 3.

While these securities are not issued by the U.S. Department of the Treasury, they do carry the full faith and credit of the U.S. government since they are backed by either the coupon or principal from a Treasury coupon security.

FEDERAL AGENCY SECURITIES

Federal agency securities can be classified by the type of issuer, those issued by *federally related institutions* and those issued by *government sponsored enterprises*. Those federal agencies that provide credit for the housing market issue two types of securities: *debentures* and *mortgage-backed securities*. Our focus here is on the former securities. We discuss mortgage-backed securities in Chapters 5 and 6.

In general, GSEs issue two types of debentures: *discount notes* and *bonds*. Discount notes are short-term obligations, with maturities ranging from overnight to 360 days. As with Treasury bills, no coupon interest is paid. Instead, the investor earns interest by buying the note at a discount. Bonds have maturities greater than 2 years. There are issues with bullet maturities and those with call provisions — long and short calls. The GSEs have also issued structured notes (discussed later when we cover medium-term notes).

Federally Related Institutions

Federally related institutions are arms of the federal government and generally do not issue securities directly in the marketplace. Federally related institutions include the Export-Import Bank of the United States, the Tennessee Valley Authority, the Commodity Credit Corporation, the Farmers Housing Administration, the General Services Administration, the Government National Mortgage Association, the Maritime Administration, the Private Export Funding Corporation, the Rural Electrification Administration, the Rural Telephone Bank, the Small Business Administration, and the Washington Metropolitan Area Transit Authority.

All federally related institutions are exempt from SEC registration. With the exception of securities of the Private Export Funding Corporation and the Tennessee Valley Authority (TVA), the securities are backed by the full faith and credit of the United States government.

In 1995, the only federally related institution to issue debenture securities was the TVA. According to the Securities Data Co., only $4.3 billion of the $224 billion issued by federal agencies was by the TVA. While the TVA was the only federally related institution to issue debentures in 1995, there are issues outstanding from other agencies.

Government Sponsored Enterprises

Government sponsored enterprises (GSEs) are privately owned, publicly chartered entities. They were created by Congress to reduce the cost of capital for certain borrowing sectors of the economy deemed to be important enough to warrant assistance. The entities in these privileged sectors include farmers, homeowners, and students. The enabling legislation dealing with GSE is amended periodically. Government sponsored enterprises issue securities directly in the marketplace.

Today there are five GSEs that issue debentures: Federal Farm Credit System, Federal Home Loan Bank System, Federal National Mortgage Association, Federal Home Loan Bank Corporation, and Student Loan Marketing Association. The Federal Farm Credit Bank System is responsible for the credit market in the agricultural sector of the economy. The Federal Home Loan Bank, Federal Home Loan Mortgage Corporation, and Federal National Mortgage Association are responsible for providing credit to the housing sectors. The Student Loan Marketing Association provides funds to support higher education.

According to the Securities Data Co., the largest GSE issuer in 1995 was the Federal Home Loan Bank ($96.5 billion), followed by the Federal National Mortgage Association ($63.8 billion), and then the Federal Home Loan Mortgage Corporation ($29.9 billion). The Federal Farm Credit System and the Student Loan Marking Corporation issued $15.7 billion and $13.8 billion, respectively, in 1995.

In addition to the debt obligations issued by these five GSEs, there are issues outstanding by one-time GSEs that have been dismantled. These include the Farm Credit Financial Association Corporation, Financing Corporation, and the Resolution Trust Corporation. The Farm Credit Financial Association Corporation was created in 1987 to address problems in the existing Farm Credit System. The Financing Corporation was created in 1987 to recapitalize the Federal Savings and Loan Insurance Corporation. Because of continuing difficulties in the savings and loan association industry, the Resolution Trust Corporation was created in 1989 to liquidate or bail out insolvent institutions.

With the exception of the securities issued by the Farm Credit Financial Assistance Corporation, GSE securities are not backed by the full faith and credit of the U.S. government, as is the case with Treasury securities. Consequently, investors purchasing GSEs are exposed to credit risk.

The price quotation convention for GSE securities is the same as that for Treasury securities. That is, the bid and ask price quotations are expressed as a percentage of par plus fractional 32nds of a point. There are some GSE issues that trade with almost the same liquidity as Treasury securities. Other issues that are supported only by a few dealers trade much like off-the-run corporate bonds. Specifically, this lack of liquidity occurs most frequently with medium-term notes which have a very small original issuance.

MUNICIPAL BONDS

Municipal securities are issued by state and local governments and by entities that they establish. All states issue municipal securities. Local governments include cities and counties. Political subdivisions of municipalities that issue securities include school districts and special districts for fire prevention, water, sewer, and other purposes. Public agencies or instrumentalities include authorities and commissions. There are both tax-exempt and taxable municipal bonds. Interest on tax-exempt municipal bonds is exempt from federal income taxation. If the bond owner resides in the same state as the issuer, the interest is typically exempt from state income taxation.

Federal credit unions are permitted to invest in municipal bonds as long as they are in the top two credit ratings assigned by a nationally recognized statistical rating organization. Before the revisions to Part 703, there was no previous minimum credit rating requirement. However, because tax-exempt municipal bonds offer a lower yield than taxable municipal bonds and the tax exemption is of no value to a credit union, federal credit unions should invest in only taxable municipal bonds. This is largely true for state chartered credit unions as well. Certain state chartered credit unions, such as those in California, may want to make a full analysis of possible tax ramifications/benefits before investing in a taxable municipal bond.

There are municipal zero-coupon bonds, floating-rate bonds, and putable bonds. Municipal bonds are issued with one of two debt retirement structures or a combination of both. Either a bond has a serial maturity structure or a term maturity structure. A serial maturity structure requires a portion of the debt obligation to be retired each year. A term maturity structure provides for the debt obligation to be repaid on a final date. Usually term bonds have maturities ranging from 20 to 40 years (although much shorter maturities are available) and retirement schedules (sinking fund provisions) that begin 5 to 10 years before the final term maturity. Municipal bonds may be called prior to the stated maturity date, either according to a mandatory sinking fund or at the option of the issuer.

Types of Municipal Bond Security Structures

An *official statement* describing the issue and the issuer is prepared for new offerings. Municipal securities have legal opinions which are summarized in the official statement. The importance of the legal opinion is twofold. First, bond counsel determines if the issue is indeed legally able to issue the securities. Second, bond counsel verifies that the issuer has properly prepared for the bond sale by having enacted various required ordinances, resolutions, and trust indentures and without violating any other laws and regulations.

There are basically two types of municipal security structures: tax-backed debt and revenue bonds. We describe each type below, as well as variants.

Tax-Backed Debt *Tax-backed debt obligations* are instruments issued by states, counties, special districts, cities, towns, and school districts that are secured by some form of tax revenue. Tax-backed debt includes general obligation debt, appropriation-backed obligations, debt obligations supported by public credit enhancement programs, and short-term debt instruments. We discuss each below.

1. *General obligation debt* The broadest type of tax-backed debt is *general obligation debt*. There are two types of general obligation pledges: unlimited and limited. An *unlimited tax general obligation debt* is the stronger form of general obligation pledge because it is secured by the issuer's unlimited taxing power. The tax revenue sources include corporate and individual income taxes, sales taxes, and property taxes. Unlimited tax general obligation debt is said to be secured by the *full faith and credit of the issuer*. A limited tax general obligation debt is a limited tax pledge because for such debt there is a statutory limit on tax rates that the issuer may levy to service the debt.

Certain general obligation bonds are secured not only by the issuer's general taxing powers to create revenues accumulated in a general fund, but also by certain identified fees, grants, and special charges, which provide additional revenues from outside the general fund. Such bonds are known as *double-barreled* in security because of the dual nature of the revenue sources. For example, the debt obligations issued by special purpose service systems may be secured by a pledge of property taxes, a pledge of special fees/operating revenue from the service provided, or a pledge of both property taxes and special fees/operating revenues (i.e., double-barreled in security).

2. *Appropriation-backed obligations* Agencies or authorities of several states have issued bonds that carry a potential state liability for making up shortfalls in the issuing entities obligation. The appropriation of funds from the state's general tax revenue must be approved by the state legislation. However, the state's pledge is not binding. Debt obligations with this nonbinding pledge of tax revenue are called *moral obligation debt*. Because a moral obligation bond requires legislative approval to appropriate the funds, it is classified as an *appropriation-backed obligation.*

The purpose of the moral obligation pledge is to enhance the creditworthiness of the issuing entity. The first moral obligation bond was issued by the Housing Finance Agency of the state of New York. Historically, most moral obligation debt has been self-supporting; that is, it has not been necessary for the state of the issuing entity to make an appropriation. In those cases in which state legislatures have been called upon to make an appropriation, they have. For example, the states of New York and Pennsylvania did this for bonds issued by their Housing Finance Agency; the state of New Jersey did this for bonds issued by the Southern Jersey Port Authority.

Another type of appropriation-backed obligation is *lease-backed debt.* There are two types of leases. One type is basically a secured long-term loan disguised as a lease. The "leased" asset is the security for the loan. In the case of a bankruptcy, the court would probably rule such an obligation as the property of the user of the leased asset and the debt obligation of the user. In contrast, the second type of lease is a true lease in which the user of the leased asset (called the lessee) makes periodic payments to the leased asset's owner (called the lessor) for the right to use the leased asset. For true leases, there must be an annual appropriation by the municipality to continue making the lease payments.

3. *Debt obligations supported by public credit enhancement programs* While a moral obligation is a form of credit enhancement provided by a state, it is not a legally enforceable or legally binding obligation of the state. There are entities that have issued debt that carries some form of public credit enhancement that is legally enforceable. This occurs when there is a guarantee by the state or a federal agency or when there is an obligation to automatically withhold and deploy state aid to pay any defaulted debt service by the issuing entity. Typically, the latter form of public credit enhancement is used for debt obligations of a state's school systems.

Here are some examples of state credit enhancement programs. Virginia's bond guarantee program authorizes the governor to withhold state aid payments to a municipality and divert those funds to pay principal and interest to a municipality's general obligation holders in the event of a default. South Carolina's constitution requires mandatory withholding of state aid by the state treasurer if a school district is not capable of meeting its general obligation debt. Texas created the Permanent School Fund to guarantee the timely payment of principal and interest of the debt obligations of qualified school districts. The fund's income is obtained from land and mineral rights owned by the state of Texas.

4. *Short-term debt instruments* Short-term debt instruments include municipal notes, commercial paper, variable-rate demand obligations, and a hybrid of the last two products.

Usually, *municipal notes* are issued for a period of 12 months, although it is not uncommon for such notes to be issued for periods as short as three months and for as long as three years. Municipal notes include *bond anticipation notes* (BANs) and *cash flow notes*. BANs are issued in anticipation of the sale of long-term bonds. The issuing entity must obtain funds in the capital market to pay off the obligation.

Cash flow notes include *tax anticipation notes* (TANs) and *revenue anticipation notes* (RANs). TANs and RANs (also known as TRANs) are issued in anticipation of the collection of taxes or other expected revenues. These are borrowings to even out irregular flows into the treasury of the issuing entity. The pledge for cash flow notes can be either a broad general obligation pledge of the issuer or a pledge from a specific revenue source. The lien position of cash flow noteholders relative to other general obligation debt which has been pledged the same revenue can be either: (1) a first lien on all pledged revenue, thereby having priority over general obligation debt which has been pledged the same revenue, (2) a lien that is in parity with general obligation debt which has been pledged the same revenue, or (3) a lien that is subordinate to the lien of general obligation debt which has been pledged the same revenue.

Commercial paper is an unsecured debt obligation of the issuer. This is a popular short-term financing vehicle used by corporations. Commercial paper is also used by municipalities to raise funds on a short-term basis ranging from 1 day to 270 days. There are two types of commercial paper issued, unenhanced and enhanced. *Unenhanced commercial paper* is a debt obligation based solely on the issuer's credit quality and liquidity capability. *Enhanced commercial paper* is a debt obligation that is credit enhanced with bank liquidity facilities (for example, a letter of credit), insurance, or a bond purchase agreement. The role of the enhancement is to reduce the risk of non-repayment of the maturing commercial paper principal by providing a source of liquidity for payment of that debt in the event no other funds of the issuer are currently available.

Variable-rate demand obligations (VRDOs) are floating-rate obligations that have a nominal long-term maturity but have a coupon rate that is either reset daily or every seven days. The investor has an option to put the issue back to the issuer at any time with seven days notice. The put price is par plus accrued interest. There are unenhanced and enhanced VRDOs.

The *commercial paper/VRDO hybrid* is customized to meet the cash flow needs of an investor. As with tax-exempt commercial paper, there is flexibility in structuring the maturity, because a remarketing agent establishes interest rates for a range of maturities. Although the instrument may have a long nominal maturity, there is a put provision as with a VRDO. Put periods can range from 1 day to over 360 days. On the put date, the investor can put back the bonds, receiving principal and interest, or the investor can elect to extend the maturity at the new interest rate and put date posted by the remarketing agent at that time. Thus the investor has two choices when initially purchasing this instrument: the interest rate and the put date. Interest is generally paid on the put date if the date is within 180 days. If the put date is more than 180 days forward, interest is paid semiannually.

Revenue Bonds The second basic type of security structure is found in a revenue bond. Revenue bonds are issued for enterprise financings that are secured by the revenues generated by the completed projects themselves, or for general public-purpose financings in which the issuers pledge to the bondholders the tax and revenue resources that were previously part of the general fund. This latter type of revenue bond is usually created to allow issuers to raise debt outside general obligation debt limits and without voter approval.

A feasibility study is performed before the endeavor is undertaken to determine whether it will be self supporting. Revenue bonds can be classified by the type of financing. These include utility revenue bonds, transportation revenue bonds, housing revenue bonds, higher education revenue bonds, health care revenue bonds, sports complex and convention center revenue bonds, seaport revenue bonds, and industrial revenue bonds.

The details of how revenue received by the enterprise will be disbursed are set forth in the trust indenture. Typically, the flow of funds for a revenue bond are as follows. First, all revenues from the enterprise are placed into a *revenue fund*. It is from the revenue fund that disbursements for expenses are made to the following funds: *operation and maintenance fund, sinking fund, debt service reserve fund, renewal and replacement fund, reserve maintenance fund*, and *surplus fund*.

Cash needed to operate the enterprise are deposited from the revenue fund to the operation and maintenance fund. Operations of the enterprise have priority over the servicing of the issue's debt. This is the typical structure of a revenue bond. The pledge of revenue to the bondholders is a *net* revenue pledge, net meaning after operation expenses. Cash required to service the debt are deposited in the sinking fund and disbursements are then made to bondholders as specified in the indenture. Any remaining cash is then distributed to the reserve funds. The purpose of the debt service reserve fund is to accumulate cash to cover any shortfall of future revenue to service the issue's debt. The specific amount that must be deposited is stated in the trust indenture. The function of the renewal and replacement fund is to accumulate cash for regularly scheduled major repairs and equipment replacement. The function of the reserve maintenance fund is to accumulate cash for extraordinary maintenance or replacement costs that might arise. Finally, if any cash remains after disbursement for operations, debt servicing, and reserves, it is deposited in the surplus fund. The issuer can use the cash in this fund in any way it deems appropriate.

There are various restrictive covenants included in the trust indenture for a revenue bond to protect the bondholders. A rate, or user-charge, covenant dictates how charges will be set on the product or service sold by the enterprise. The covenant could specify that the minimum charges be set so as to satisfy both expenses and debt servicing, or a higher rate to provide for a certain amount of reserves. An additional bonds covenant indicates whether additional bonds with the same lien may be issued. If additional bonds with the same lien are issued, conditions that must be satisfied are specified. Other covenants would specify that the facility may not be sold, how much insurance must be maintained, requirements for recordkeeping and for the auditing of the enterprise's financial statements by an independent accounting firm, and requirements for maintaining the facilities in good order.

Hybrid Securities Some municipal bonds that have the basic characteristics of general obligation bonds and revenue bonds have more issue-specific structures as well. Three important examples are insured bonds, bank-backed bonds, and refunded bonds.

Insured bonds are backed by insurance policies written by commercial insurance companies, as well as by the credit of the municipal issuer. Municipal bond insurance is a contractual commitment by an insurance company to pay the bondholder any bond principal and/or coupon interest that is due on a stated maturity date but that has not been paid by the bond issuer. Once issued, this municipal bond insurance usually extends for the term of the bond issue, and it cannot be cancelled by the insurance company. Insured bonds are probably the most common issuance form for taxable municipal bonds, but are frequently utilized in a tax-exempt issuance as well.

Most insured municipal bonds are insured by one of the following insurance companies that are primarily in the business of insuring municipal bonds: AMBAC Indemnity Corporation; Capital Guaranty Insurance Company; Connie Lee Insurance Company; Financial Guaranty Insurance Company; Financial Security Assurance, Inc.; and, Municipal Bond Investors Insurance Corporation.

Municipal obligations have been increasingly supported by various types of credit facilities provided by commercial banks. The support is in addition to the issuer's cash flow revenues.

Bank-backed municipal bonds are supported by either a letter of credit, irrevocable line or credit, or a revolving line of credit. A *letter-of-credit agreement* is the strongest type of support available from a commercial bank. Under this arrangement, the bank is required to advance funds to the trustee if a default has occurred. An *irrevocable line of credit* is not a guarantee of the bond issue though it does provide a level of security. A *revolving line of credit* is a liquidity-type credit facility that provides a source of liquidity for payment of maturing debt in the event no other funds of the issuer are currently available. Because a bank can cancel a revolving line of credit without notice if the issuer fails to meet certain covenants, bond security depends entirely on the creditworthiness of the municipal issuer. Such is not the case with insured bonds.

Refunded bonds if properly structured have the highest credit quality. Although originally issued as either revenue or general obligation bonds, municipal bonds are sometimes refunded. A refunding usually occurs when the original bonds are escrowed or collateralized by direct obligations guaranteed by the U.S. government. By this it is meant that a portfolio of securities guaranteed by the U.S. government are placed in trust. The portfolio of securities is assembled such that the cash flow from all the securities matches the obligations that the issuer must pay. For example, suppose that a municipality has a 7%, $100 million issue with 12 years remaining to maturity. The municipality's obligation is to make payments of $3.5 million every six months for the next 12 years and $100 million 12 years from now. If the issuer wants to refund this issue, a portfolio of U.S. government obligations can be purchased that has a cash flow of $3.5 million every six months for the next 12 years and $100 million 12 years from now.

Once this portfolio of securities whose cash flow matches that of the municipality's obligation is in place, the refunded bonds are no longer secured as either general obligation or revenue bonds. The bonds are now supported by the portfolio of securities held in an escrow fund. Such bonds, if escrowed with securities guaranteed by the U.S. government, have little if any credit risk. They are the safest municipal bond investments available.

The escrow fund for a refunded municipal bond can be structured so that the refunded bonds are to be called at the first possible call date or a subsequent call date established in the original bond indenture. Such bond's are known as *prerefunded municipal bonds*. While refunded bonds are usually retired at their first or subsequent call date, some are structured to match the debt obligation to the retirement date. Such bonds are known as *escrowed-to-maturity bonds*.

Credit Risk

While municipal bonds at one time were considered second in safety only to U.S. Treasury securities, today there are new concerns about the credit risks of municipal securities. The first concern came out of the New York City billion-dollar financial crisis in 1975. On February 25, 1975, the state of New York's Urban Development Corporation defaulted on a $100 million note issue that was the obligation of New York City; many market participants had been convinced that the state of New York would not allow the issue to default. Although New York City was able later to obtain a $140 million revolving credit from banks to cure the default, lenders became concerned that the city would face difficulties in repaying its accumulated debt, which stood at $14 billion on March 31, 1975. This financial crisis sent a loud and clear warning to investors in general — regardless of supposedly ironclad protection for the bondholder, when issuers such as large cities have severe financial difficulties, the financial stakes of public employee unions, vendors, and community groups may be dominant forces in balancing budgets.

The second reason for concern about municipal securities credit risk is the proliferation in this market of innovative financing techniques to secure new bond issues. In addition to the established general obligation bonds and revenue bonds, there are now more non-voter-approved, innovative, and legally untested security mechanisms. These innovative financing mechanisms include moral obligation bonds and commercial bank-backed letters of credit bonds, to name a few. What distinguishes these newer bonds from the more traditional general obligation and revenue bonds is that there is no history of court decisions or other case law that firmly establishes the rights of the bondholders and the obligations of the issuers. It is not possible to determine in advance the probable legal outcome if the newer financing mechanisms were to be challenged in court. This is illustrated most dramatically by the bonds of the Washington Public Power Supply System (WPPSS) where bondholder rights to certain revenues were not upheld by the highest court in the state of Washington.

The third reason is the impact on the creditworthiness of both general obligation and revenue bonds that the scaling down of federal grants and aid programs have had. At the same time, there has been an increase in federal-mandated services. As an example of the change in federal funding policies, amendments to the Clean Water Act in the early 1980s reduced the total federal contribution to local waste-treatment programs from $90 billion projected under the old law to $36 billion. Additionally, after October 1, 1984, the federal matching contribution to local sewerage constructions projects declined from 75% to 55% of the costs. For two decades prior, many state and local governments had grown dependent on this and other federal grant programs as direct subsidies to their local economies as well.

The fourth reason for the concern with credit risk is that the U.S. economy is undergoing a fundamental change, which is resulting in a decline of various sectors of the economy. This decline has widespread implications for entire regions of the country. Many general obligations and revenue bond issuers can be expected to undergo significant economic deterioration that could adversely impact their tax collections and wealth indicators such as personal income, real estate property values, and retail sales.

Finally, there is a concern that financial managers or treasurers of investment funds of municipalities may not be managing those funds prudently. Investment funds are targeted for short-term operating needs and long-term capital projects. The concern is not that a financial manager is earning a below-market rate using a conservative investment policy; rather, the concern is that the financial manager is pursuing a high-risk investment strategy that can result in a loss of principal that is so large that it jeopardizes the issuer's ability to meet its debt obligations. Such policies were followed by some financial managers as interest rates declined to low levels and these strategies sought to generate additional interest income so as to reduce the need to raise taxes. Financial managers who pursued such high-risk investment strategies that benefited from a decline in interest rates did extremely well when interest rates declined. However, when interest rates rose, the losses realized where devastating to some municipalities. Orange County, California is not only the best-known example of a municipality that defaulted because of the imprudent management of investment funds, but is the largest municipal default to date as a result of the losses in its investment portfolio.

While municipal bonds do expose a credit union to credit risk, they offer the opportunity to enhance return. There are some types of municipal securities that we discuss below (refunded bonds) that are effectively guaranteed by the U.S. government. There are others that are insured by an insurance company. We will discuss insured bonds below. Insured bonds expose the investor to the credit risk of the insurer. Nevertheless, they offer a credit union another level of credit protection.

There is a wide range of credit quality in the municipal bond market. Investors rely on the credit ratings that are assigned by the nationally recognized statistically rating organizations. The two dominant companies with respect to rating municipal debt obligations are Standard & Poor's and Moody's. Below we discuss the factors that should be considered in assessing the credit risk of an issue.[2]

Tax-Backed Debt In assessing the credit risk of tax-backed debt, there are four basic categories that should be considered. The first category includes information on the issuer's debt structure to determine the overall debt burden. The debt burden usually is composed of the respective direct and overlapping debts per capita as well as the respective direct and overlapping debts as percentages of real estate valuations and personal incomes.

The second category relates to the issuer's ability and political discipline to maintain sound budgetary policy. The focus of attention here usually is on the issuer's general operating funds and whether it has maintained at least balanced budgets over three to five years.

The third category involves determining the specific local taxes and intergovernmental revenues available to the issuer, as well as obtaining historical information both on tax collection rates, which are important when looking at property tax levies, and on the dependence of local budgets on specific revenue sources.

The fourth and last category of information necessary to the credit analysis is an assessment of the issuer's overall socioeconomic environment. The determinations that have to be made here include trends of local employment distribution and composition, population growth, real estate property valuation, and personal income, among other economic factors.

Standard & Poor's and Moody's consider these four informational categories in arriving at their respective credit ratings of general obligation bonds. However, these two rating companies have major differences in their respective

[2] For a further discussion of how to evaluate the credit risk of a municipal obligation, see Sylvan G. Feldstein and Frank J. Fabozzi, *Dow Jones-Irwin Guide to Municipal Bonds* (Homewood, IL: Dow Jones-Irwin, 1987).

approaches toward these four categories. They also bring other differences in conceptual factors to bear before assigning their respective general obligation credit ratings. The differences between the rating companies are very important since at times they can result in dramatically different credit ratings for the same issuer's bonds.

The rating companies have stated in their publications what criteria guide their respective credit-rating approaches. It is also possible to infer what they emphasize from reviewing their credit reports and rating decisions on individual issues. It appears that Moody's tends to focus on the debt burden and budgetary operations of the issuer; Standard & Poor's considers the issuer's economic environment as the most important element in its analysis.

The commercial rating companies differ in how they apply their analytical tools to the rating of state and local government general obligation bonds. Moody's basically believes that state and local bonds are not fundamentally different. Moody's applies the same debt- and budgetary-related concerns to state general obligation bonds issued by counties, school districts, towns, and cities. This commercial rating company has even assigned ratings below A to state general obligation bonds. For example, in May 1982, Moody's assigned a rating of Baa1 to the state of Michigan on the basis of the weak local economy and the state's budgetary problems at the time.

Unlike Moody's, Standard & Poor's seems to make more of a distinction between state and local government general obligation bonds. Because states have broader legal powers in the areas of taxation and policy-making that do not require home-rule approvals, broader revenue bases, and more diversified economies, Standard & Poor's seems to view state general obligation bonds as being significantly stronger than those of their respective underlying jurisdictions. Standard & Poor's has only given one rating below A to the general obligation bonds of a state (Louisiana) bonds. Of the 40 state general obligation bonds that both commercial rating companies rated, Moody's gave ratings in the AA range or better to 35 states while Moody's gave ratings of Aa or better to only 33 states.

On the whole, for reasons just cited, Standard & Poor's seems to tend to have a higher credit assessment of state general obligation bonds than does Moody's. Furthermore, Moody's views these broader revenue resources as making states more vulnerable in difficult economic times to demands by local governments for increased financial aid.

There is a difference in the attitude of the two commercial rating companies in assessing the importance of the automatic withholding of state aid to pay debt service of defaulted local government general obligation bonds. Standard & Poor's views this as a very positive credit feature. Although Standard & Poor's does review the budgetary operations of the local government issuer to be sure there are no serious budgetary problems, the assigned rating reflects the general obligation credit rating of the state involved, the legal base of the withholding mechanism, the historical background and long-term state legislative support for the pledged state aid program, and the specified coverage of the state aid monies available to maximum debt-service requirements on the general obligation bonds. Normally, Standard & Poor's applies a blanket rating to all local general obligation bonds covered by the specific state aid withholding mechanism. The rating is one or two notches below the rating of that state's particular general obligation bonds.

Although Moody's recognizes the state aid withholding mechanisms in its credit reviews, it believes that its assigned rating must in the first instance reflect the underlying ability of the issuer to make timely debt-service payments. In contrast, Standard & Poor's considers the state aid withholding mechanism equally as important a credit factor as the underlying budget, economic, and debt-related characteristics of the bond issuer.

Revenue Bonds While there are numerous security structures for revenue bonds, the underlying principle in rating is whether the project being financed will generate sufficient cash flow to satisfy the obligations due bondholders. In assessing the credit risk for both types of revenue bonds, the trust indenture and legal opinion should provide legal comfort in the following bond-security areas: (1) the limits of the basic security, (2) the flow-of-funds structure, (3) the rate, or user-charge, covenant, (4) the priority-of-revenue claims, (5) the additional-bonds tests, and (6) other relevant covenants.

BANK OBLIGATIONS

There are three types of bank obligations in which a credit union may invest: certificates of deposit (CD), deposits notes, and bank notes. In Chapter 2, we discussed CDs, distinguishing between domestic CDs and EuroCDs. CDs can be further divided into non-negotiable and negotiable CDs.

Non-negotiable CDs cannot be sold prior to the maturity date. That is, these CDs have no secondary market for resale before maturity. Additionally, there is usually a loss or forfeiture of several months interest if the CD is liquidated early. For many years, credit unions invested in one type of non-negotiable CD — a $100,000 CD, known as a "jumbo CD," and this is still a common investment vehicle, especially among smaller credit unions with less than $10 million in assets. This non-negotiable CD is fully insured by the Federal Deposit Insurance Corporation (FDIC) as to the return of the principal and interest invested up to $100,000. Interest on a jumbo CD is paid monthly. Interest on these CDs is commonly calculated based on a "365/365" basis and occasionally on a "30/360" basis. We'll explain what this means later when we discuss yields.

A *negotiable CD* is one that can be sold in the market prior to the maturity date. That is, a negotiable CD is a marketable security. Interest is calculated on an "actual/360" basis (also called a "365/360" basis). Negotiable CDs are for amounts in excess of $100,000. As a result, they carry credit risk. The credit risk exposure is the excess of the maturity value over $100,000. For accepting this credit risk, a credit union is rewarded in the form of a higher yield than a non-negotiable CD offered by the same institution and with the same maturity. Therefore, the trade off is as follows: a credit union can obtain a higher yield and the flexibility of being able to sell the CD before maturity by investing in a negotiable CD but must accept credit risk for the amount invested in excess of $100,000.

This trade-off relative to non-negotiable CDs also occurs for deposit notes. *Deposit notes* are exactly like a negotiable CD (insured up to $100,000) except for the fact that the interest is accrued on a "30/360" basis. This is the way interest is calculated on corporate bonds and, as a result, made deposit notes more attractive to foreign investors who were accustomed to such a convention. As a result, the liquidity for these instruments was enhanced.

Bank notes are senior, unsecured obligations of a bank, not a bank holding company. A bank holding company is a corporation and corporate bonds and notes are not permissible investments for federal credit unions. However, bank notes are not corporate bonds because they are issued by the bank itself. Even though they are reported as "other liabilities" on the bank's balance sheet, they nonetheless rank *pari passu* with the uninsured depositors of the bank. The NCUA requires for a bank note to be a permissible investment that it meet several criteria including the stipulation that it must qualify as a deposit under the Federal Reserves' Regulation D. Research by one of the authors has indicated that bank notes are considered to be deposits for Regulation D purposes and this has been confirmed in discussions with the Federal Reserve. (A credit union should obtain its own opinion regarding this.) Like deposit notes, bank notes pay interest on a 30/360 basis. There is credit risk for bank notes as there is for negotiable CDs and deposit notes. However, the amount of invested funds exposed to credit risk is greater for bank notes since the first $100,000 invested is not insured.

Credit Risk

Negotiable bank CDs, deposit notes, and bank notes expose a credit union to credit risk. Hence, we refer to these instruments as *credit-sensitive bank obligations*, as opposed to fully insured CDs. The creditworthiness of a bank issuing a credit-sensitive bank obligation is generally measured by its credit rating as determined through the analytical efforts of a credit rating agency. As discussed earlier in this chapter, there are six nationally recognized statistical rating organizations and only one of these (Thomson BankWatch) follows financial institutions exclusively. Four of the rating agencies (S&P, Moody's, Duff & Phelps, and Fitch) are general credit rating companies that rate a wider range of debt instruments of corporate America and its geographically diverse governmental bodies. The last of the six (IBCA, Ltd.) only rates international banks.

In its proposed revision to Part 703, the NCUA makes a distinction as to its minimum acceptable credit rating for an investment of over $100,000 in a credit-sensitive bank obligation. The NCUA cites a minimum acceptable credit rating of B/C (or its equivalent). The rating of B/C references a hierarchy of ratings and it should be noted that the B/C rating is unique to Thomson BankWatch.

Yields on Bank Obligations

The yield on bank obligations is higher than same-maturity Treasury obligations. The premium reflects credit risk faced by an investor in negotiable CDs, deposit notes, and bank notes, as well as the poorer liquidity relative to Treasury obligations. The amount of the yield premium depends on the credit rating of the issuing bank.

Complicating yield comparisons among bank obligations, as well as in comparing yields on bank obligations with other debt instruments described in this chapter, is the day count convention for calculating yield. Negotiable CDs pay interest based on an "actual/360" basis or "365/360" basis. The 360 in the denominator is the number of days assumed in a year. The numerator indicates how the number of days in the investment period over which interest is calculated is determined. The term "actual" or "365" means that the actual number of days in the period is counted. In contrast, the interest for deposit notes and bank notes is calculated on a "30/360" basis, which is the same way that interest is calculated on corporate bonds. A 30/360 basis calculation means that a month is assumed to have 30 days, regardless of the actual number of days in the month.

To understand the difference between the "365/360" basis and "30/360" basis, suppose that $1 million is invested for three months paying 5%. Suppose that the actual number of days in that 3-month period is 92. Then, using the 365/360 basis, the calculated interest would be:

$$\$1,000,000 \times 0.05 \times (92/360) = \$12,777.78$$

Using a 30/360 basis, the calculated interest would be:

$$\$1,000,000 \times 0.05 \times (90/360) = \$12,500.00$$

Notice that if this is a 1-year maturity instrument, using the 365/360 basis would produce an amount greater by simply multiplying $1 million by 5%.

For a non-negotiable CD, the "365/365" basis is the most common day count convention used. This means that the actual number of days in the year and the actual number of days in the period are used. So, for our $1 million 3-month investment paying 5%, the calculated interest is:

$$\$1,000,000 \times 0.05 \times (92/365) = \$12,602.74$$

While there are formulas to convert the yield based on one day count convention for calculating interest into another, by far the simplest way to compare alternative investments is by looking at the total dollars received per dollar invested. Since instruments make periodic interest payments, it is necessary to make some assumption as to what can be earned by reinvesting those interest payments. This exercise will show how sensitive the investment selection will be to the assumption of the reinvestment of interest. From the calculated total dollars received per dollar invested, a return measure can be calculated. This measure is called the *total return*, which we discuss further in Chapter 11.

The key here is that calculating the total dollars received per dollar invested over some specified maturity date will always indicate the best vehicle in terms of return. Reliance on formulas to convert yield numbers to some market convention is not a useful exercise and, in fact, may give misleading results.

CORPORATE BONDS

As the name indicates, corporate bonds are issued by corporations. Federal credit unions are not permitted to invest in corporate bonds. State chartered credit unions may be entitled to invest depending on the specific state regulation concerning the investment powers of credit unions.

Corporate bonds are classified by the type of issuer. The four general classifications used by bond information services are: (1) utilities, (2) transportations, (3) industrials, and (4) banks and finance companies. Finer breakdowns are often made to create more homogeneous groupings. For example, utilities are subdivided into electric power companies, gas distribution companies, water companies, and communication companies. Transportations are divided further into airlines, railroads, and trucking companies. Industrials are the catchall class, and the most heterogeneous of the groupings with respect to investment characteristics. Industrials include all kinds of manufacturing, merchandising, and service companies. In recent years, industrials have raised the largest amount of public debt, followed by financial institutions and then utilities.

The features of corporate bonds were described in Chapter 2, including embedded options. The rating systems shown in Exhibit 1 are used for corporate bonds.

Security for Bonds

Either real property or personal property may be pledged to offer security beyond that of the general credit standing of the issuer. With a *mortgage bond*, the issuer has granted the bondholders a lien against the pledged assets. A lien is a legal right to sell mortgaged property to satisfy unpaid obligations to bondholders. In practice, foreclosure and sale of mortgaged property is unusual. If a default occurs, there is usually a financial reorganization of the issuer in which provision is made for settlement of the debt to bondholders. The mortgage lien is important, though, because it gives the mortgage bondholders a very strong bargaining position relative to other creditors in determining the terms of a reorganization. Although a lien placed against mortgages, these bonds are not mortgage-backed securities which are discussed in the next two chapters and should not be confused with those securities.

Some companies do not own fixed assets or other real property and so have nothing on which they can give a mortgage lien to secure bondholders. Instead, they own securities of other companies; they are holding companies and the other companies are subsidiaries. To satisfy the desire of bondholders for security, the issuer grants investors a lien on stocks, notes, bonds or whatever other kind of financial asset they own. These assets are termed "collateral" (or personal property), and bonds secured by such assets are called *collateral trust bonds*.

Debenture bonds are not secured by a specific pledge of property, but that does not mean that holders have no claim on property of issuers or on their earnings. Debenture bondholders have the claim of general creditors on all assets of the issuer not pledged specifically to secure other debt. Furthermore, they even have a claim on pledged assets to the extent that these assets have value greater than necessary to satisfy secured creditors. *Subordinated debenture bonds* are issues that rank after secured debt, after debenture bonds, and often after some general creditors in its claim on assets and earnings.

It is important to recognize that while a superior legal status will strengthen a bondholder's chance of recovery in case of default, it will not absolutely prevent bondholders from suffering financial loss when the issuer's ability to generate cash flow adequate to pay its obligations is seriously eroded. Claims against a weak lender are oftentimes satisfied for less than face value.

Bankruptcy and Creditor Rights

Corporate bonds are "senior" corporate securities. By senior we mean that the holder of the security has priority over the equity owners in the case of bankruptcy of a corporation. And, as we have explained, there are creditors who have priority over other creditors.

The law governing bankruptcy in the United States is the Bankruptcy Reform Act of 1978. One purpose of the act is to set forth the rules for a corporation to be either liquidated or reorganized. The *liquidation* of a corporation means that all the assets will be distributed to the holders of claims of the corporation and no corporate entity will survive. In a *reorganization*, a new corporate entity will result. Some holders of the claim of the bankrupt corporation will receive cash in exchange for their claims, others may receive new securities in the corporation that results from the reorganization, and others may receive a combination of both cash and new securities in the resulting corporation.

Another purpose of the bankruptcy act is to give a corporation time to decide whether to reorganize or liquidate and then the necessary time to formulate a plan to accomplish either a reorganization or liquidation. When a corporation files for bankruptcy this is achieved because the act grants the corporation protection from creditors who seek to collect their claims.[3] A company that files for protection under the bankruptcy act generally becomes a "debtor-in-possession," and continues to operate its business under the supervision of the court.

The bankruptcy act is comprised of 15 chapters, each chapter covering a particular type of bankruptcy. Of particular interest to us are two of the chapters,

---

[3] The petition for bankruptcy can be filed either by the company itself, in which case it is called a *voluntary bankruptcy*, or be filed by its creditors, in which case it is called an *involuntary bankruptcy*.

Chapter 7 and Chapter 11. Chapter 7 deals with the liquidation of a company; Chapter 11 deals with the reorganization of a company.

When a company is liquidated, creditors receive distributions based on the "absolute priority rule" to the extent assets are available. The absolute priority rule is the principle that senior creditors are paid in full before junior creditors are paid anything. For secured creditors and unsecured creditors, the absolute priority rule guarantees their seniority to equity holders.

In liquidations, the absolute priority rule generally holds. In contrast, there is a good body of literature that argues that strict absolute priority has not been upheld by the courts or the SEC in the case of reorganizations. Studies of actual reorganizations under Chapter 11 have found that the violation of absolute priority is the rule rather than the exception. Consequently, while investors in the debt of a corporation may feel that they have priority over the equity owners and priority over other classes of debtors, the actual outcome of a bankruptcy may be far different from what the terms of the debt agreement state.

MEDIUM-TERM NOTES

A medium-term note (MTN) is a debt instrument issued by federal agencies and corporations with the unique characteristic that notes are offered continuously to investors by an agent of the issuer. Investors can select from several maturity ranges: 9 months to 1 year, more than 1 year to 18 months, more than 18 months to 2 years, and so on up to 30 years. MTNs are rated by the nationally recognized statistical rating organizations using the rating systems shown in Exhibit 1.

The term "medium-term note" to describe this debt instrument is misleading. Traditionally, the term "note" or "medium-term" was used to refer to debt issues with a maturity greater than 1 year but less than 15 years. Certainly this is not a characteristic of MTNs since they have been sold with maturities from nine months to 30 years, and even longer. For example, in July 1993, Walt Disney Corporation issued a security with a 100-year maturity off its medium-term note shelf registration.

The issuer posts rates over a range of maturities: for example, nine months to 1 year, 1 year to 18 months, 18 months to 2 years, and annually thereafter. Usually, an issuer will post rates as a spread over a Treasury security of comparable maturity. For example, in the 2 to 3 year maturity range, the offering rate may be 35 basis points over the 2-year Treasury. Rates will not be posted for maturity ranges that the issuer does not desire to sell. The rate offering schedule can be changed at any time by the issuer either in response to changing market conditions or because the issuer has raised the desired amount of funds at a given maturity. In the latter case, the issuer can either not post a rate for that maturity range or lower the rate.

Structured MTNs

At one time the typical MTN was a fixed-rate debenture that was noncallable. It is common today for issuers of MTNs to couple their offerings with transactions in the derivative markets (options, futures/forwards, swaps, caps, and floors) so as to create debt obligations with more interesting risk/return but sometimes complex features than are otherwise not available in the bond market. Specifically, an issue can have a floating-rate over all or part of the life of the security and the coupon reset formula can be based on a benchmark interest rate, equity index or individual stock price, a foreign exchange rate, or a commodity index. There are even MTNs with coupon reset formulas that vary inversely with a benchmark interest rate. MTNs can have various embedded options included.

MTNs created when the issuer simultaneously transacts in the derivative markets are called *structured notes*. By using the derivative markets in combination with an offering, borrowers are able to create investment vehicles that are more customized for institutional investors to satisfy their investment objectives, but who may be forbidden from using derivatives for hedging. Moreover, it allows institutional investors who are restricted to investing in investment grade debt issues the opportunity to participate in other asset classes to make a market play. Hence, structured notes are sometimes referred to as "rule busters." For example, an investor who buys an MTN whose coupon rate is tied to the performance of the S&P 500 is participating in the equity market without owning common stock. If the coupon rate is tied to a foreign stock market index, the investor is participating in the equity market of a foreign country without owning foreign common stock. In exchange for creating a structured note product, borrowers can reduce their funding costs.

Federal credit unions are permitted to invest in structured notes as long as the issuer is a federal agency and the features of the issue do not violate Part 703. For example, in the case of a floating-rate MTN, the coupon formula can only be based on a domestic interest rate index or LIBOR. State chartered credit unions can invest in issues by corporations if permitted by state statutes. However, it is important to keep in mind that while the credit risk associated with a structured note issued by a federal agency may be minimal, there can be substantial price risk for even a note that has a permissible reference rate. For example, a structured note can be a callable step-up note or a range note.

It must be emphasized that structured notes are complex financial instruments which require sophisticated analysis and insight. Generally speaking, the typical credit union can find superior value in many other areas of the bond market without needing to delve into structured notes.

ASSET-BACKED SECURITIES

Asset-backed securities are securities backed by one of the following types of loan obligations: (1) fully amortizing installment loans, (2) leases, (3) receivables, and (4) revolving lines of credit. Federal credit unions are not permitted to invest in asset-backed securities; whether state chartered federally insured credit unions are permitted to invest depends on state regulations governing these entities.

The two key features of an asset-backed security is its cash flow and its credit risk. We discuss each below.

Cash Flow

For asset-backed securities backed by installment loans, borrowers pay regularly scheduled monthly loan payments (interest and scheduled principal repayments) and may make prepayments. Thus, these securities are amortizing securities and they have an embedded option — the prepayment option. The two most common types of asset-backed securities are those backed by automobile loans and home equity loans.

For securities backed by automobile loans, prepayments result from: (1) sales and trade-ins requiring full payoff of the loan, (2) repossession and subsequent sale of the automobile, (3) loss or destruction of the vehicle, (4) payoff of the loan with cash to save interest cost, and (5) refinancing of the loan at a lower interest cost. Refinancings are of minor importance for automobile loans. Moreover, the interest rates for the automobile loans underlying several issues are substantially below market rates if they are offered by manufacturers as part of a sales promotion. There is good historical information on the other causes of prepayments. Therefore, the cash flow of securities backed by automobile loans do not have a great deal of uncertainty despite prepayments.

For asset-backed securities backed by home equity loans prepayments occur for the same reasons that we describe in the next two chapters for mortgage-backed securities. Unlike asset-backed securities backed by automobile loans, home equity loan-backed securities are affected by prepayments due to refinancings.

For credit card receivable asset-backed securities, interest is paid to holders of credit card-backed securities monthly. Most issues have a fixed interest rate, but there are floating-rate issues. In contrast to the other asset-backed securities just discussed, the principal is not amortized. Instead, for a specified period of time, referred to as the *lockout period*, the principal payments made by credit card borrowers are retained by the trustee and reinvested in additional receivables. After the lockout period, the principal is no longer reinvested but paid to investors. The lockout period can vary from 18 months to 10 years. There are provisions in credit card receivable-backed securities that requires earlier amortization of the principal if certain events occur. One such event is a significant increase in the losses on the underlying receivables.

Credit Risk

Asset-backed securities expose investors to credit risk. The nationally recognized statistical rating organizations that rate corporate and municipal debt issues also rate asset-backed securities. In analyzing the credit quality of the pool of loans, the rating companies look at whether the loans were properly originated, comply with consumer lending laws, the characteristics of the loans, and the underwriting standards used by the originator.

All asset-backed securities are credit enhanced. Credit enhancement is used to provide greater protection to investors against losses (i.e., defaults by the borrowers of the underlying loans). The amount of credit enhancement necessary depends on two factors. The first factor is the historical loss experience on similar loans made by the lender. The second factor is the rating sought by the issuer. For a given historical loss experience, more credit enhancement is needed to obtain a triple A rating than to obtain a single A rating.

Credit enhancement can take one or more of the following forms: third-party guarantees, reserve funds or cash collateral, recourse to the issuer, over collateralization, and senior/subordinated structures. A third-party guarantee can be either a letter of credit from a bank or a policy from an insurance company. The rating of the third-party guarantor must be at least as high as the rating sought. Thus, if the third-party guarantor has a single A rating, a triple A rating for the asset-backed security can not be obtained by using only this guarantee.

A reserve fund or cash collateral is a fund established by the issuer of the asset-backed security that may be used to make principal and interest payments when there are losses. Recourse to the issuer specifies that if there are losses, security holders can look to the investor to make up all or part of the losses.

Over collateralization involves establishing a pool of assets with a greater principal amount than the principal amount of the asset-backed securities. For example, the principal amount of an issue may be $100 million but the principal amount of the pool of assets is $102 million.

In a senior/subordinated structure two classes of asset-backed securities are issued. The senior class has priority over the subordinated class with respect to the payment of principal and interest from the pool of assets. Thus, it is the subordinated piece that accepts the greater credit risk and provides protection for the senior class. The protection is greater, the larger the amount of the principal of the subordinated class relative to the senior class. Thus, for a $100 million issue, greater protection against losses is afforded the senior class if the principal for that class is $70 million and the subordinated class is $30 than if it is $80 million for the senior class and $20 million for the subordinated class.

Today, the most common type of credit enhancement is the cash collateral and the senior/subordinated structure. In automobile loan-backed securities, credit enhancement typically consists of a combination of subordination, partially funded reserve account, and a mechanism to build in some over collateralization. The amount of credit enhancement necessary to obtain a particular credit rating is based on a cash flow analysis of the security structure undertaken by a commercial rating company from whom a rating is sought.[4]

---

[4] For a discussion of how one rating company, Fitch Investors Service, assesses the credit risk of an asset-backed security, see Mary Griffin Metz and Suzanne Mistretta, "Evaluating Credit Risk of Asset-Backed Securities," Chapter 27 in Frank J. Fabozzi (ed.), *The Handbook of Fixed Income Securities* (Burr Ridge, IL: Irwin Professional Publishing, 1995), p. 602.

CORPORATE CREDIT UNIONS

Corporate credit unions are entities which serve the investment and liquidity needs of natural person credit unions. They differ in their membership constituency from natural person credit unions, serving other credit unions as opposed to individual members. Their role in the credit union movement to date has been of critical importance, if not historic, in funding the prolific growth experienced by credit unions.

The corporate credit union system exists on a regional basis and is indigenous to almost every state in the country. In recent years, certain larger corporate credit unions have succeeded in expanding their field of membership beyond the confines of their own state border. This is reflective of increased national competition for servicing the investment needs of credit unions. Unfortunately, this competition was also the impetus for the largest credit union failure in history — Capital Corporate FCU — due to inappropriate investment practices by management.

This single feature did not go unnoticed by friendly and unfriendly competition of credit unions in the financial industry and in Congress. This has led to much stricter scrutiny of credit unions in general, and corporate credit unions in particular. The revisions to Part 703 for natural person credit unions and Part 704 for corporate credit unions are, without question, a regulatory response to the failure of Capital Corporate FCU and a direct outgrowth of the failure.

Prior to this failure, credit unions "assumed" all was well with their particular corporate credit union. The unfortunate losses borne by depositors and shareholders/owners of Capital Corporate FCU underscore the need for due diligence in all credit union practices, *not* just those investments *outside* their corporate. As stated by Steve Tolen, author of *Credit Union Investment Strategies*:[5]

> In dealing with corporate credit unions, the CU movement has a tradition of making exceptions to what would otherwise be considered prudent asset concentration levels. If a credit union decides to exceed normal asset concentration levels with *any* institution, it should make an effort to support that decision by performing a higher level of due diligence. This should include an analysis of the institutions credit quality. In the case of corporate credit unions that means assessing the investment portfolio, since a corporate credit union's credit depends largely on the quality of its investment portfolio. *Relying on ratings of corporate commercial paper issues (if any) can result in false conclusions.*" (original emphasis supplied — no emphasis added).

Corporate credit unions still serve a very vital role for credit unions across the country. Increased competition for short-term alternatives from banks

---

[5] Steve Tolen, *Credit Union Investment Strategies* (Madison, WI: Credit Union Executive Society, 1994), p. 14.

and other sources as well as the revision of Part 704 will place a strain on the corporate credit union system. However, their natural and historical role will not and should not diminish. Their convenience, cooperative spirit, and familiarity will always place them in an advantageous posture in the market. They are especially appropriate for the placement of overnight and short-term (less than six months) funds. Above all else, the overriding message must be that a natural person credit union has an unyielding fiduciary duty to the members it serves and should not allow the political affiliations of trade association membership by its management or board to cloud the basic rules of financial prudence and integrity in its evaluation of corporate credit union investment opportunities.

INVESTMENT COMPANY SHARES

Investment companies sell shares to the public and invest the proceeds in a diversified portfolio of securities. Each share that they sell represents a proportionate interest in a portfolio of securities. A federal credit union may invest in an investment company which is registered with the Securities and Exchange Commission under the Investment Company Act of 1940. However, the portfolio of the investment company is restricted to include investments that are permissible for federal credit unions. Part 703 only allows investment in such a company up to the capital of a credit union.

Types of Investment Companies

There are two types of investment companies: open-end funds and closed-end funds.

An *open-end fund*, more popularly referred to as a *mutual fund*, continually stands ready to sell new shares to the public and to redeem its outstanding shares on demand at a price equal to an appropriate share of the value of its portfolio, which is computed daily at the close of the market. A mutual fund's share price is based on its *net asset value (NAV) per share*, which is found by subtracting from the market value of the portfolio the mutual fund's liabilities and then dividing by the number of mutual fund shares outstanding.

Mutual fund shares are offered directly from the mutual fund company or through a broker on its behalf. Shares are quoted on a bid-offer basis. The *offer price* is the price at which the mutual fund will sell the shares. It is equal to the net asset value per share plus any sales commission that the mutual fund may charge. The sales commission is referred to as a "load." A *load fund* is one that tends to impose large commissions, typically ranging from 8.5% on small amounts invested down to 1% on amounts of $500,000 or over. A mutual fund that does not impose a sales commission is called a *no-load fund*. No-load mutual funds compete directly with load funds and appeal to investors who object to paying a commission (particularly because there is no empirical evidence that suggests that load funds have outperformed no-load funds after accounting for the load charge). The relative attraction of no-load funds has forced many mutual funds to convert to no-load status. (Some funds have adopted a so-called "low-load" strategy, that is, charging a relatively small load of around 3%-3.5% and proportionately small loads below 1% for amounts of $500,000 to $1 million or more.) For no-load funds, the offer price is the same as the net asset value per share.

In contrast to mutual funds, closed-end funds sell shares like any other corporation and usually do not redeem their shares. Shares of closed-end funds sell on either an organized exchange, such as the New York Stock Exchange, or in the over-the-counter market. The price of a share in a closed-end fund is determined by supply and demand, so the price can fall below or rise above the net asset value per share.

Structure and Expenses of a Fund

A fund is structured with a board of directors, a financial advisor responsible for managing the portfolio, and a distributing and selling organization. Funds enter into contracts with a financial advisor to manage the fund, typically, a company that specializes in the management of funds.

The financial advisor to the fund charges a *management fee*, also called an *investment advisory fee*. Funds incur other costs in addition to the management fee. These include the expenses for maintaining shareholder records, providing shareholders with financial statements, custodial and accounting services. These expenses are referred to as *other expenses* in the industry. The management fee and other expenses are referred to as *annual fund operating expenses*.

The annual fund operating expenses must be specified in the prospectus. The management fee is known. How much the other expenses will be are not known. However, an estimate is provided in the prospectus based on the fund's historical expenses. For credit unions, the evaluation of the fee structure is an essential prerequisite to placing investment dollars in any type of fund. Furthermore, a credit union should seek advice, if necessary, to determine if the funds shouldn't be placed directly instead of paying fees to the fund.

KEY POINTS

1. The four nationally recognized statistical rating organizations that rate all types of debt are (1) Duff and Phelps Credit Rating Co., (2) Fitch Investors Service, (3) Moody's Investors Service, and (4) Standard & Poor's Corporation.

2. Two nationally recognized statistical rating organizations that primarily rate only banks are Thomson BankWatch and IBCA Ltd.

3. Investment grade bonds are issues that are assigned a rating in the top four categories while those rated below the top four categories are referred to as non-investment grade bonds.

4. U.S. Treasury coupon securities include notes and bonds and these securities do not expose investors to credit risk.

5. STRIPS are zero-coupon Treasury securities created by dealers and do not expose investors to credit risk.

6. Federal agencies are categorized as either federally related institutions or government sponsored enterprises.

7. Those federal agencies that provide credit for the housing market issue debentures and mortgage-backed securities.

8. Federally related institutions are arms of the federal government and generally do not issue securities directly in the marketplace.

9. With the exception of securities of the Private Export Funding Corporation and the Tennessee Valley Authority, federally related institution securities are backed by the full faith and credit of the United States government.

10. Government sponsored enterprises (GSEs) are privately owned, publicly chartered entities that were created by Congress to reduce the cost of capital for certain borrowing sectors of the economy deemed to be important enough to warrant assistance.

11. The five GSEs that issue debentures are the Federal Farm Credit System, Federal Home Loan Bank System, Federal National Mortgage Association, Federal Home Loan Bank Corporation, and Student Loan Marketing Association.

12. In general, GSEs issue two types of debentures: discount notes (short-term obligations with maturities ranging from overnight to 360 days issued on a discount basis) and bonds (which have maturities greater than 2 years).

13. There are GSE issues with bullet maturities and those with call provisions as well as structured notes.

14. With the exception of the securities issued by the Farm Credit Financial Assistance Corporation, GSE securities are not backed by the full faith and credit of the U.S. government, and therefore expose investors to credit risk.

15. Municipal securities are issued by state and local governments and their authorities, with the coupon interest on most issues being exempt from federal income taxes.

16. Credit unions are permitted to invest in municipal securities if the issue is rated in the top two ratings.

17. Because credit unions do not benefit from the tax advantage of tax-exempt municipal bonds, investments in this sector should be restricted to taxable municipal bonds.

18. There are basically two types of municipal security structures: tax-backed debt and revenue bonds.

19. Tax-backed debt obligations are instruments issued by states, counties, special districts, cities, towns, and school districts that are secured by some form of tax revenue.

20. Tax-backed debt includes general obligation debt (the broadest type of tax-backed debt), appropriation-backed obligations (moral obligation bonds and lease-backed bonds), debt obligations supported by public credit enhancement programs, and short-term debt instruments.

21. An unlimited tax general obligation debt is secured by the issuer's unlimited taxing power where the tax revenue sources include corporate and individual income taxes, sales taxes, and property taxes, and such issues are said to be secured by the full faith and credit of the issuer.

22. A limited tax general obligation debt is a limited tax pledge because for such debt there is a statutory limit on tax rates that the issuer may levy to service the debt.

23. A general obligation bond is said to be double-barreled in security when it is secured not only by the issuer's general taxing powers to create revenues accumulated in a general fund, but also by certain identified fees, grants, and special charges, which provide additional revenues from outside the general fund.

24. A moral obligation bond is a bond issued by an agency or authority that carries a nonbinding pledge by the state for making up shortfalls in the issuing entities obligation if approved by the state legislature.

25. A public credit enhancement obligation is one in which there is a guarantee by the state or a federal agency or when there is an obligation to automatically withhold and deploy state aid to pay any defaulted debt service by the issuing entity.

26. Short-term debt instruments include municipal notes, commercial paper, variable-rate demand obligations, and a hybrid of the last two products.

27. Municipal notes include bond anticipation notes (BANs) and cash flow notes (tax anticipation notes (TANs), revenue anticipation notes (RANs), and TRANs).

28. There are two types of commercial paper issued by municipalities: unenhanced commercial paper (a debt obligation issued based solely on the issuer's credit quality and liquidity capability) and enhanced commercial paper (a debt obligation that is credit enhanced with bank liquidity facilities, insurance, or a bond purchase agreement).

29. Variable-rate demand obligations (VRDOs) are floating-rate obligations that have a nominal long-term maturity but have a coupon rate that is either reset daily or every seven days with an option to put the issue back to the trustee at any time with seven days notice.

30. Revenue bonds are issued for enterprise financings that are secured by the revenues generated by the completed projects themselves, or for general public-purpose financings in which the issuers pledge to the bondholders the tax and revenue resources that were previously part of the general fund.

31. Typically taxable municipal bonds are insured bonds, that is, bonds that are in addition to being secured by the issuer's revenue, are backed by insurance policies written by commercial insurance companies.

32. There are three basic types of bank support: letter of credit, irrevocable line or credit, and revolving line of credit.

33. Refunded bonds are no longer secured as either general obligation or revenue bonds but are supported by a portfolio of securities held in an escrow fund and if escrowed with securities guaranteed by the U.S. government, refunded bonds are the safest municipal bond investments available.

34. In assessing the credit risk of a municipal security, investors typically rely on the credit ratings that are assigned by the nationally recognized statistically rating organizations, the two dominant companies in rating municipal securities being Standard & Poor's and Moody's.

35. In assessing the credit risk of tax-backed debt, the following four basic informational categories should be considered: (1) information on the issuer's debt structure to determine the overall debt burden; (2) information on the issuer's ability and political discipline to maintain sound budgetary policy; (3) information on the specific local taxes and intergovernmental revenues available to the issuer; and (4) information on the issuer's overall socioeconomic environment.

36. While Standard & Poor's and Moody's use the four informational categories in arriving at their respective credit ratings of general obligation bonds, there are major differences in their respective approaches toward these four categories.

37. While there are numerous security structures for revenue bonds, the underlying principle in rating is whether the project being financed will generate sufficient cash flow to satisfy the obligations due bondholders.

38. Bank obligations include non-negotiable CDs, negotiable bank CDs, deposit notes, and bank notes.

39. Non-negotiable CDs such as $100,000 or jumbo CDs are fully insured as to the return of the principal and interest invested up to $100,000.

40. Negotiable CDs, deposit notes, and banks are marketable instruments but expose a credit union to credit risk.

41. There is a trade-off between the higher yield and marketability provided by investing in negotiable CDs, deposit notes, and bank notes, and credit risk.

42. In its proposed revision to Part 703, The NCUA cites a minimum acceptable credit rating of B/C (or its equivalent) for bank obligations in excess of $100,000.

43. Deposit notes are exactly like a negotiable bank CDs except for the fact that the interest is accrued on a 30/360 basis.

44. Bank notes are senior, unsecured obligations of a bank (not a bank holding company), pay interest on a 30/360 basis, and rank *pari passu* with uninsured depositors of the bank.

45. For a bank note to be a permissible investment, the NCUA requires that it meet several criteria including the stipulation that it must qualify as a deposit under the Federal Reserves' Regulation D.

46. Corporate bonds are obligations of corporations in which federal credit unions may not invest but in which state chartered credit unions might be able to invest.

47. While in theory when a company is reorganized, creditors receive distributions based on the "absolute priority rule" to the extent assets are available, in most instances this rule is violated.

48. A medium-term note (MTN) is a debt instrument with the unique characteristic that notes are offered continuously to investors by an agent of the issuer and investors can select from several maturity ranges.

49. Structured notes are created when issuers couple their offering with transactions in the derivative markets to create medium-term notes with coupon rates that depend on various economic or financial outcomes.

50. While a structured note may be issued by a federal agency and have permissible features, a credit union is still exposed to price risk if the note must be sold prior to the maturity date.

51. Investments in corporate credit unions need to be treated with the same due diligence as any other credit union investment.

52. A share of an investment company represents a proportionate interest in a portfolio of securities.

53. A federal credit union may invest in an investment company which is registered with the SEC if the investment company's portfolio is restricted to include investments that are permissible for federal credit unions.

54. There are two types of investment companies: open-end funds and closed-end funds.

Chapter 5

Mortgage Passthrough Securities

The objectives of this chapter are to:

1. explain what a mortgage loan is;

2. describe the different types of mortgage loans;

3. describe the cash flow of a mortgage loan;

4. explain what prepayments are;

5. explain what is meant by prepayment risk;

6. explain what a mortgage passthrough security is;

7. explain the investment characteristics of mortgage passthrough securities;

8. describe the different types of agency passthrough securities and their features;

9. explain the importance of prepayments to the estimation of the cash flow of a passthrough security;

10. describe the industry convention for determining the cash flow of a passthrough security;

11. understand why the particular form of prepayment risk that a credit union faces is extension risk; and,

12. explain what is meant by the average life of a mortgage-backed security.

Mortgage-backed securities are securities backed by a pool of mortgage loans. Mortgage-backed securities include the following securities: (1) mortgage passthrough securities, (2) collateralized mortgage obligations, and (3) stripped mortgage-backed securities. The latter two mortgage-backed securities are referred to as *derivative mortgage-backed securities* because they are created from mortgage passthrough securities. Part 703 permits credit unions to invest in mortgage passthrough securities and collateralized mortgage obligations that pass certain stress tests. Credit unions, however, are not permitted to invest in stripped mortgage-backed securities. In this chapter, we will discuss the various types of mortgage passthrough securities. The next chapter covers collateralized mortgage obligations. Chapter 7 covers the stress tests that a credit union is required to perform.

MORTGAGE LOANS

Mortgage loans are the raw material for the creation of mortgage-backed securities. A mortgage loan is a loan secured by the collateral of some specified real estate property which obliges the borrower to make a predetermined series of payments. The mortgage gives the lender the right, if the borrower defaults (i.e. fails to make the contracted payments), to "foreclose" on the loan and seize the property in order to ensure that the debt is paid off.

The types of real estate properties that can be mortgaged are divided into two broad categories: residential and non-residential properties. The former category includes houses, condominiums, cooperatives, and apartments. Residential real estate can be subdivided into single-family (one-to-four family) residences and multifamily residences (apartment buildings in which more than four families reside). Non-residential property includes commercial and farm properties. Our focus in this chapter is on single-family residential mortgage loans since these are the only types of mortgage loans in which a credit union may invest. Specifically, Part 703 prohibits credit unions from investing in commercial loans and mortgage-backed securities backed by such loans.

Types of Mortgage Loans

There are many types of mortgage designs available in the United States. A mortgage design is a specification of the interest rate, term of the mortgage, and the manner in which the borrowed funds are repaid. Below we describe the three most popular mortgage designs: (1) the fixed-rate level-payment fully amortized mortgage, (2) the adjustable-rate mortgage, and (3) the balloon mortgage. These mortgage loans are amortizing instruments.

Fixed-Rate Level-Payment Fully Amortized Mortgage The interest rate on the mortgage loan is called the *mortgage rate* or the *contract rate*. The basic idea behind the design of the fixed-rate level-payment fully amortized mortgage (fixed-rate level-payment mortgage hereafter) is that the borrower pays interest and repays principal in equal installments over an agreed-upon period of time, called the maturity or term of the mortgage. Thus at the end of the term, the loan has been fully amortized. The frequency of payment is typically monthly, and the prevailing term of the mortgage is typically from 15 to 30 years.

Each monthly mortgage payment for a fixed-rate level-payment mortgage is due on the first of each month and consists of:

1. interest of $\frac{1}{12}$ of the fixed annual interest rate times the amount of the outstanding mortgage balance at the beginning of the previous month, and
2. a repayment of a portion of the outstanding mortgage balance.

The difference between the monthly mortgage payment and the portion of the payment that represents interest equals the amount that is applied to reduce the outstanding mortgage balance. The monthly mortgage payment is designed so that after the last scheduled monthly payment of the loan is made, the amount of the outstanding mortgage balance is zero (i.e. the mortgage is fully repaid).

To illustrate a fixed-rate level-payment mortgage, consider a 30-year (360-month), $100,000 mortgage with an 8.125% mortgage rate. The monthly mortgage payment would be $742.50. Exhibit 1 shows for selected months how each monthly mortgage payment is divided between interest and repayment of principal. At the beginning of month 1, the mortgage balance is $100,000, the amount of the original loan. The mortgage payment for month 1 includes interest on the $100,000 borrowed for the month. Since the interest rate is 8.125%, the monthly interest rate is 0.0067708 (0.08125 divided by 12). Interest for month 1 is therefore $677.08 ($100,000 times 0.0067708). The $65.41 difference between the monthly mortgage payment of $742.50 and the interest of $677.08 is the portion of the monthly mortgage payment that represents repayment of principal. This $65.41 in month 1 reduces the mortgage balance.

The mortgage balance at the end of month 1 (beginning of month 2) is then $99,934.59 ($100,000 minus $65.41). The interest for the second monthly mortgage payment is $676.64, the monthly interest rate (0.0066708) times the mortgage balance at the beginning of month 2 ($99,934.59). The difference between the $742.50 monthly mortgage payment and the $676.64 interest is $65.86, representing the amount of the mortgage balance paid off with that monthly mortgage payment. Notice that the last mortgage payment in month 360 is sufficient to pay off the remaining mortgage balance.

As Exhibit 1 clearly shows, *the portion of the monthly mortgage payment applied to interest declines each month and the portion applied to reducing the mortgage balance increases.* The reason for this is that as the mortgage balance is reduced with each monthly mortgage payment, the interest on the mortgage balance declines. Since the monthly mortgage payment is fixed, an increasingly larger portion of the monthly payment is applied to reduce the principal in each subsequent month.

Exhibit 1: Amortization Schedule for a Fixed-Rate Level-Payment Mortgage

Mortgage loan: $100,000
Mortgage rate: 8.125%
Monthly payment: $742.50
Term of loan: 30 years (360 months)

	Beginning of Month Mortgage Balance	Mortgage Payment	Scheduled Repayment	Interest	End of Month Mortgage Balance
1	$100,000.00	$742.50	$677.08	$65.41	$99,934.59
2	99,934.59	742.50	676.64	65.86	99,868.73
3	99,868.73	742.50	676.19	66.30	99,802.43
4	99,802.43	742.50	675.75	66.75	99,735.68
25	98,301.53	742.50	665.58	76.91	98,224.62
26	98,224.62	742.50	665.06	77.43	98,147.19
27	98,147.19	742.50	664.54	77.96	98,069.23
74	93,849.98	742.50	635.44	107.05	93,742.93
75	93,742.93	742.50	634.72	107.78	93,635.15
76	93,635.15	742.50	633.99	108.51	93,526.64
141	84,811.77	742.50	574.25	168.25	84,643.52
142	84,643.52	742.50	573.11	169.39	84,474.13
143	84,474.13	742.50	571.96	170.54	84,303.59
184	76,446.29	742.50	517.61	224.89	76,221.40
185	76,221.40	742.50	516.08	226.41	75,994.99
186	75,994.99	742.50	514.55	227.95	75,767.04
233	63,430.19	742.50	429.48	313.02	63,117.17
234	63,117.17	742.50	427.36	315.14	62,802.03
235	62,802.03	742.50	425.22	317.28	62,484.75
289	42,200.92	742.50	285.74	456.76	41,744.15
290	41,744.15	742.50	282.64	459.85	41,284.30
291	41,284.30	742.50	279.53	462.97	40,821.33
321	25,941.42	742.50	175.65	566.85	25,374.57
322	25,374.57	742.50	171.81	570.69	24,803.88
323	24,803.88	742.50	167.94	574.55	24,229.32
358	2,197.66	742.50	14.88	727.62	1,470.05
359	1,470.05	742.50	9.95	732.54	737.50
360	737.50	742.50	4.99	737.50	0.00

Adjustable-Rate Mortgages An adjustable-rate mortgage (ARM) is a loan in which the mortgage rate is reset periodically based on some reference rate. This mortgage design represents an approach applied to many other instruments, such as bank loans. By using a reference rate that is a short-term rate, depository institutions are able to improve the matching of their returns to their cost of funds.

Outstanding ARMs call for resetting the mortgage rate either every month, six months, year, two years, three years or five years. In recent years ARMs typically have had reset periods of six months, one year or five years. The mortgage rate at the reset date is equal to a reference rate plus a spread. The spread is typically between 125 and 200 basis points, reflecting market conditions, and the features of the ARM.

Two categories of reference rates have been used in ARMs: (1) market-determined rates and (2) calculated rates based on the cost of funds for thrifts. Market-determined rates have been limited to Treasury-based rates. The reference rate will have an important impact on the performance of an ARM and how they are priced.

Cost of funds index for thrifts are calculated based on the monthly weighted average interest cost for liabilities of thrifts. The most popular is the Eleventh Federal Home Loan Bank Board District Cost of Funds Index (COFI). The Eleventh District includes the states of California, Arizona, and Nevada. The cost of funds is calculated by first computing the monthly interest expenses for all thrifts included in the Eleventh District. The interest expenses are summed and then divided by the average of the beginning and ending monthly balance. The index value is reported with a one month lag. For example, June's Eleventh District COFI is reported in July. The mortgage rate for a mortgage based on the Eleventh District COFI is usually reset based on the previous month's reported index rate. For example, if the reset date is August, the index rate reported in July will be used to set the mortgage rate. Consequently, there is a two month lag by the time the average cost of funds is reflected in the mortgage rate. This obviously is an advantage to the borrower when interest rates are rising and a disadvantage to the investor. The opposite is true when interest rates are falling.

A pure ARM is one that resets periodically and has no other terms that affect the monthly mortgage payment. However, the monthly mortgage payment, and hence, the investor's cash flow, are affected by other terms. These are due to (1) periodic caps and (2) lifetime rate caps and floors. Periodic caps limit the amount that the mortgage rate may increase or decrease at the reset date. The periodic rate cap is expressed in percentage points. The most common rate cap on annual reset loans is 2%. Most ARMs have an upper limit on the mortgage rate that can be charged over the life of the loan. This lifetime loan cap is expressed in terms of the initial rate, the most common lifetime cap being 5% to 6%. For example, if the initial mortgage rate is 7% and the lifetime cap is 5%, the maximum interest rate that the lender can charge over the life of the loan is 12%. Many ARMs also have a lower limit (floor) on the interest rate that can be charged over the life of the loan.

Balloon Mortgages A *balloon mortgage* is one in which the borrower is given long-term financing by the lender but at specified future dates the mortgage rate is renegotiated. Thus, the lender is providing long-term funds for what is effectively a short-term borrowing, how short depending on the frequency of the renegotiation period. Effectively it is a short-term balloon loan in which the lender or other entity agrees to provide financing for the remainder of the term of the mortgage. The balloon payment is the original amount borrowed less the amount amortized.

Servicing and the Cash Flow

Every mortgage loan must be serviced. Servicing of a mortgage loan involves collecting monthly payments and forwarding proceeds to owners of the loan; sending payment notices to mortgagors; reminding mortgagors when payments are overdue; maintaining records of principal balances; administering an escrow balance for real estate taxes and insurance purposes; initiating foreclosure proceedings if necessary; and, furnishing tax information to mortgagors when applicable.

The servicer of the mortgage loan must be compensated. The compensation is a portion of the mortgage's contract rate. For example, the servicing fee may be 50 basis points. Consequently, the interest rate that the investor receives is the contract rate less the servicing fee. So, for example, if the contract rate is 8.125% and the servicing fee is 0.5% (50 basis points), the interest rate that the investor receives is 7.625%.

Prepayments and Cash Flow Uncertainty

Our illustration of the cash flow from a fixed-rate level-payment mortgage assumes that the homeowner does not pay off any portion of the mortgage balance prior to the scheduled due date. But homeowners do pay off all or part of their mortgage balance prior to the maturity date. Payments made in excess of the scheduled principal repayments are called *prepayments.*

Prepayments occur for one of several reasons. First, homeowners prepay the entire mortgage when they sell their home. The sale of a home may occur because of (1) a change of employment that necessitates moving, (2) the purchase of a more expensive home ("trading up"), or (3) a divorce in which the settlement requires sale of the marital residence. Second, the borrower may be moved to pay off part of the mortgage balance as market rates fall below the mortgage rate. Third, in the case of homeowners who cannot meet their mortgage obligations, the property is repossessed and sold. The proceeds of such a sale are used to pay off the mortgage in the case of a conventional mortgage. For an insured mortgage, the insurer will pay off the mortgage balance. Finally, if property is destroyed by fire or if another insured catastrophe occurs, the insurance proceeds are used to pay off the mortgage. We'll look more closely at the factors that affect prepayment behavior in Chapter 7.

The effect of prepayments is that the amount and timing of the cash flow from a mortgage is not known with certainty. This risk is referred to as *prepayment risk*. For example, all that the investor in a $100,000, 8.125% 30-year FHA-insured mortgage knows is that as long as the loan is outstanding, interest will be received and the principal will be repaid at the scheduled date each month; then at the end of the 30 years, the investor would have received $100,000 in principal payments. What the investor does not know — the uncertainty — is for how long the loan will be outstanding, and therefore what the timing of the principal payments will be. This is true for all mortgage loans, not just fixed-rate level-payment mortgages.

Thus, the monthly cash flow of a mortgage is equal to:

1. net interest (i.e., interest after servicing fee);
2. regularly scheduled principal repayment; and,
3. prepayments.

Credit Risk

The two primary factors in determining whether the funds will be lent are the (1) *payment-to-income* (PTI) ratio, and (2) the *loan-to-value* (LTV) ratio. The former is the ratio of monthly payments to monthly income and is a measure of the ability of the applicant to make monthly payments (both mortgage and real estate tax payments). The lower this ratio, the greater the likelihood that the applicant will be able to meet the required payments.

The difference between the purchase price of the property and the amount borrowed is the borrower's down payment. The LTV is the ratio of the amount of the loan to the market (or appraised) value of the property. The lower this ratio, the greater the protection the lender has if the applicant defaults on the payments and the lender must repossess and sell the property. For example, if an applicant wants to borrow $150,000 on property with an appraised value of $200,000, the LTV is 75%. Suppose the applicant subsequently defaults on the mortgage. The lender can then repossess the property and sell it to recover the amount owed. But the amount that will be received by the lender depends on the market value of the property. In our example, even if conditions in the housing market are weak, the lender will still be able to recover the proceeds lent if the value of the property declines by $50,000. Suppose instead that the applicant wanted to borrow $180,000 for the same property. The LTV would then be 90%. If the lender had to sell the property because the applicant defaults, there is less protection for the lender.

When the lender makes the loan based on the credit of the borrower and on the collateral for the mortgage, the mortgage is said to be a *conventional mortgage*. The lender also may take out mortgage insurance to guarantee the fulfillment of the borrower's obligations. The cost of mortgage insurance is paid to the guarantor by the mortgage originator, but it is passed along to the borrower in the form of higher mortgage payments.

There are two types of mortgage-related insurance. The first type is originated by the lender to insure against default by the borrower and is called *mort-*

gage insurance. It is usually required by lenders on loans with loan-to-value (LTV) ratios greater than 80%. The amount insured will be some percentage of the loan and may decline as the LTV ratio declines. While the insurance is required by the lender, the cost of the insurance is borne by the borrower, usually through a higher contract rate.

There are two forms of mortgage insurance: insurance provided by a government agency and private mortgage insurance. The federal agencies that provide this insurance to qualified borrowers are the Federal Housing Administration (FHA), the Veterans Administration (VA), and the Federal Farmers Administration (FmHA). Private mortgage insurance can be obtained from a mortgage insurance company.

The second type of mortgage-related insurance is acquired by the borrower, usually with a life insurance company, and is typically called *credit life*. Unlike mortgage insurance, this type is not required by the lender. The policy provides for a continuation of mortgage payments after the death of the insured person, which allows the survivors to continue living in the house. Since the insurance coverage decreases as the mortgage balance declines, this type of mortgage insurance is simply a term policy.

While both types of insurance have a beneficial effect on the creditworthiness of the borrower, the first type is more important from the lender's perspective. Mortgage insurance is sought by the lender when the borrower is viewed as being capable of meeting the monthly mortgage payments, but does not have enough funds for a large down payment. For example, suppose a borrower seeks financing of $100,000 to purchase a single-family residence for $110,000, thus making a down payment of $10,000. The LTV ratio is 90.9%, exceeding the uninsured maximum LTV of 80%. Even if the lender's credit analysis indicates that the borrower's PTI is acceptable, the mortgage loan cannot be extended. However, if a private mortgage insurance company insures a portion of the loan, then the lender is afforded protection. Mortgage insurance companies will write policies to insure a maximum of 20% of loans with an LTV ranging from 80% to 90%, and a maximum of 25% of loans with an LTV ranging from 90% to 95%. The lender is still exposed to default by the borrower on the noninsured portion of the mortgage loan and, in the case of private mortgage insurers, exposed to the risk that the insurer will default.

MORTGAGE PASSTHROUGH SECURITIES

A *mortgage passthrough security* is created when one or more holders of mortgages form a collection (pool) of mortgages and sell shares or participation certificates in the pool. A pool may consist of several thousand or only a few mortgages.

The three major types of passthrough securities are guaranteed by agencies created by Congress to increase the supply of capital to the residential mortgage market and to provide support for an active secondary market: Government National Mortgage Association ("Ginnie Mae"), Federal Home Loan Mortgage Corporation ("Freddie Mac"), and Federal National Mortgage Association ("Fannie Mae"). The securities associated with these three entities are known as *agency passthrough securities*.

While Fannie Mae and Freddie Mac are commonly referred to as "agencies" of the U.S. government, as explained in Chapter 4, both are corporate instrumentalities of the U.S. government. That is, they are government sponsored enterprises. Their guarantee does not carry the full faith and credit of the U.S. government. In contrast, Ginnie Mae is a federally related institution because it is part of the Department of Housing and Urban Development. As such, its guarantee carries the full faith and credit of the U.S. government.

There are also *nonagency passthroughs*. These securities do not carry the implicit or explicit guarantee of the U.S. government. They are issued by private entities such as Citibank and the Residential Funding Corporation. Credit Unions are permitted to invest in nonagency passthroughs as long as they qualify in terms of the tests explained in Chapter 7 and they are rated in at least the top two rating categories. To obtain a rating, the issuer must enhance the credit. The credit enhancement mechanisms described in the previous chapter for asset-backed securities have been used for nonagency passthroughs.

The cash flow of a mortgage passthrough security depends on the cash flow of the underlying mortgages. As we explained in the previous section, the cash flow consists of monthly mortgage payments representing interest, the scheduled repayment of principal, and any prepayments.

Payments are made to security holders each month. The monthly cash flow for a passthrough is less than the monthly cash flow of the underlying mortgages by an amount equal to the servicing fee and other fees. The other fees are those charged by the issuer or guarantor of the passthrough for guaranteeing the issue (discussed later). The coupon rate on a passthrough, called the *passthrough coupon rate*, is less than the mortgage rate on the underlying pool of mortgage loans by an amount equal to the servicing and guaranteeing fees.

Not all of the mortgages that are included in a pool of mortgages that are securitized have the same mortgage rate and the same maturity. Consequently, when describing a passthrough security, a weighted average coupon rate and a weighted average maturity are determined. A *weighted average coupon rate*, or WAC, is found by weighting the mortgage rate of each mortgage loan in the pool by the amount of the mortgage outstanding. A *weighted average maturity*, or WAM, is found by weighting the remaining number of months to maturity for each mortgage loan in the pool by the amount of the mortgage outstanding.

Features of Agency Passthroughs

Features of agency passthroughs vary not only by agency but also by program offered. The key features of a passthrough will have an impact on its prepayment characteristics. These general features, summarized below and discussed further when we review the various agency programs, can be classified into five groups: (1) the type of guarantee, (2) the numbers of lenders whose mortgage loans are permitted in a pool, (3) the mortgage design of the loans, (4) the characteristics of the mortgage loans in the pools, and (5) the payment procedure.

Type of Guarantee An agency can provide two types of guarantees. One type of guarantee is the timely payment of both interest and principal, meaning the interest and principal will be paid when due, even if any of the mortgagors fail to make their monthly mortgage payments. Passthroughs with this type of guarantee are referred to as *fully-modified passthroughs*. The second type guarantees both interest and principal payments; however, it only guarantees the timely payment of interest. The scheduled principal is passed through as it is collected with a guarantee that the scheduled payment will be made no later than a specified date. Passthroughs with this type of guarantee are called *modified passthroughs*.

Number of Lenders Permitted in a Pool A pool may consist of mortgages originated by a single lender or multiple lenders. A single-lender pool has mortgage loans concentrated in one geographical area or a few states. In multiple-lender pools, the underlying mortgage loans have a greater geographical diversification of borrowers.

Mortgage Design of the Loans Earlier in this chapter, we described different types of mortgage designs. Agency passthroughs have pools of loans with various mortgage designs.

Characteristics of the Mortgage Loans in the Pool Not all mortgage loans are permitted in a pool that collateralizes a passthrough. The underwriting standards established by the agency specify the permissible loans. These key underwriting standards are summarized below.

> *Mortgage Loans Permitted in the Pool:* Mortgage loans can be classified as government-insured loans and conventional loans.
> *Maximum Size of a Loan:* For agency securities, the loan limits are reset annually.
> *Amount of Seasoning Permitted:* The seasoning of a mortgage loan refers to the time which has passed since the loan was originated.
> *Assumability of Mortgages:* If a mortgage loan may be taken over by another borrower, the loan is said to be assumable.
> *Maturity:* Programs are available with mortgage loans of different maturities. For example, a pool can have a stated maturity of 30 years, even though not all of the mortgage loans in the pool have a maturity of 30 years, since seasoned loans may be included.

Net Interest Spread Permitted: The contract rate on a mortgage loan is also called the coupon rate or gross coupon rate. The net coupon rate is the difference between the coupon rate and fees for servicing and agency guarantee. The net interest spread that is permitted for a mortgage loan to qualify for inclusion in a pool varies.

Payment Procedure Differences in payment procedures involve payment delays and the method of payment. Payment delays for passthroughs occur for two reasons. First, monthly mortgage payments made by homeowners are made in arrears. That is, the payment for the funds borrowed in, say, March are due on the first of the month of April, the normal delay when investing in mortgage loans. When the payments are received, they must be processed and the checks mailed to passthrough investors. The actual delay for passthrough investors — that is, the number of days that payment is delayed beyond the normal delay — varies with the agency and agency program. The "stated delay" of a passthrough is the normal delay plus the actual delay. If the payment is made on the 15th of the month, then the actual delay is 14 days, since the monthly payment would have been due on the first of the month. If the stated delay for a passthrough is 44 days, then the actual delay is 14 days.

By method of payment, we mean how many monthly checks an investor who owns several pools of an agency passthrough will receive. There can be either one check for all pools or multiple checks.

Government National Mortgage Association MBS
Ginnie Mae passthroughs are guaranteed by the full faith and credit of the U.S. government. For this reason, Ginnie Mae passthroughs are viewed as risk-free in terms of credit risk, just like Treasury securities. The security guaranteed by Ginnie Mae is called a *mortgage-backed security* (MBS). Ginnie Mae MBSs are issued under one of two programs: GNMA I and GNMA II.

Type of Guarantee All Ginnie Mae MBS are fully modified passthroughs.

Number of Lenders Permitted in a Pool Only single-lender pools are permitted under the GNMA I program; both single-lender and multiple-lender pools are allowed in the GNMA II program. Single-lender pools issued under the GNMA II program are called *custom pools*; multiple-lender pools are called *jumbo pools*.

Mortgage Design of the Loans Under the two programs, passthroughs with different types of mortgage designs are issued. The large majority of GNMA MBS are backed by single-family mortgages, where a single-family mortgage is a loan for a 1-to-4 family primary residence with a fixed-rate level-payment mortgage. A Ginnie Mae MBS of this type is referred to as a "GNMA SF MBS." All GNMA ARMs are issued within the GNMA II program.

Characteristics of the Mortgage Loans in the Pool The key underwriting standards for the mortgage loans are summarized below.

> *Mortgage Loans Permitted in the Pool:* Only mortgage loans insured or guaranteed by either the Federal Housing Administration, the Veterans Administration or the Farmers Home Administration can be included in a mortgage pool guaranteed by Ginnie Mae.
>
> *Maximum Size of a Loan:* The maximum loan size is set by Congress, based on the maximum amount that the FHA, VA, or FmHA may guarantee. The maximum for a given loan varies with the region of the country and type of residential property. At the time of this writing, the maximum FHA loan is $124,875 for regions of the country designated as high cost regions; for a VA loan it is $144,000.
>
> *Amount of Seasoning Permitted:* In both programs, only newly originated mortgage loans may be included in a pool. These are defined as mortgage loans that have been seasoned less than 24 months.
>
> *Assumability of Mortgages:* Assumable mortgages are permitted in a GNMA pool.
>
> *Maturity:* Within the single-family MBS, there are pools that consist of 30-year and 15-year mortgages that collateralize the security. The 15-year pools are commonly referred to as "midgets."
>
> *Net Spread Permitted:* In the GNMA I program, the net interest spread permitted is 50 basis points; for the GNMA II program, the net interest spread may vary from 50 to 150 basis points.

Payment Procedure The stated delay for GNMA I and II programs are 45 and 50 days, respectively. Thus, corresponding actual delays are 14 and 19 days. The method of payment also differs for the two programs. In the GNMA I program, payments are made by the individual servicers. In the GNMA II program, payments from all pools owned by an investor are consolidated and paid in one check by the central paying agent, Chemical Bank.

Federal Home Loan Mortgage Corporation PC

The second type of agency passthrough is that issued by Freddie Mac, called a *participation certificate* (PC). Although a guarantee of Freddie Mac is not a guarantee by the U.S. government, most market participants view Freddie Mac PCs as similar, although not identical, in creditworthiness to Ginnie Mae passthroughs.

Freddie Mac has two programs from which it creates PCs: the Cash Program and the Guarantor/Swap Program. The underlying loans for both programs are conventional mortgages (i.e., mortgages not backed by a government agency). In the cash program the mortgages that back the PC include individual conventional one- to four-family mortgage loans that Freddie Mac purchases from mortgage originators, pools, and sells. Under the Guarantor/Swap Program, Freddie Mac allows originators to swap pooled mortgages for PCs backed by those mortgages. For example, a thrift may have $50 million of mortgages. It can swap these mortgages for a Freddie Mac PC whose underlying mortgage pool is the $50 million mortgage pool the thrift swapped for the PC. The PCs created under the first program are called *Cash PCs* or *Regular PCs*, under the second program they are called *Swap PCs*.

Type of Guarantee Freddie Mac offers both modified passthroughs and fully modified passthroughs. Non-Gold PCs that have been issued as part of its Cash program and almost all that have been issued as part of the Guarantor/Swap program are modified passthroughs. There are a very small number of non-Gold PCs in the latter program that are fully modified passthroughs. All Gold PCs issued are fully modified passthroughs.

For modified PCs issued by Freddie Mac, the scheduled principal is passed through as it is collected, with Freddie Mac only guaranteeing that the scheduled payment will be made no later than one year after it is due.

Number of Lenders Permitted in a Pool There are only multiple-lender pools in the Cash program. In the Guarantor/Swap program, there are both single-lender and multiple-lender pools.

Mortgage Design of the Loans There are pools with fixed-rate level-payment mortgage loans, adjustable-rate mortgage loans, and balloon mortgage loans. A wide variety of ARM PCs are issued under both the Cash and Guarantor/Swap programs. There are Treasury-indexed ARM pools and cost-of-funds-indexed ARM pools. The latter includes the 11th District Cost of Funds, as well as the National Cost of Funds, and the Federal Home Loan Bank Contract Rate.

Characteristics of the Mortgage Loans in the Pool The key underwriting standards for the mortgage loans are summarized below.

> *Mortgage Loans Permitted in the Pool:* The majority of PCs are backed by conventional mortgage loans. There are a few PCs backed by FHA and VA guaranteed mortgage loans.
> *Maximum Size of a Loan:* For both Freddie Mac and Fannie Mae, the maximum loan size is set each year based on the annual percentage change in the average price of conventionally financed homes as determined by the Federal Home Loan Bank Board. The maximum loan for a one-to-four family residence depends on the number of units. At the time of this writing, the maximum loans are as follows: one unit, $187,600; two units, $239,950; three units, $290,000; and four units $360,450.[1]
> *Amount of Seasoning Permitted:* There are no limits on seasoning for either program.

---

[1] For property in the states of Alaska and Hawaii, the corresponding loan limits are 50% higher.

Assumability of Mortgages: No assumable mortgages are permitted in a Freddie Mac pool.

Maturity: There are 30-year and 15-year Freddie Mac Regular and Swap PCs. The 15-year Regular PCs are called "gnomes" and Swap PCs are called "non-gnomes."

Net Interest Spread Permitted: In general, the net interest spread can be 50 to 250 basis points for both programs.

Payment Procedure The stated delay and actual delay for non-Gold PCs issued as part of either program is 75 and 44 days, respectively. The Gold PCs have a shorter payment delay; the stated delay is 45 days while the actual delay is 14 days. One monthly check is received in both programs for all pools an investor owns.

Federal National Mortgage Association MBS

The passthroughs issued by Fannie Mae are called *mortgage-backed securities* (MBSs). Like a Freddie Mac PC, a Fannie Mae MBS is not the obligation of the U.S. government. Fannie Mae also has a swap program similar to that of Freddie Mac.

There are four standard MBS programs established by Fannie Mae, which we discuss below. In addition to its regular programs, Fannie Mae issues securities known as "boutique" securities. These are securities that are issued through negotiated transactions and not backed by one of the mortgage loan types in its regular program.

Type of Guarantee All Fannie Mae MBSs are fully modified passthroughs.

Number of Lenders Permitted in a Pool There are only multiple-lender pools in the Cash program. In this program Fannie Mae purchases mortgage loans from various lenders and then creates a pool to collateralize the MBSs. In Fannie Mae's Guarantor/Swap program there are both single-lender and multiple-lender pools.

Mortgage Design of the Loans Three of the four standard programs have pools backed by mortgage loans that are fixed-rate level-payment mortgages. The fourth standard program is a MBS collateralized by adjustable-rate mortgage loans. In its boutique program, the passthroughs can be backed by either fixed-rate or adjustable-rate conventional mortgage loans. In the former case, there are boutique securities in which the underlying mortgage loans are balloons.

Characteristics of the Mortgage Loans in the Pool The key underwriting standards for the mortgage loans are summarized below.

Mortgage Loans Permitted in the Pool: Two of the four standard programs are backed by conventional mortgages. One is backed by FHA-insured or VA-guaranteed mortgages. The two programs backed by conventional mortgages are called *Conventional MBSs*. The MBS that are backed by FHA-insured or VA-guaranteed mortgages are called *Government MBS*.

Maximum Size of a Loan: The maximum loan size is the same as for Freddie Mac PCs.

Amount of Seasoning Permitted: There are no limits on seasoning.

Assumability of Mortgages: No assumable mortgages are permitted in a Fannie Mae pool.

Maturity: The two programs backed by conventional mortgages are 30-year and 15-year MBS, commonly referred to as the *Conventional Long-Term* and *Conventional Intermediate-Term MBS*, respectively. The 15-year MBSs are also known as "dwarfs." The MBS that are backed by 30-year FHA-insured or VA-guaranteed mortgages are called *Government Long-Term MBS.*

Net Interest Spread Permitted: In general, the net interest spread can be 50 to 250 basis points for both programs.

Payment Procedure The stated delay is 55 days and the actual delay 24 days.

PREPAYMENT CONVENTIONS AND CASH FLOW

In order to value a passthrough security, it is necessary to project its cash flow. The difficulty is that the cash flow is unknown because of prepayments. The only way to project a cash flow is to make some assumption about the prepayment rate over the life of the underlying mortgage pool. Two conventions have been used as a benchmark for prepayment rates — the conditional prepayment rate and the Public Securities Association Prepayment Benchmark.

Conditional Prepayment Rate

One convention for projecting prepayments and the cash flow of a passthrough assumes that some fraction of the remaining mortgage balance in the pool is prepaid each month for the remaining term of the mortgage. The prepayment rate assumed for a pool, called the *conditional prepayment rate* (CPR), is based on the characteristics of the pool (including its historical prepayment experience) and the current and expected future economic environment.

The CPR is an annual prepayment rate. To estimate monthly prepayments, the CPR must be converted into a monthly prepayment rate, commonly referred to as a *single-monthly mortality rate* (SMM). A formula can be used to determine the SMM for a given CPR:

$$\text{SMM} = 1 - (1 - \text{CPR})^{1/12} \tag{1}$$

Suppose that the CPR used to estimate prepayments is 6%. The corresponding SMM is:

$$\begin{aligned} \text{SMM} &= 1 - (1 - 0.06)^{1/12} \\ &= 1 - (0.94)^{0.08333} = 0.005143 \end{aligned}$$

An SMM of w% means that approximately w% of the remaining mortgage balance at the beginning of the month, less the scheduled principal payment, will prepay that month. That is,

Prepayment for month t = SMM

$$\times \text{(Beginning mortgage balance for month t}$$
$$- \text{Scheduled principal payment for month t)} \qquad (2)$$

For example, suppose that an investor owns a passthrough in which the remaining mortgage balance at the beginning of some month is $290 million. Assuming that the SMM is 0.5143% and the scheduled principal payment is $3 million, the estimated prepayment for the month is:

$$0.005143 \times (\$290,000,000 - \$3,000,000) = \$1,476,041$$

PSA Prepayment Benchmark

The Public Securities Association (PSA) prepayment benchmark is expressed as a monthly series of annual prepayment rates. The PSA benchmark assumes that prepayment rates are low for newly originated mortgages and then will speed up as the mortgages become seasoned.

The PSA benchmark assumes the following prepayment rates for 30-year mortgages:

(1) a CPR of 0.2% for the first month, increased by 0.2% per year per month for the next 30 months when it reaches 6% per year, and
(2) a 6% CPR for the remaining months.

This benchmark, referred to as "100% PSA" or simply "100 PSA," is graphically depicted in Exhibit 2. Mathematically, 100 PSA can be expressed as follows:

if $t \leq 30$ then CPR = 6% (t/30)
if $t > 30$ then CPR = 6%

where t is the number of months since the mortgage originated.

Slower or faster speeds are then referred to as some percentage of PSA. For example, 50 PSA means one-half the CPR of the PSA benchmark prepayment rate; 150 PSA means 1.5 times the CPR of the PSA benchmark prepayment rate; 300 PSA means three times the CPR of the benchmark prepayment rate. A prepayment rate of 0 PSA means that no prepayments are assumed.

The CPR is converted to an SMM using equation (1). For example, the SMMs for month 5, month 20, and months 31 through 360 assuming 100 PSA are calculated as follows:

Exhibit 2: Graphical Depiction of 100 PSA

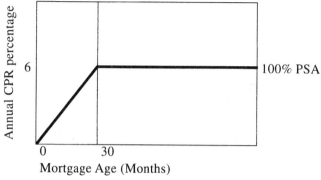

for month 5: CPR $= 6\%(5/30) = 1\% = 0.01$

$$SMM = 1 - (1 - 0.01)^{1/12}$$

$$= 1 - (0.99)^{0.083333} = 0.000837$$

for month 20: CPR $= 6\%(20/30) = 4\% = 0.04$

$$SMM = 1 - (1 - 0.04)^{1/12}$$

$$= 1 - (0.96)^{0.083333} = 0.003396$$

for month 31-360: CPR $= 6\%$

$$SMM = 1 - (1 - 0.06)^{1/12}$$

$$= 1 - (0.94)^{0.083333} = 0.005143$$

The SMMs for month 5, month 20, and months 31 through 360 assuming 165 PSA are computed as follows:

for month 5: CPR $= 6\%(5/30) = 1\% = 0.01$

$$165\,PSA = 1.65(0.01) = 0.0165$$

$$SMM = 1 - (1 - 0.0165)^{1/12}$$

$$= 1 - (0.9835)^{0.083333} = 0.001386$$

for month 20: CPR $= 6\%(20/30) = 4\% = 0.04$

$$165\,PSA = 1.65(0.04) = 0.066$$

$$SMM = 1 - (1 - 0.066)^{1/12}$$

$$= 1 - (0.934)^{0.083333} = 0.005674$$

for months 31-360: CPR = 6%

$$165 \text{ PSA} = 1.65(0.06) = 0.099$$

$$\text{SMM} = 1 - (1 - 0.099)^{1/12}$$

$$= 1 - (0.901)^{0.083333} = 0.007828$$

Notice that the SMM assuming 165 PSA is not just 1.65 times the SMM assuming 100 PSA. It is the CPR that is a multiple of the CPR assuming 100 PSA.

Illustration of Monthly Cash Flow Construction

We now show how to construct a monthly cash flow for a hypothetical passthrough given a PSA assumption. For the purpose of this illustration, the underlying mortgages for this hypothetical passthrough are assumed to be fixed-rate level-payment mortgages with a weighted average coupon (WAC) rate of 8.125%. It will be assumed that the passthrough rate is 7.5% with a weighted average maturity (WAM) of 357 months.

Exhibit 3 shows the cash flow for selected months assuming 100 PSA. The cash flow is broken down into three components: (1) interest (based on the passthrough rate), (2) the regularly scheduled principal repayment, and (3) prepayments based on 100 PSA.

Let's walk through Exhibit 3 column by column.

Column 1: This is the month.

Column 2: This column gives the outstanding mortgage balance at the beginning of the month. It is equal to the outstanding balance at the beginning of the previous month reduced by the total principal payment in the previous month.

Column 3: This column shows the SMM for 100 PSA. Two things should be noted in this column. First, for month 1, the SMM is for a passthrough that has been seasoned three months. That is, the CPR is 0.8%. This is because the WAM is 357. Second, from month 27 on, the SMM is 0.00514 which corresponds to a CPR of 6%.

Column 4: The total monthly mortgage payment is shown in this column. Notice that the total monthly mortgage payment declines over time as prepayments reduce the mortgage balance outstanding. There is a formula to determine what the monthly mortgage balance will be for each month given prepayments.[2]

Column 5: The monthly interest paid to the passthrough investor is found in this column. This value is determined by multiplying the outstanding mortgage balance at the beginning of the month by the passthrough rate of 7.5% and dividing by 12.

---

[2] The formula is presented in Chapter 20 of Frank J. Fabozzi, *Fixed Income Mathematics: Analytical and Statistical Techniques* (Chicago: Probus Publishing, 1993).

Exhibit 3: Monthly Cash Flow for a $400 Million Passthrough with a 7.5% Passthrough Rate, a WAC of 8.125%, and a WAM of 357 Months Assuming 100 PSA

Month	Outstanding Balance	SMM	Mortgage Payment	Net Interest	Scheduled Principal	Prepayment	Total Principal	Cash Flow
1	400,000,000	0.00067	2,975,868	2,500,000	267,535	267,470	535,005	3,035,005
2	399,464,995	0.00084	2,973,877	2,496,656	269,166	334,198	603,364	3,100,020
3	398,861,631	0.00101	2,971,387	2,492,885	270,762	400,800	671,562	3,164,447
4	398,190,069	0.00117	2,968,399	2,488,688	272,321	467,243	739,564	3,228,252
5	397,450,505	0.00134	2,964,914	2,484,066	273,843	533,493	807,335	3,291,401
6	396,643,170	0.00151	2,960,931	2,479,020	275,327	599,514	874,841	3,353,860
7	395,768,329	0.00168	2,956,453	2,473,552	276,772	665,273	942,045	3,415,597
8	394,826,284	0.00185	2,951,480	2,467,664	278,177	730,736	1,008,913	3,476,577
9	393,817,371	0.00202	2,946,013	2,461,359	279,542	795,869	1,075,410	3,536,769
10	392,741,961	0.00219	2,940,056	2,454,637	280,865	860,637	1,141,502	3,596,140
11	391,600,459	0.00236	2,933,608	2,447,503	282,147	925,008	1,207,155	3,654,658
12	390,393,304	0.00254	2,926,674	2,439,958	283,386	988,948	1,272,333	3,712,291
13	389,120,971	0.00271	2,919,254	2,432,006	284,581	1,052,423	1,337,004	3,769,010
14	387,783,966	0.00288	2,911,353	2,423,650	285,733	1,115,402	1,401,134	3,824,784
15	386,382,832	0.00305	2,902,973	2,414,893	286,839	1,177,851	1,464,690	3,879,583
16	384,918,142	0.00322	2,894,117	2,405,738	287,900	1,239,739	1,527,639	3,933,378
17	383,390,502	0.00340	2,884,789	2,396,191	288,915	1,301,033	1,589,949	3,986,139
18	381,800,553	0.00357	2,874,992	2,386,253	289,884	1,361,703	1,651,587	4,037,840
19	380,148,966	0.00374	2,864,730	2,375,931	290,805	1,421,717	1,712,522	4,088,453
20	378,436,444	0.00392	2,854,008	2,365,228	291,678	1,481,046	1,772,724	4,137,952
21	376,663,720	0.00409	2,842,830	2,354,148	292,503	1,539,658	1,832,161	4,186,309
22	374,831,559	0.00427	2,831,201	2,342,697	293,279	1,597,525	1,890,804	4,233,501
23	372,940,755	0.00444	2,819,125	2,330,880	294,005	1,654,618	1,948,623	4,279,503
24	370,992,132	0.00462	2,806,607	2,318,701	294,681	1,710,908	2,005,589	4,324,290
25	368,986,543	0.00479	2,793,654	2,306,166	295,307	1,766,368	2,061,675	4,367,841
26	366,924,868	0.00497	2,780,270	2,293,280	295,883	1,820,970	2,116,852	4,410,133
27	364,808,016	0.00514	2,766,461	2,280,050	296,406	1,874,688	2,171,094	4,451,144
28	362,636,921	0.00514	2,752,233	2,266,481	296,879	1,863,519	2,160,398	4,426,879
29	360,476,523	0.00514	2,738,078	2,252,978	297,351	1,852,406	2,149,758	4,402,736
30	358,326,766	0.00514	2,723,996	2,239,542	297,825	1,841,347	2,139,173	4,378,715
100	231,249,776	0.00514	1,898,682	1,445,311	332,928	1,187,608	1,520,537	2,965,848
101	229,729,239	0.00514	1,888,917	1,435,808	333,459	1,179,785	1,513,244	2,949,052
102	228,215,995	0.00514	1,879,202	1,426,350	333,990	1,172,000	1,505,990	2,932,340
103	226,710,004	0.00514	1,869,538	1,416,938	334,522	1,164,252	1,498,774	2,915,712
104	225,211,230	0.00514	1,859,923	1,407,570	335,055	1,156,541	1,491,596	2,899,166
105	223,719,634	0.00514	1,850,357	1,398,248	335,589	1,148,867	1,484,456	2,882,703
200	109,791,339	0.00514	1,133,751	686,196	390,372	562,651	953,023	1,639,219
201	108,838,316	0.00514	1,127,920	680,239	390,994	557,746	948,740	1,628,980
202	107,889,576	0.00514	1,122,119	674,310	391,617	552,863	944,480	1,618,790
203	106,945,096	0.00514	1,116,348	668,407	392,241	548,003	940,243	1,608,650
204	106,004,852	0.00514	1,110,607	662,530	392,866	543,164	936,029	1,598,560
205	105,068,823	0.00514	1,104,895	656,680	393,491	538,347	931,838	1,588,518

Exhibit 3 (Concluded)

Month	Outstanding Balance	SMM	Mortgage Payment	Net Interest	Scheduled Principal	Prepayment	Total Principal	Cash Flow
300	32,383,611	0.00514	676,991	202,398	457,727	164,195	621,923	824,320
301	31,761,689	0.00514	673,510	198,511	458,457	160,993	619,449	817,960
302	31,142,239	0.00514	670,046	194,639	459,187	157,803	616,990	811,629
303	30,525,249	0.00514	666,600	190,783	459,918	154,626	614,545	805,328
304	29,910,704	0.00514	663,171	186,942	460,651	151,462	612,113	799,055
305	29,298,591	0.00514	659,761	183,116	461,385	148,310	609,695	792,811
350	4,060,411	0.00514	523,138	25,378	495,645	18,334	513,979	539,356
351	3,546,432	0.00514	520,447	22,165	496,435	15,686	512,121	534,286
352	3,034,311	0.00514	517,770	18,964	497,226	13,048	510,274	529,238
353	2,524,037	0.00514	515,107	15,775	498,018	10,420	508,437	524,213
354	2,015,600	0.00514	512,458	12,597	498,811	7,801	506,612	519,209
355	1,508,988	0.00514	509,823	9,431	499,606	5,191	504,797	514,228
356	1,004,191	0.00514	507,201	6,276	500,401	2,591	502,992	509,269
357	501,199	0.00514	504,592	3,132	501,199	0	501,199	504,331

Column 6: This column gives the regularly scheduled principal repayment. This is the difference between the total monthly mortgage payment [the amount shown in column (4)] and the gross coupon interest for the month. The gross coupon interest is 8.125% multiplied by the outstanding mortgage balance at the beginning of the month, then divided by 12.

Column 7: The prepayment for the month is reported in this column. The prepayment is found by using equation (2). For example, in month 100, the beginning mortgage balance is $231,249,776, the scheduled principal payment is $332,298, and the SMM at 100 PSA is 0.00514301 (only 0.00514 is shown in the exhibit to save space), so the prepayment is:

$$0.00514301 \times (\$231,249,776 - \$332,928) = \$1,187,608$$

Column 8: The total principal payment, which is the sum of columns (6) and (7), is shown in this column.

Column 9: The projected monthly cash flow for this passthrough is shown in this last column. The monthly cash flow is the sum of the interest paid to the passthrough investor [column (5)] and the total principal payments for the month [column (8)].

Exhibit 4 shows selected monthly cash flows for the same passthrough assuming 165 PSA.

PRICE QUOTATIONS

Passthroughs are quoted in the same manner as U.S. Treasury coupon securities. A quote of 94-05 means 94 and 5/32nd of par value, or 94.15625% of par value.

Exhibit 4: Monthly Cash Flow for a $400 Million Passthrough with a 7.5% Passthrough Rate, a WAC of 8.125%, and a WAM of 357 Months Assuming 165 PSA

Month	Outstanding Balance	SMM	Mortgage Payment	Net Interest	Scheduled Principal	Prepayment	Total Principal	Cash Flow
1	400,000,000	0.00111	2,975,868	2,500,000	267,535	442,389	709,923	3,209,923
2	399,290,077	0.00139	2,972,575	2,495,563	269,048	552,847	821,896	3,317,459
3	398,468,181	0.00167	2,968,456	2,490,426	270,495	663,065	933,560	3,423,986
4	397,534,621	0.00195	2,963,513	2,484,591	271,873	772,949	1,044,822	3,529,413
5	396,489,799	0.00223	2,957,747	2,478,061	273,181	882,405	1,155,586	3,633,647
6	395,334,213	0.00251	2,951,160	2,470,839	274,418	991,341	1,265,759	3,736,598
7	394,068,454	0.00279	2,943,755	2,462,928	275,583	1,099,664	1,375,246	3,838,174
8	392,693,208	0.00308	2,935,534	2,454,333	276,674	1,207,280	1,483,954	3,938,287
9	391,209,254	0.00336	2,926,503	2,445,058	277,690	1,314,099	1,591,789	4,036,847
10	389,617,464	0.00365	2,916,666	2,435,109	278,631	1,420,029	1,698,659	4,133,769
11	387,918,805	0.00393	2,906,028	2,424,493	279,494	1,524,979	1,804,473	4,228,965
12	386,114,332	0.00422	2,894,595	2,413,215	280,280	1,628,859	1,909,139	4,322,353
13	384,205,194	0.00451	2,882,375	2,401,282	280,986	1,731,581	2,012,567	4,413,850
14	382,192,626	0.00480	2,869,375	2,388,704	281,613	1,833,058	2,114,670	4,503,374
15	380,077,956	0.00509	2,855,603	2,375,487	282,159	1,933,203	2,215,361	4,590,848
16	377,862,595	0.00538	2,841,068	2,361,641	282,623	2,031,931	2,314,554	4,676,195
17	375,548,041	0.00567	2,825,779	2,347,175	283,006	2,129,159	2,412,164	4,759,339
18	373,135,877	0.00597	2,809,746	2,332,099	283,305	2,224,805	2,508,110	4,840,210
19	370,627,766	0.00626	2,792,980	2,316,424	283,521	2,318,790	2,602,312	4,918,735
20	368,025,455	0.00656	2,775,493	2,300,159	283,654	2,411,036	2,694,690	4,994,849
21	365,330,765	0.00685	2,757,296	2,283,317	283,702	2,501,466	2,785,169	5,068,486
22	362,545,596	0.00715	2,738,402	2,265,910	283,666	2,590,008	2,873,674	5,139,584
23	359,671,922	0.00745	2,718,823	2,247,950	283,545	2,676,588	2,960,133	5,208,083
24	356,711,789	0.00775	2,698,575	2,229,449	283,338	2,761,139	3,044,477	5,273,926
25	353,667,312	0.00805	2,677,670	2,210,421	283,047	2,843,593	3,126,640	5,337,061
26	350,540,672	0.00835	2,656,123	2,190,879	282,671	2,923,885	3,206,556	5,397,435
27	347,334,116	0.00865	2,633,950	2,170,838	282,209	3,001,955	3,284,164	5,455,002
28	344,049,952	0.00865	2,611,167	2,150,312	281,662	2,973,553	3,255,215	5,405,527
29	340,794,737	0.00865	2,588,581	2,129,967	281,116	2,945,400	3,226,516	5,356,483
30	337,568,221	0.00865	2,566,190	2,109,801	280,572	2,917,496	3,198,067	5,307,869
100	170,142,350	0.00865	1,396,958	1,063,390	244,953	1,469,591	1,714,544	2,777,933
101	168,427,806	0.00865	1,384,875	1,052,674	244,478	1,454,765	1,699,243	2,751,916
102	166,728,563	0.00865	1,372,896	1,042,054	244,004	1,440,071	1,684,075	2,726,128
103	165,044,489	0.00865	1,361,020	1,031,528	243,531	1,425,508	1,669,039	2,700,567
104	163,375,450	0.00865	1,349,248	1,021,097	243,060	1,411,075	1,654,134	2,675,231
105	161,721,315	0.00865	1,337,577	1,010,758	242,589	1,396,771	1,639,359	2,650,118
200	56,746,664	0.00865	585,990	354,667	201,767	489,106	690,874	1,045,540
201	56,055,790	0.00865	580,921	350,349	201,377	483,134	684,510	1,034,859
202	55,371,280	0.00865	575,896	346,070	200,986	477,216	678,202	1,024,273
203	54,693,077	0.00865	570,915	341,832	200,597	471,353	671,950	1,013,782
204	54,021,127	0.00865	565,976	337,632	200,208	465,544	665,752	1,003,384
205	53,355,375	0.00865	561,081	333,471	199,820	459,789	659,609	993,080

Exhibit 4 (Concluded)

Month	Outstanding Balance	SMM	Mortgage Payment	Net Interest	Scheduled Principal	Prepayment	Total Principal	Cash Flow
300	11,758,141	0.00865	245,808	73,488	166,196	100,269	266,465	339,953
301	11,491,677	0.00865	243,682	71,823	165,874	97,967	263,841	335,664
302	11,227,836	0.00865	241,574	70,174	165,552	95,687	261,240	331,414
303	10,966,596	0.00865	239,485	68,541	165,232	93,430	258,662	327,203
304	10,707,934	0.00865	237,413	66,925	164,912	91,196	256,107	323,032
305	10,451,827	0.00865	235,360	65,324	164,592	88,983	253,575	318,899
350	1,235,674	0.00865	159,202	7,723	150,836	9,384	160,220	167,943
351	1,075,454	0.00865	157,825	6,722	150,544	8,000	158,544	165,266
352	916,910	0.00865	156,460	5,731	150,252	6,631	156,883	162,614
353	760,027	0.00865	155,107	4,750	149,961	5,277	155,238	159,988
354	604,789	0.00865	153,765	3,780	149,670	3,937	153,607	157,387
355	451,182	0.00865	152,435	2,820	149,380	2,611	151,991	154,811
356	299,191	0.00865	151,117	1,870	149,091	1,298	150,389	152,259
357	148,802	0.00865	149,809	930	148,802	0	148,802	149,732

There are many seasoned issues of the same agency with the same coupon rate outstanding at any given time. Each issue is backed by a different pool of mortgages. For example, there are many seasoned pools of GNMA 8's. One issue may be backed by a pool of mortgages all for California properties, while another may be backed by a pool of mortgages for primarily New York homes. Others may be backed by a pool of mortgages on homes in several regions of the country.

Which pool are dealers referring to when they talk about, say, GNMA 8's? They are not referring to any specific pool. They mean a "generic" security even though the prepayment characteristics of passthroughs of underlying pools from different parts of the country are different. Thus, the projected PSA prepayment rates for passthrough securities reported by dealer firms are for generic passthroughs. A particular pool purchased may have a materially different prepayment speed from the generic benchmark. Moreover, when an investor purchases a passthrough without specifying a pool number, the seller can deliver the worst-paying pools from the securities it holds. Credit unions should be particularly cognizant of this fact and avoid purchasing such pools without specifying what is acceptable criteria for the receipt of a TBA pool. Furthermore, it is unclear whether the prohibition against certain when issued trading will extend to the purchase of TBA pools under the revised Part 703.

EXTENSION RISK AND CONTRACTION RISK

An investor who owns passthrough securities does not know what the cash flow will be because that depends on prepayments. That is, the investor faces prepayment risk. To understand the significance of prepayment risk for a credit union, suppose a credit union buys a 10% Ginnie Mae at a time when mortgage rates are 8%. Let's consider what will happen to prepayments if mortgage rates rise to 12%.

The price of the passthrough, like the price of any bond, will decline. But again it will decline more because the higher rates will tend to slow down the rate of prepayment, in effect increasing the amount invested at the coupon rate, which is lower than the market rate. Prepayments will slow down, because homeowners will not refinance or partially prepay their mortgages when mortgage rates are higher than the contract rate of 8%. Of course this is just the time when a credit union want prepayments to speed up so that they can reinvest the prepayments at the higher market interest rate (12%). This adverse consequence of rising mortgage rates is called *extension risk.*

Banks and savings and loan associations are also concerned with extension risk. However, there are other institutional investors concerned with a different form of prepayment risk, called *contraction risk.* For example, a pension fund that purchases a passthrough security is concerned that if market rates drop below the coupon rate, prepayments will accelerate. This will shorten the life of the passthrough, forcing the pension fund to reinvest the unanticipated principal received at a lower rate. Credit Unions tend to be more liquid when rates are low and prepayments are accelerating. Thus, credit unions also experience the adverse consequence of reinvesting these funds at a lower rate.

Therefore, prepayment risk encompasses contraction risk and extension risk. Some institutional investors are concerned with extension risk and others with contraction risk when they purchase a passthrough security. Is it possible to alter the cash flow of a passthrough so as to reduce the contraction risk and extension risk for institutional investors? This can be done, as we shall see in the next chapter when we discuss collateralized mortgage obligations.

COMPARISON TO TREASURY SECURITIES

Mortgage passthroughs are often compared to Treasury securities. When we speak of comparing a mortgage passthrough security to a comparable Treasury, what does "comparable" mean? The stated maturity of a mortgage passthrough security is an inappropriate measure because of prepayments. Instead, market participants have used two measures: Macaulay duration and average life. As we explain in Chapter 10, Macaulay duration is a weighted-average term to maturity where the weights are the present value of the cash flows. The more commonly used measure is the average life.

The *average life* of a mortgage-backed security is the average time to receipt of principal payments (scheduled principal payments and projected prepayments), weighted by the amount of principal expected. Mathematically, the average life is expressed as follows:

$$\text{Average life} = \sum_{t=1}^{T} \frac{t \times \text{Principal expected at time t}}{12(\text{Total principal})}$$

where T is the number of months.

The average life of a passthrough depends on the PSA prepayment assumption. To see this, the average life is shown below for different prepayment speeds for the passthrough we used to illustrate the cash flow for 100 PSA and 165 PSA in Exhibits 3 and 4:

PSA speed	50	100	165	200	300	400	500	600	700
Average life	15.11	11.66	8.76	7.68	5.63	4.44	3.68	3.16	2.78

KEY POINTS

1. A mortgage loan is a loan secured by the collateral of some specified real estate property which obliges the borrower to make a predetermined series of payments.

2. The basic idea behind the design of the fixed-rate level-payment fully amortized mortgage is that the borrower pays interest and repays principal in equal installments over the life of the loan, such that at maturity the loan balance is zero.

3. An adjustable-rate mortgage (ARM) is a loan in which the mortgage rate is reset periodically in accordance with some appropriately chosen reference rate plus a spread.

4. There are two categories of reference rates that have been used in ARMs — market-determined rates and calculated rates based on the cost of funds for thrifts.

5. In a balloon mortgage the borrower is given long-term financing by the lender, but at a specified future date the mortgage rate is renegotiated.

6. In all mortgage loans, the portion of the monthly mortgage payment applied to interest declines each month and the portion applied to reducing the mortgage balance increases.

7. The interest rate on a mortgage loan that the investor receives is the contract rate less the servicing fee.

8. Prepayments are mortgage payments made in excess of the scheduled principal repayment.

9. The monthly cash flow of a mortgage is the sum of the net interest (i.e., interest after servicing fee), regularly scheduled principal repayment, and prepayments.

10. The effect of prepayments is that the amount and timing of the cash flow from a mortgage is unknown.

11. The uncertainty of the cash flow due to prepayments is called prepayment risk.

12. The two primary factors in determining whether the funds will be lent are the payment-to-income ratio and the loan-to-value.

13. A conventional mortgage is one in which the lender makes the loan based on the credit of the borrower and on the collateral for the mortgage.

14. Mortgage insurance is usually required by lenders on loans with a loan-to-value ratio in excess of 80%.

15. The two forms of mortgage insurance are private mortgage insurance and government agency mortgage insurance provided by the Federal Housing Administration, the Veterans Administration, and the Federal Farmers Administration.

16. A mortgage passthrough security is created when one or more holders of mortgages form a collection (pool) of mortgages and sell shares or participation certificates in the pool.

17. The three agencies that issue passthroughs are the Government National Mortgage Association ("Ginnie Mae"), Federal Home Loan Mortgage Corporation ("Freddie Mac"), and Federal National Mortgage Association ("Fannie Mae").

18. Ginnie Mae passthroughs are guaranteed by the full faith and credit of the U.S. government while the guarantee of Fannie Mae and Freddie Mac is not.

19. The cash flow of a mortgage passthrough security depends on the cash flow of the underlying mortgages and includes the aggregate monthly mortgage payments representing interest net of servicing fees and guarantee fees, the scheduled repayment of principal, and any prepayments.

20. The key features of a passthrough that affect their investment characteristics are the type of guarantee, the numbers of lenders whose mortgage loans are permitted in a pool, the mortgage design of the loans, the characteristics of the mortgage loans in the pools, and the payment procedure.

21. A projection of prepayments is necessary to determine the cash flow of a passthrough security.

22. The two conventions have been used as a benchmark for prepayment rates are the conditional prepayment rate and Public Securities Association Prepayment Benchmark.

23. The PSA prepayment benchmark is a series of conditional prepayment rates and is simply a market convention that describes in general the pattern of prepayments.

24. A measure commonly used to estimate the life of a passthrough is its average life.

25. Typically, dealers do not refer to any specific pool but a "generic" security and therefore a particular pool purchased may have a materially different prepayment speed from the generic benchmark.

26. The prepayment risk associated with investing in mortgage passthrough securities can be decomposed into contraction risk and extension risk.

27. Extension risk is the primary risk for credit unions.

Chapter 6

Collateralized Mortgage Obligations

The objectives of this chapter are to:

1. explain how a collateralized mortgage obligation is created;

2. show how the different types of bond classes are created;

3. explain how a CMO distributes prepayment risk among bond classes;

4. explain which bond classes provide better protection against extension risk;

5. demonstrate the greater prepayment protection provided for planned amortization class bonds.

6. explain the substantial prepayment risk for support bonds;

7. discuss the credit risk of CMOs; and,

8. explain what a REMIC is.

An investor in a mortgage passthrough security is exposed to prepayment risk. Some institutional investors are concerned with extension risk and others with contraction risk when they invest in a passthrough. As an example, credit unions are primarily concerned with extension risk. This problem can be mitigated by redirecting the cash flows of passthrough securities to different bond classes, called *tranches*, so as to create securities that have different exposure to prepayment risk and therefore different risk/return patterns than the passthrough securities from which they were created. When the cash flows of mortgage-related products are redistributed to different bond classes, the resulting securities are called *collateralized mortgage obligations* (CMO). The creation of a CMO cannot eliminate prepayment risk; it can only distribute the various forms of this risk among different classes of bondholders.

In this chapter we shall look at the wide range of CMO structures.

SEQUENTIAL-PAY TRANCHES

The first CMO was created in 1983 and was structured so that each class of bond would be retired sequentially. Such structures are referred to as *sequential-pay* CMOs.

To illustrate a sequential-pay CMO, we discuss FAF-01,[1] a hypothetical deal made up to illustrate the basic features of the structure. The collateral for this hypothetical CMO is a hypothetical passthrough with a total par value of $400 million and the following characteristics: (1) the passthrough coupon rate is 7.5%, (2) the weighted average coupon (WAC) is 8.125%, and (3) the weighted average maturity (WAM) is 357 months. This is the same passthrough that we used in the previous chapter to illustrate the cash flow of a passthrough based on some PSA assumption.

From this $400 million of collateral, four bond classes or tranches are created. Their characteristics are summarized in Exhibit 1. The total par value of the four tranches is equal to the par value of the collateral (i.e., the passthrough security). In this simple structure, the coupon rate is the same for each tranche and also the same as the coupon rate on the collateral. There is no reason why this must be so, and, in fact, typically the coupon rate varies by tranche.

Now remember that a CMO is created by redistributing the cash flow — interest and principal — to the different tranches based on a set of payment rules. The payment rules at the bottom of Exhibit 1 describe how the cash flow from the passthrough (i.e., collateral) is to be distributed to the four tranches. There are separate rules for the payment of the coupon interest and the payment of principal, the principal being the total of the regularly scheduled principal payment and any prepayments.

---

[1] All CMO structures are given a name. In our illustration we use FAF.

Exhibit 1: FAF-01: A Hypothetical Four-Tranche Sequential-Pay Structure

Tranche	Par Amount	Coupon Rate
A	$194,500,000	7.5%
B	36,000,000	7.5
C	96,500,000	7.5
D	73,000,000	7.5
Total	$400,000,000	

Payment rules:

1. *For payment of periodic coupon interest:* Disburse periodic coupon interest to each tranche on the basis of the amount of principal outstanding at the beginning of the period.

2. *For disbursement of principal payments:* Disburse principal payments to tranche A until it is completely paid off. After tranche A is completely paid off, disburse principal payments to tranche B until it is completely paid off. After tranche B is completely paid off, disburse principal payments to tranche C until it is completely paid off. After tranche C is completely paid off, disburse principal payments to tranche D until it is completely paid off.

In FAF-01, each tranche receives periodic coupon interest payments based on the amount of the outstanding balance. The disbursement of the principal, however, is made in a special way. A tranche is not entitled to receive principal until the entire principal of the tranche before it has been paid off. More specifically, tranche A receives all the principal payments until the entire principal amount owed to that tranche, $194,500,000, is paid off; then tranche B begins to receive principal and continues to do so until it is paid the entire $36,000,000. Tranche C then receives principal, and when it is paid off, tranche D starts receiving principal payments.

While the priority rules for the disbursement of the principal payments are known, the precise amount of the principal in each period is not. This will depend on the cash flow, and therefore principal payments, of the collateral, which depends on the actual prepayment rate of the collateral. An assumed PSA speed allows the cash flow to be projected. Exhibit 4 in the previous chapter shows the cash flow (interest, regularly scheduled principal repayment, and prepayments) assuming 165 PSA. Assuming that the collateral does prepay at 165 PSA, the cash flow available to all four tranches of FAF-01 will be precisely the cash flow shown in Exhibit 4 of the previous chapter.

To demonstrate how the priority rules for FAF-01 work, Exhibit 2 shows the cash flow for selected months assuming the collateral prepays at 165 PSA. For each tranche, the exhibit shows: (1) the balance at the end of the month, (2) the principal paid down (regularly scheduled principal repayment plus prepayments), and (3) interest. In month 1, the cash flow for the collateral consists of a principal payment of $709,923 and interest of $2.5 million (0.075 times $400 million divided by 12). The interest payment is distributed to the four tranches based on the amount of the par value outstanding. So, for example, tranche A receives $1,215,625 (0.075 times $194,500,000 divided by 12) of the $2.5 million. The principal, however, is all distributed to tranche A. Therefore, the cash flow for tranche A in month 1 is $1,925,548. The principal balance at the end of month 1 for tranche A is $193,790,076 (the original principal balance of $194,500,000 less the principal payment of $709,923). No principal payment is distributed to the three other tranches because there is still a principal balance outstanding for tranche A. This will be true for months 2 through 80.

After month 81, the principal balance will be zero for tranche A. For the collateral, the cash flow in month 81 is $3,318,521, consisting of a principal payment of $2,032,196 and interest of $1,286,325. At the beginning of month 81 (end of month 80), the principal balance for tranche A is $311,926. Therefore, $311,926 of the $2,032,196 of the principal payment from the collateral will be disbursed to tranche A. After this payment is made, no additional principal payments are made to this tranche as the principal balance is zero. The remaining principal payment from the collateral, $1,720,271, is disbursed to tranche B. According to the assumed prepayment speed of 165 PSA, tranche B then begins receiving principal payments in month 81.

Exhibit 2 shows that tranche B is fully paid off by month 100, when tranche C then begins to receive principal payments. Tranche C is not fully paid off until month 178, at which time tranche D begins receiving the remaining principal payments. The maturity (i.e., the time until the principal is fully paid off) for these four tranches assuming 165 PSA would be 81 months for tranche A, 100 months for tranche B, 178 months for tranche C, and 357 months for tranche D.

The *principal pay down window* for a tranche is the time period between the beginning and the ending of the principal payments to that tranche. So, for example, for tranche A, the principal pay down window would be month 1 to month 81 assuming 165 PSA. For tranche B it is from month 82 to month 100. The window is also specified in terms of the length of the time from the beginning of the principal pay down window to the end of the principal pay down window. For tranche A, the window would be stated as 80 months, for tranche B 19 months.

Let's look at what has been accomplished by creating the CMO. The average life of the passthrough is 8.76 years, assuming a prepayment speed of 165 PSA. Exhibit 3 reports the average life of the collateral and the four tranches assuming different prepayment speeds. Notice that the four tranches have average lives that are both shorter and longer than the collateral thereby attracting investors who have a preference for an average life different from that of the collateral.

There is still a major problem: there is considerable variability of the average life for the tranches. We'll see how this can be tackled later on. However, there is some protection provided for each tranche against prepayment risk. This is because prioritizing the distribution of principal (i.e., establishing the payment rules for principal) effectively protects the shorter-term tranche A in this structure against extension risk. This protection must come from somewhere, so it comes from the three other tranches. Similarly, tranches C and D provide protection against extension risk for tranches A and B. At the same time, tranches C and D benefit because they are provided protection against contraction risk, the protection coming from tranches A and B.

Exhibit 2: Monthly Cash Flow for Selected Months for FAF-01 Assuming 165 PSA

Month	Tranche A			Tranche B		
	Balance	Principal	Interest	Balance	Principal	Interest
1	194,500,000	709,923	1,215,625	36,000,000	0	225,000
2	193,790,077	821,896	1,211,188	36,000,000	0	225,000
3	192,968,181	933,560	1,206,051	36,000,000	0	225,000
4	192,034,621	1,044,822	1,200,216	36,000,000	0	225,000
5	190,989,799	1,155,586	1,193,686	36,000,000	0	225,000
6	189,834,213	1,265,759	1,186,464	36,000,000	0	225,000
7	188,568,454	1,375,246	1,178,553	36,000,000	0	225,000
8	187,193,208	1,483,954	1,169,958	36,000,000	0	225,000
9	185,709,254	1,591,789	1,160,683	36,000,000	0	225,000
10	184,117,464	1,698,659	1,150,734	36,000,000	0	225,000
11	182,418,805	1,804,473	1,140,118	36,000,000	0	225,000
12	180,614,332	1,909,139	1,128,840	36,000,000	0	225,000
75	12,893,479	2,143,974	80,584	36,000,000	0	225,000
76	10,749,504	2,124,935	67,184	36,000,000	0	225,000
77	8,624,569	2,106,062	53,904	36,000,000	0	225,000
78	6,518,507	2,087,353	40,741	36,000,000	0	225,000
79	4,431,154	2,068,807	27,695	36,000,000	0	225,000
80	2,362,347	2,050,422	14,765	36,000,000	0	225,000
81	311,926	311,926	1,950	36,000,000	1,720,271	225,000
82	0	0	0	34,279,729	2,014,130	214,248
83	0	0	0	32,265,599	1,996,221	201,660
84	0	0	0	30,269,378	1,978,468	189,184
85	0	0	0	28,290,911	1,960,869	176,818
95	0	0	0	9,449,331	1,793,089	59,058
96	0	0	0	7,656,242	1,777,104	47,852
97	0	0	0	5,879,138	1,761,258	36,745
98	0	0	0	4,117,880	1,745,550	25,737
99	0	0	0	2,372,329	1,729,979	14,827
100	0	0	0	642,350	642,350	4,015
101	0	0	0	0	0	0
102	0	0	0	0	0	0
103	0	0	0	0	0	0
104	0	0	0	0	0	0
105	0	0	0	0	0	0

Exhibit 2 (Concluded)

	Tranche C			Tranche D		
Month	Balance	Principal	Interest	Balance	Principal	Interest
1	96,500,000	0	603,125	73,000,000	0	456,250
2	96,500,000	0	603,125	73,000,000	0	456,250
3	96,500,000	0	603,125	73,000,000	0	456,250
4	96,500,000	0	603,125	73,000,000	0	456,250
5	96,500,000	0	603,125	73,000,000	0	456,250
6	96,500,000	0	603,125	73,000,000	0	456,250
7	96,500,000	0	603,125	73,000,000	0	456,250
8	96,500,000	0	603,125	73,000,000	0	456,250
9	96,500,000	0	603,125	73,000,000	0	456,250
10	96,500,000	0	603,125	73,000,000	0	456,250
11	96,500,000	0	603,125	73,000,000	0	456,250
12	96,500,000	0	603,125	73,000,000	0	456,250
95	96,500,000	0	603,125	73,000,000	0	456,250
96	96,500,000	0	603,125	73,000,000	0	456,250
97	96,500,000	0	603,125	73,000,000	0	456,250
98	96,500,000	0	603,125	73,000,000	0	456,250
99	96,500,000	0	603,125	73,000,000	0	456,250
100	96,500,000	1,072,194	603,125	73,000,000	0	456,250
101	95,427,806	1,699,243	596,424	73,000,000	0	456,250
102	93,728,563	1,684,075	585,804	73,000,000	0	456,250
103	92,044,489	1,669,039	575,278	73,000,000	0	456,250
104	90,375,450	1,654,134	564,847	73,000,000	0	456,250
105	88,721,315	1,639,359	554,508	73,000,000	0	456,250
175	3,260,287	869,602	20,377	73,000,000	0	456,250
176	2,390,685	861,673	14,942	73,000,000	0	456,250
177	1,529,013	853,813	9,556	73,000,000	0	456,250
178	675,199	675,199	4,220	73,000,000	170,824	456,250
179	0	0	0	72,829,176	838,300	455,182
180	0	0	0	71,990,876	830,646	449,943
181	0	0	0	71,160,230	823,058	444,751
182	0	0	0	70,337,173	815,536	439,607
183	0	0	0	69,521,637	808,081	434,510
184	0	0	0	68,713,556	800,690	429,460
185	0	0	0	67,912,866	793,365	424,455
350	0	0	0	1,235,674	160,220	7,723
351	0	0	0	1,075,454	158,544	6,722
352	0	0	0	916,910	156,883	5,731
353	0	0	0	760,027	155,238	4,750
354	0	0	0	604,789	153,607	3,780
355	0	0	0	451,182	151,991	2,820
356	0	0	0	299,191	150,389	1,870
357	0	0	0	148,802	148,802	930

Exhibit 3: Average Life for the Collateral and the Four Tranches of FAF-01

Prepayment speed (PSA)	Average life for				
	Collateral	Tranche A	Tranche B	Tranche C	Tranche D
50	15.11	7.48	15.98	21.02	27.24
100	11.66	4.90	10.86	15.78	24.58
165	8.76	3.48	7.49	11.19	20.27
200	7.68	3.05	6.42	9.60	18.11
300	5.63	2.32	4.64	6.81	13.36
400	4.44	1.94	3.70	5.31	10.34
500	3.68	1.69	3.12	4.38	8.35
600	3.16	1.51	2.74	3.75	6.96
700	2.78	1.38	2.47	3.30	5.95

ACCRUAL BONDS

In FAF-01, the payment rules for interest provide for all tranches to be paid interest each month. In many sequential-pay CMO structures, at least one tranche does not receive current interest. Instead, the interest for that tranche would accrue and be added to the principal balance. Such a bond class is commonly referred to as an *accrual tranche*, or a *Z bond* (because the bond is similar to a zero-coupon bond). The interest that would have been paid to the accrual tranche class is then used to speed up the pay down of the principal balance of earlier bond tranches.

To see this, consider FAF-02, a hypothetical CMO structure with the same collateral as FAF-01 and with four tranches, each with a coupon rate of 7.5%. The difference is in the last tranche, Z, which is an accrual tranche. The structure for FAF-02 is shown in Exhibit 4.

Exhibit 5 shows cash flows for selected months for tranches A and B. Let's look at month 1 and compare it to month 1 in Exhibit 2. Both cash flows are based on 165 PSA. The principal payment from the collateral is $709,923. In FAF-01, this is the principal paydown for tranche A. In FAF-02, the interest for tranche Z, $456,250, is not paid to that tranche but instead is used to pay down the principal of tranche A. So, the principal payment to tranche A in Exhibit 5 is $1,166,173, the collateral's principal payment of $709,923 plus the interest of $456,250 that was diverted from tranche Z.

The expected final maturity for tranches A, B, and C has shortened as a result of the inclusion of tranche Z. The final payout for tranche A is 64 months rather than 81 months; for tranche B it is 77 months rather than 100 months; and for tranche C it is 112 rather than 178 months.

The average lives for tranches A, B, and C are shorter in FAF-02 compared to FAF-01 because of the inclusion of the accrual bond. For example, at 165 PSA, the average lives are as follows:

Structure	Tranche A	Tranche B	Tranche C
FAF-02	2.90	5.86	7.87
FAF-01	3.48	7.49	11.19

The reason for the shortening of the non-accrual tranches is that the interest that would be paid to the accrual bond is being allocated to the other tranches. Tranche Z in FAF-02 will have a longer average life than tranche D in FAF-01.

Thus, shorter term tranches and a longer term tranche are created by including an accrual bond. The accrual bond has appeal to investors who are concerned with reinvestment risk. Since there are no coupon payments to reinvest, reinvestment risk is eliminated until all the other tranches are paid off.

Essentially, credit unions are discouraged from investing in an accrual tranche CMO. Currently, credit unions are permitted to purchase accrual/Z bonds for hedging purposes only. However, the NCUA has noted that credit unions who have held these bonds in the past have been unable to demonstrate that they were using them as a hedge. Such being the case, credit unions will be prohibited from buying these tranches in the future. Existing holdings of these securities are permitted under a grandfathering provision in the revision to Part 703 depending on safety and soundness concerns being met. CMO testing, described in the next chapter, is critical to determine the legality of such bonds. In any event, credit unions should avoid these bonds, but it is important to understand their role in a CMO structure.

Exhibit 4: FAF-02: A Hypothetical Four-Tranche Sequential-Pay Structure with An Accrual Bond Class

Tranche	Par Amount	Coupon rate
A	$194,500,000	7.5%
B	36,000,000	7.5
C	96,500,000	7.5
Z (Accrual)	73,000,000	7.5
Total	$400,000,000	

Payment rules:

1. *For payment of periodic coupon interest:* Disburse periodic coupon interest to tranches A, B, and C on the basis of the amount of principal outstanding at the beginning of the period. For tranche Z, accrue the interest based on the principal plus accrued interest in the previous period. The interest for tranche Z is to be paid to the earlier tranches as a principal paydown.

2. *For disbursement of principal payments:* Disburse principal payments to tranche A until it is completely paid off. After tranche A is completely paid off, disburse principal payments to tranche B until it is completely paid off. After tranche B is completely paid off, disburse principal payments to tranche C until it is completely paid off. After tranche C is completely paid off, disburse principal payments to tranche Z until the original principal balance plus accrued interest is completely paid off.

Exhibit 5: Monthly Cash Flow for Selected Months for Tranches A and B of FAF-02 Assuming 165 PSA

Month	Tranche A			Tranche B		
	Balance	Principal	Interest	Balance	Principal	Interest
1	194,500,000	1,150,965	972,500	36,000,000	0	195,000
2	193,349,035	1,265,602	966,745	36,000,000	0	195,000
3	192,083,433	1,379,947	960,417	36,000,000	0	195,000
4	190,703,486	1,493,906	953,517	36,000,000	0	195,000
5	189,209,581	1,607,383	946,048	36,000,000	0	195,000
6	187,602,197	1,720,286	938,011	36,000,000	0	195,000
7	185,881,911	1,832,519	929,410	36,000,000	0	195,000
8	184,049,392	1,943,990	920,247	36,000,000	0	195,000
9	182,105,402	2,054,604	910,527	36,000,000	0	195,000
10	180,050,798	2,164,271	900,254	36,000,000	0	195,000
11	177,886,528	2,272,897	889,433	36,000,000	0	195,000
12	175,613,631	2,380,393	878,068	36,000,000	0	195,000
60	16,303,583	3,079,699	81,518	36,000,000	0	195,000
61	13,223,884	3,061,796	66,119	36,000,000	0	195,000
62	10,162,088	3,044,105	50,810	36,000,000	0	195,000
63	7,117,983	3,026,624	35,590	36,000,000	0	195,000
64	4,091,359	3,009,352	20,457	36,000,000	0	195,000
65	1,082,007	1,082,007	5,410	36,000,000	1,910,280	195,000
66	0	0	0	34,089,720	2,975,428	184,653
67	0	0	0	31,114,292	2,958,773	168,536
68	0	0	0	28,155,519	2,942,321	152,509
69	0	0	0	25,213,198	2,926,071	136,571
70	0	0	0	22,287,128	2,910,020	120,722
71	0	0	0	19,377,107	2,894,169	104,959
72	0	0	0	16,482,938	2,878,515	89,283
73	0	0	0	13,604,423	2,863,057	73,691
74	0	0	0	10,741,366	2,847,794	58,182
75	0	0	0	7,893,572	2,832,724	42,757
76	0	0	0	5,060,849	2,817,846	27,413
77	0	0	0	2,243,003	2,243,003	12,150
78	0	0	0	0	0	0
79	0	0	0	0	0	0
80	0	0	0	0	0	0

Exhibit 6: FAF-03: A Hypothetical Five-Tranche Sequential-Pay Structure with Floater, Inverse Floater, and Accrual Bond Classes

Tranche	Par amount	Coupon rate
A	$194,500,000	7.50%
B	36,000,000	7.50%
FL	72,375,000	1-mo. LIBOR + 0.50
IFL	24,125,000	28.50 − 3 × (1-mo. LIBOR)
Z (Accrual)	73,000,000	7.50%
Total	$400,000,000	

Payment rules:

1. *For payment of periodic coupon interest:* Disburse periodic coupon interest to tranches A, B, FL, and IFL on the basis of the amount of principal outstanding at the beginning of the period. For tranche Z, accrue the interest based on the principal plus accrued interest in the previous period. The interest for tranche Z is to be paid to the earlier tranches as a principal paydown. The maximum coupon rate for FL is 10%; the minimum coupon rate for IFL is 0%.

2. *For disbursement of principal payments:* Disburse principal payments to tranche A until it is completely paid off. After tranche A is completely paid off, disburse principal payments to tranche B until it is completely paid off. After tranche B is completely paid off, disburse principal payments to tranches FL and IFL until they are completely paid off. The principal payments between tranches FL and IFL should be made in the following way: 75% to tranche FL and 25% to tranche IFL. After tranches FL and IFL are completely paid off, disburse principal payments to tranche Z until the original principal balance plus accrued interest is completely paid off.

FLOATING-RATE TRANCHES

A floating-rate tranche can be created from a fixed-rate tranche by creating a floater and an inverse floater. We will illustrate the creation of a floating-rate and inverse floating-rate tranche using the hypothetical CMO structure FAF-02, which is a four-tranche sequential-pay structure with an accrual bond. We can select any of the tranches from which to create a floating-rate and inverse floating-rate tranche. In fact, we can create these two securities for more than one of the four tranches or for only a portion of one tranche.

In this case, we create a floater and an inverse floater from tranche C. The par value for this tranche is $96.5 million, and we create two tranches that have a combined par value of $96.5 million. We refer to this CMO structure with a floater and an inverse floater as FAF-03. It has five tranches, designated A, B, FL, IFL, and Z, where FL is the floating-rate tranche and IFL is the inverse floating-rate tranche. Exhibit 6 describes FAF-03. Any reference rate can be used to create a floater and the corresponding inverse floater. The reference rate for setting the coupon rate for FL and IFL in FAF-03 is 1-month LIBOR.

The amount of the par value of the floating-rate tranche will be some portion of the $96.5 million. There are an infinite number of ways to cut up the $96.5 million between the floater and inverse floater, and final partitioning will be driven by the demands of investors. In the FAF-03 structure, we made the floater from $72,375,000 or 75% of the $96.5 million. The coupon formula on the floater is 1-month LIBOR plus 50 basis points. So, for example, if LIBOR is 3.75% at the coupon reset date, the coupon rate on the floater is 3.75% + 0.5%, or 4.25%. There is a cap on the coupon rate for the floater (discussed later).

Unlike floating-rate notes whose principal is unchanged over the life of the instrument, the floater's principal balance declines over time as principal repayments are made. The principal payments to the floater are determined by the principal payments from the tranche from which the floater is created. In our CMO structure, this is tranche C.

Since the floater's par value is $72,375,000 of the $96.5 million, the balance is the inverse floater. Assuming that 1-month LIBOR is the reference rate, the coupon formula for the inverse floater takes the following form:

$$K - L \times (1\text{-month LIBOR})$$

In FAF-03, K is set at 28.50% and L at 3. Thus, if 1-month LIBOR is 3.75%, the coupon rate for the month is:

$$28.50\% - 3 \times 3.75\% = 17.25\%$$

K is the cap or maximum coupon rate for the inverse floater. In FAF-03, the cap for the inverse floater is 28.50%.

The L or multiple in the coupon formula for the inverse floater is called the *coupon leverage*. The higher the coupon leverage, the more the inverse floater's coupon rate changes for a given change in 1-month LIBOR. For example, a coupon leverage of 3.0 means that a 1-basis point change in 1-month LIBOR will change the coupon rate on the inverse floater by 3 basis points.

As in the case of the floater, the principal paydown of an inverse floater will be a proportionate amount of the principal pay down of tranche C.

Because 1-month LIBOR is always positive, the coupon rate paid to the floating-rate tranche cannot be negative. If there are no restrictions placed on the coupon rate for the inverse floater, however, it is possible for the coupon rate for that tranche to be negative. To prevent this, a floor can be placed on the coupon rate. In many structures, the floor is set at zero. Once a floor is set for the inverse floater, a cap is imposed on the floater. In FAF-03, a floor of zero is set for the inverse floater. The floor results in a cap for the floater of 10%.

The cap for the floater and the inverse floater, the floor for the inverse floater, the coupon leverage, and the index spread are not determined independently. Given four of these variables, the fifth will be determined.

PLANNED AMORTIZATION CLASS TRANCHES

In March 1987, the M.D.C. Mortgage Funding Corporation CMO Series 0 included a class of bonds referred to as "stabilized mortgage reduction term bonds" or "SMRT" bonds; another class in its CMO Series P was referred to as "planned amortization class bonds" or "PAC" bonds. The Oxford Acceptance Corporation III Series C CMOs included a class of bonds referred to as a "planned redemption obligation bonds" or "PRO" bonds. The characteristic common to these three bonds is that, if the prepayments are within a specified range, the cash flow pattern is known.

The greater predictability of the cash flow for these classes of bonds, now referred to exclusively as *PAC* bonds, occurs because there is a principal repayment schedule that must be satisfied. PAC bondholders have priority over all other tranches in the CMO structure in receiving principal payments from the underlying collateral. The greater certainty of the cash flow for the PAC bonds comes at the expense of the non-PAC classes, called the *support* or *companion* bonds. It is these bonds that absorb the prepayment risk. Because PAC bonds have protection against both extension risk and contraction, they are said to provide *two-sided prepayment protection*.

To illustrate how to create a PAC bond, we will use as collateral a $400 million passthrough with a coupon rate of 7.5%, an 8.125% WAC, and a WAM of 357 months. The second column of Exhibit 7 shows the principal payment (regularly scheduled principal repayment plus prepayments) for selected months assuming a prepayment speed of 90 PSA, and the next column shows the principal payments for selected months assuming that the passthrough prepays at 300 PSA.

The last column of Exhibit 7 gives the *minimum* principal payment if the collateral speed is 90 PSA or 300 PSA for months 1 to 349. (After month 349, the outstanding principal balance will be paid off if the prepayment speed is between 90 PSA and 300 PSA.) For example, in the first month, the principal payment would be $508,169.52 if the collateral prepays at 90 PSA and $1,075,931.20 if the collateral prepays at 300 PSA. Thus, the minimum principal payment is $508,169.52, as reported in the last column of Exhibit 7. In month 103, the minimum principal payment is also the amount if the prepayment speed is 90 PSA, $1,446,761, compared to $1,458,618.04 for 300 PSA. In month 104, however, a prepayment speed of 300 PSA would produce a principal payment of $1,433,539.23, which is less than the principal payment of $1,440,825.55 assuming 90 PSA. So, $1,433,539.23 is reported in the last column of Exhibit 7. In fact, from month 104 on the minimum principal payment is the one that would result assuming a prepayment speed of 300 PSA.

In fact, if the collateral prepays at any constant speed between 90 PSA and 300 PSA over its life, the minimum principal payment would be the amount reported in the last column of Exhibit 7. For example, if we had included principal payment figures assuming a prepayment speed of 200 PSA, the minimum principal payment would not change: from month 11 through month 103, the minimum principal payment is that generated from 90 PSA, but from month 104 on, the minimum principal payment is that generated from 300 PSA.

Exhibit 7: Monthly Principal Payment for $400 Million
7.5% Coupon Passthrough with an 8.125% WAC and a 357
WAM Assuming Prepayment Rates of 90 PSA and 300 PSA

Month	At 90% PSA	At 300% PSA	PAC schedule
		Minimum principal payment	
1	508,169.52	1,075,931.20	508,169.52
2	569,843.43	1,279,412.11	569,843.43
3	631,377.11	1,482,194.45	631,377.11
4	692,741.89	1,683,966.17	692,741.89
5	753,909.12	1,884,414.62	753,909.12
6	814,850.22	2,083,227.31	814,850.22
7	875,536.68	2,280,092.68	875,536.68
8	935,940.10	2,474,700.92	935,940.10
9	996,032.19	2,666,744.77	996,032.19
10	1,055,784.82	2,855,920.32	1,055,784.82
11	1,115,170.01	3,041,927.81	1,115,170.01
12	1,174,160.00	3,224,472.44	1,174,160.00
13	1,232,727.22	3,403,265.17	1,232,727.22
14	1,290,844.32	3,578,023.49	1,290,844.32
15	1,348,484.24	3,748,472.23	1,348,484.24
16	1,405,620.17	3,914,344.26	1,405,620.17
17	1,462,225.60	4,075,381.29	1,462,225.60
18	1,518,274.36	4,231,334.57	1,518,274.36
101	1,458,719.34	1,510,072.17	1,458,719.34
102	1,452,725.55	1,484,126.59	1,452,725.55
103	1,446,761.00	1,458,618.04	1,446,761.00
104	1,440,825.55	1,433,539.23	1,433,539.23
105	1,434,919.07	1,408,883.01	1,408,883.01
211	949,482.58	213,309.00	213,309.00
212	946,033.34	209,409.09	209,409.09
213	942,601.99	205,577.05	205,577.05
346	618,684.59	13,269.17	13,269.17
347	617,071.58	12,944.51	12,944.51
348	615,468.65	12,626.21	12,626.21
349	613,875.77	12,314.16	3,432.32
350	612,292.88	12,008.25	0
351	610,719.96	11,708.38	0
352	609,156.96	11,414.42	0
353	607,603.84	11,126.28	0
354	606,060.57	10,843.85	0
355	604,527.09	10,567.02	0
356	603,003.38	10,295.70	0
357	601,489.39	10,029.78	0

Exhibit 8: FAF-04 CMO Structure with One PAC Bond and One Support Bond

Tranche	Par amount	Coupon rate
P (PAC)	$243,800,000	7.5%
S (Support)	156,200,000	7.5
Total	400,000,000	

Payment rules:

1. *For payment of periodic coupon interest:* Disburse periodic coupon interest to each tranche on the basis of the amount of principal outstanding at the beginning of the period.

2. *For disbursement of principal payments:* Disburse principal payments to tranche P based on its schedule of principal repayments. Tranche P has priority with respect to current and future principal payments to satisfy the schedule. Any excess principal payments in a month over the amount necessary to satisfy the schedule for tranche P are paid to tranche S. When tranche S is completely paid off, all principal payments are to be made to tranche P regardless of the schedule.

This characteristic of the collateral allows for the creation of a PAC bond, assuming that the collateral prepays over its life at a speed between 90 PSA to 300 PSA. A schedule of principal repayments that the PAC bondholders are entitled to receive before any other bond class in the CMO structure is specified. The monthly schedule of principal repayments is as specified in the last column of Exhibit 7, which shows the minimum principal payment. While there is no assurance that the collateral will prepay between these two speeds over its life, a PAC bond can be structured to assume that it will.

Exhibit 8 shows a CMO structure, FAF-04, created from the $400 million, 7.5% coupon passthrough with a WAC of 8.125% and a WAM of 357 months. There are just two tranches in this structure: a 7.5% coupon PAC bond created assuming 90 to 300 PSA with a par value of $243.8 million, and a support bond with a par value of $156.2 million. The two speeds used to create a PAC bond are called the *initial PAC collars* (or *initial PAC bands*); in our case 90 PSA is the lower collar and 300 PSA the upper collar.

Exhibit 9 reports the average life for the PAC bond and the support bond in FAF-04 assuming various *actual* prepayment speeds. Notice that between 90 PSA and 300 PSA, the average life for the PAC bond is stable at 7.26 years. However, at slower or faster PSA speeds, the schedule is broken, and the average life changes, lengthening when the prepayment speed is less than 90 PSA and shortening when it is greater than 300 PSA. Even so, there is much greater variability for the average life of the support bond.

Exhibit 9: Average Life for PAC Bond and Support Bond in FAF-04 Assuming Various Prepayment Speeds

Prepayment rate (PSA)	PAC Bond (P)	Support Bond (S)
0	15.97	27.26
50	9.44	24.00
90	7.26	18.56
100	7.26	18.56
150	7.26	12.57
165	7.26	11.16
200	7.26	8.38
250	7.26	5.37
300	7.26	3.13
350	6.56	2.51
400	5.92	2.17
450	5.38	1.94
500	4.93	1.77
700	3.70	1.37

Sequential-Pay PAC Bonds

Most CMO PAC structures have more than one class of PAC bonds. We created six PAC bonds from FAF-04, which we call FAF-05. Information about this CMO structure is described in Exhibit 10. The total par value of the six PAC bonds is equal to $243.8 million, which is the amount of the single PAC bond in FAF-04.

Exhibit 11 shows the average life for the six PAC bonds and the support bond in FAF-05 at various prepayment speeds. From a PAC bond in FAF-04 with an average life of 7.26, we have created six bonds with an average life as short as 2.58 years (P-A) and as long as 16.92 years (P-F) if prepayments stay within 90 PSA and 300 PSA.

As expected, the average lives are stable if the prepayment speed is between 90 PSA and 300 PSA. Notice that even outside this range the average life is stable for several of the PAC bonds. For example, the PAC P-A bond is stable even if prepayment speeds are as high as 400 PSA. For the PAC P-B, the average life does not vary when prepayments are in the initial collar until prepayments are greater than 350 PSA. Why is it that the shorter the PAC, the more protection it has against faster prepayments?

To understand why this is so, remember that there are $156.2 million in support bonds that are protecting the $85 million of PAC P-A. Thus, even if prepayments are faster than the initial upper collar, there may be sufficient support bonds to assure the satisfaction of the schedule. In fact, as can been from Exhibit 11, even if prepayments are at 400 PSA over the life of the collateral, the average life is unchanged.

Exhibit 10: FAF-05 CMO Structure with Six PAC Bonds and One Support Bond

Tranche	Par amount	Coupon rate
P-A	$85,000,000	7.5%
P-B	8,000,000	7.5
P-C	35,000,000	7.5
P-D	45,000,000	7.5
P-E	40,000,000	7.5
P-F	30,800,000	7.5
S	156,200,000	7.5
Total	$400,000,000	

Payment rules:

1. *For payment of periodic coupon interest:* Disburse periodic coupon interest to each tranche on the basis of the amount of principal outstanding at the beginning of the period.

2. *For disbursement of principal payments:* Disburse principal payments to tranches P-A to P-F based on their respective schedules of principal repayments. Tranche P-A has priority with respect to current and future principal payments to satisfy the schedule. Any excess principal payments in a month over the amount necessary to satisfy the schedule for tranche P-A are paid to tranche S. Once tranche P-A is completely paid off, tranche P-B has priority, then tranche P-C, etc. When tranche S is completely paid off, all principal payments are to be made to the remaining PAC tranches in order of priority regardless of the schedule.

Exhibit 11: Average Life for the Six PAC Bonds in FAF-05 Assuming Various Prepayment Speeds

Prepayment rate (PSA)	PAC Bonds					
	P-A	P-B	P-C	P-D	P-E	P-F
0	8.46	14.61	16.49	19.41	21.91	23.76
50	3.58	6.82	8.36	11.30	14.50	18.20
90	2.58	4.72	5.78	7.89	10.83	16.92
100	2.58	4.72	5.78	7.89	10.83	16.92
150	2.58	4.72	5.78	7.89	10.83	16.92
165	2.58	4.72	5.78	7.89	10.83	16.92
200	2.58	4.72	5.78	7.89	10.83	16.92
250	2.58	4.72	5.78	7.89	10.83	16.92
300	2.58	4.72	5.78	7.89	10.83	16.92
350	2.58	4.72	5.94	6.95	9.24	14.91
400	2.57	4.37	4.91	6.17	8.33	13.21
450	2.50	3.97	4.44	5.56	7.45	11.81
500	2.40	3.65	4.07	5.06	6.74	10.65
700	2.06	2.82	3.10	3.75	4.88	7.51

Now consider PAC P-B. The support bonds are providing protection for both the $85 million of PAC P-A and $93 million of PAC P-B. As can be seen from Exhibit 11, prepayments could be 350 PSA and the average life is still unchanged. From Exhibit 11 it can be seen that the degree of protection against extension risk increases the shorter the PAC. Thus, while the initial collar may be 90 to 300 PSA, the *effective collar* is wider for the shorter PAC tranches.

Effective Collars and Actual Prepayments

The creation of a mortgage-backed security cannot make prepayment risk disappear. This is true for both a passthrough and a CMO. Thus, the reduction in prepayment risk (both extension risk and contraction risk) that a PAC offers must come from somewhere.

Where does the prepayment protection come from? It comes from the support bonds. It is the support bonds that forego principal payments if the collateral prepayments are slow; support bonds do not receive any principal until the PAC bonds receive the scheduled principal repayment. This reduces the risk that the PAC bonds will extend. Similarly, it is the support bonds that absorb any principal payments in excess of the scheduled principal payment that are made. This reduces the contraction risk of the PAC bonds. *Thus, the key to the prepayment protection offered by a PAC bond is the amount of support bonds outstanding. If the support bonds are paid off quickly because of faster-than-expected prepayments, then there is no longer any protection for the PAC bonds.* In fact, in FAF-05, if the support bond is paid off, the structure is effectively reduced to a sequential-pay CMO. In such cases, the schedule is unlikely to be maintained, and the structure is referred to as a *busted PAC*.

The support bonds can be thought of as bodyguards for the PAC bondholders. When the bullets fly — i.e., prepayments occur — it is the bodyguards that get killed off first. The bodyguards are there to absorb the bullets. Once all the bodyguards are killed off (i.e., the support bonds paid off with faster-than-expected payments), the PAC bonds must fend for themselves: they are exposed to all the bullets.

With the bodyguard metaphor for the support bonds in mind, let's consider two questions asked by CMO buyers:

1. Will the schedule of principal repayments be satisfied if prepayments are faster than the initial upper collar?
2. Will the schedule of principal repayments be satisfied as long as prepayments stay within the initial collar?

Let's address the first question. The initial upper collar for FAF-04 is 300 PSA? Suppose that actual prepayments are 500 PSA for seven consecutive months; will this disrupt the schedule of principal repayments? The answer is: It depends!

There are two pieces of information we will need to answer this question. First, when does the 500 PSA occur? Second, what has been the actual prepayment experience up to the time that prepayments are 500 PSA? For example, suppose six years from now is when the prepayments reach 500 PSA, and also suppose that for the next six years the actual prepayment speed has been 90 PSA every month. What this means is that there are more bodyguards (i.e., support bonds) around than was expected when the PAC was structured at the initial collar. In establishing the schedule of principal repayments, it was assumed that the bodyguards would be killed off at 300 PSA. But the actual prepayment experience results in them being killed off at only 90 PSA. Thus, six years from now when the 500 PSA is assumed to occur, there are more bodyguards than expected. Thus, a 500 PSA for seven consecutive months may have no effect on the ability of the schedule of principal repayments to be met.

In contrast, suppose that the actual prepayment experience for the next six years is 300 PSA (the upper collar of the initial PAC collar). In this case, there are no extra bodyguards around. As a result, any prepayment speeds faster than 300 PSA, such as 500 PSA in our example, jeopardize satisfaction of the principal repayment schedule and increase extension risk. This does not mean that the schedule will be broken. What it does mean is that the prepayment protection is reduced.

It should be clear from these observations that the initial collars are not particularly useful in assessing the prepayment protection for a seasoned PAC bond. This is most important to understand, as it is common for CMO buyers to compare prepayment protection of PACs in different CMO structures, and conclude that the greater protection is offered by the one with the wider collar. This approach is inadequate because it is actual prepayment experience that determines the degree of prepayment protection, as well as the expected future prepayment behavior of the collateral.

The way to determine this protection is to calculate the effective collar for a seasoned PAC bond. An effective collar for a seasoned PAC is the lower and the upper PSA that can occur in the future and still allow maintenance of the schedule of principal repayments.

The effective collar changes every month. An extended period over which actual prepayments are below the upper range of the initial PAC collar will result in an increase in the upper range of the effective collar. This is because there will be more bodyguards around than anticipated. An extended period of prepayments slower than the lower range of the initial PAC collar will raise the lower range of the effective collar. This is because it will take faster prepayments to make up the shortfall of the scheduled principal payments not made plus the future scheduled principal payments.

The PAC schedule may not be satisfied even if the actual prepayments never fall outside of the initial collar. This may seem surprising since our previous analysis indicated that the average life would not change if prepayments are at either extreme of the initial collar. However, recall that all of our previous analysis has been based on a single PSA speed for the life of the structure.

If we vary the PSA speed over time rather than keep it constant over the life of the CMO, we can see what happens to the effective collar if the prepayments are at the initial upper collar for a certain number of months.[2] Exhibit 12 shows the average life two years from now for the PAC bond in FAF-04 assuming that prepayments are 300 PSA for the first 24 months. Notice that the average life is stable at six years if the prepayments for the following months are between 115 PSA and 300 PSA. That is, the effective PAC collar is no longer the initial collar. Instead, the lower collar has shifted upward. This means that the protection from year 2 on is for 115 to 300 PSA, a narrower band than initially even though the earlier prepayments did not exceed the initial upper collar.

Providing Greater Prepayment Protection for PACs

One way to provide greater protection for PAC bonds is to issue fewer PAC bonds relative to support bonds. In FAF-05, for example, rather than creating the six PAC bonds with a total par value of $243.8 million, we could use only $158.8 million of the $400 million of collateral to create these bonds, by reducing the amount of each of the six PAC bonds. An alternative is not to issue one of the PAC bonds, typically the shorter-term one. For example, suppose that we create only the last five of the six PAC bonds in FAF-05. The $85 million for PAC P-A is then used to create more support bonds. Such a CMO structure with no principal payments to a PAC bond class in the earlier years is referred to as a *lockout structure*.

A lockout structure provides greater prepayment protection to all PAC bonds in the CMO structure. One way to provide greater prepayment protection to only some PAC bonds is to alter the principal payment rules for distributing principal once all the support bonds have been paid off. In FAF-05, for example, once the support bond in this structure is paid off, the structure effectively becomes a sequential-pay structure. For PAC P-A this means that while there is protection against extension risk, as this tranche receives principal payments before the other five PAC bonds, there is no protection against contraction risk.

Exhibit 12: Average Life Two Years from Now for PAC Bond of FAF-04 Assuming Prepayments of 300 PSA for First 24 Months

PSA from Year 2 on	Average Life
95	6.43
105	6.11
115	6.01
120	6.00
125	6.00
300	6.00
305	5.62

---

[2] When an analysis is performed by varying the PSA speed, it is referred to as *vector analysis*.

To provide greater protection to PAC P-A, the payment rules after all support bonds have been paid off can be specified so that any principal payments in excess of the scheduled amount will be paid to the last PAC bond, P-F. Thus, PAC P-F is exposed to greater contraction risk, which provides the other five PAC bonds with more protection against contraction risk. The principal payment rules would also specify that once the support bond and PAC P-F bond are paid off, then all principal payments in excess of the scheduled amounts to earlier tranches are to be paid to the next to the last PAC bond, PAC P-E in our example.

A CMO structure requiring any excess principal payments to be made to the longer PAC bonds after all support bonds are paid off is called a *reverse PAC structure*.

Other PAC Tranches

Earlier we described how the collateral can be used to create a CMO with accrual bonds, floaters, and inverse floaters. These same types of bond classes can be created from a PAC bond. The difference between the bond classes described and those created from a PAC bond is simply the prepayment protection offered by the PAC structure.

TARGETED AMORTIZATION CLASS BONDS

A *targeted amortization class*, or TAC, bond resembles a PAC bond in that both have a schedule of principal repayment. The difference between a PAC bond and a TAC bond is that the former has a wide PSA range over which the schedule of principal repayment is protected against contraction risk and extension risk. A TAC bond, in contrast, has a single PSA rate from which the schedule of principal repayment is protected. As a result, the prepayment protection afforded the TAC bond is less than that for a PAC bond. The creation of a bond with a schedule of principal repayments based on a single prepayment rate results in protection against contraction risk but not extension risk. Thus, while PAC bonds are said to have two-sided prepayment protection, TAC bonds have one-sided prepayment protection. Such a bond would not be acceptable to a credit union which seeks protection against extension risk.

Some institutional investors are interested in protection against extension risk but are willing to accept contraction risk. This is the opposite protection from that sought by the buyers of TAC bonds. The structures created to provide such protection are referred to as *reverse TAC bonds*.

VERY ACCURATELY DETERMINED MATURITY BONDS

Accrual or Z-bonds have been used in CMO structures as support for bonds called *very accurately determined maturity* (VADM) or *guaranteed final maturity bonds*.

In this case, the interest accruing (i.e., not being paid out) on a Z bond is used to pay the interest and principal on a VADM bond. This effectively provides protection against extension risk even if prepayments slow down, since the interest accruing on the Z bond will be sufficient to pay off the scheduled principal and interest on the VADM bond. Thus, the maximum final maturity can be determined with a high degree of certainty. If prepayments are high, resulting in the supporting Z bond being paid off faster, however, a VADM bond can shorten.

A VADM is similar in character to a reverse TAC. For structures with similar collateral, however, a VADM bond offers greater protection against extension risk. Moreover, most VADMs will not shorten significantly if prepayments speed up. Thus, they offer greater protection against contraction risk compared to a reverse TAC with the same underlying collateral. Compared to PACs, VADM bonds have greater absolute protection against extension risk, and while VADM bonds do not have as much protection against contraction risk, as noted previously, the structures that have included these bonds are such that contraction risk is generally not significant.

SUPPORT BONDS

The support bonds — or bodyguards — are the bonds that provide prepayment protection for the PAC tranches. *Consequently, support tranches expose investors to the greatest level of prepayment risk.* Because of this, investors must be particularly careful in assessing the cash flow characteristics of support bonds to reduce the likelihood of adverse portfolio consequences due to prepayments.

The support bond typically is divided into different bond classes. All the bond classes we have discussed earlier are available, including sequential-pay support bond classes, floater and inverse floater support bond classes, and accrual support bond classes.

The support bond can even be partitioned so as to create support bond classes with a schedule of principal repayments. That is, support bond classes that are PAC bonds can be created. In a structure with a PAC bond and a support bond with a PAC schedule of principal repayments, the former is called a PAC I bond or Level I PAC bond and the latter a PAC II bond or Level II PAC bond. While PAC II bonds have greater prepayment protection than the support bond classes without a schedule of principal repayments, the prepayment protection is less than that provided PAC I bonds.

CREDIT RISK

A CMO can be viewed as a business entity. The assets of this business are the collateral; that is, the passthrough securities or pool of mortgage loans backing the deal. The collateral for a CMO is held in trust for the exclusive benefit of all the bondholders. The liabilities are the payments due to the CMO bond classes. The liability obligation consists of the par value and periodic interest payment that is owed to each class of bond. The CMO or, equivalently, the business, is structured so that, even under the worst possible consequences concerning prepayments, all the liabilities will be satisfied.

Credit risk exposure depends on who the issuer of the CMO is. An issuer is either (1) a government sponsored enterprise (such as Freddie Mac or Fannie Mae) or (2) a private non-GSE entity. CMOs issued by the two government sponsored enterprises are referred to as *agency CMOs*. Those issued by a private entity can be divided into two types. A private entity that issues a CMO but whose underlying collateral is a pool of passthroughs guaranteed by an agency is called a *private-label CMO*. If the collateral for a CMO is a pool of whole loans the structure is referred to as a *whole-loan CMO*.

The guarantee of a government sponsored enterprise depends on the financial capacity of the agency. CMOs issued by private entities are rated by commercial rating agencies. Credit unions can invest in agency CMOs and nonagency CMOs that are rated at least in the two highest rating categories (Aaa/AAA to Aa3/AA−). However, a CMO tranche must pass the tests explained in the next chapter.

KEY POINTS

1. Collateralized mortgage obligations are bond classes created by redirecting the cash flows of passthroughs.

2. The creation of a CMO cannot eliminate prepayment risk, it can only transfer the various forms of this risk (contraction and extension) among different classes of bonds called tranches.

3. In a CMO there are rules for the distribution of interest and principal from the collateral to the bond classes.

4. In a sequential-pay CMO structure the tranches are retired in sequence.

5. The principal pay down window for a tranche is the time period between the beginning and the ending of the principal payments to that tranche.

6. An accrual bond is one in which the interest for that tranche accrues and is added to the principal balance.

7. A floating-rate tranche is created from a fixed-rate tranche by creating a floater and an inverse floater.

8. Unlike a floating-rate note whose principal is unchanged over the life of the instrument, the floater tranche's principal balance declines over time as principal prepayments are made.

9. A floating-rate tranche has a cap.

10. An inverse floater is a tranche that has a coupon rate that changes every month in the opposite direction of the change in the reference rate.

11. A planned amortization class (PAC) has a principal schedule that must be met monthly before any other tranche in the structure may receive principal payments.

12. A planned amortization class tranche has reduced average life variability with the better prepayment protection provided by the support tranches.

13. If the support bonds of a CMO structure are fully paid off, the PAC bonds no longer have prepayment protection.

14. An effective collar for a seasoned PAC is the lower and the upper PSA that can occur in the future and still allow maintenance of the schedule of principal repayments.

15. The effective collar for a PAC differs from its initial collar as the amount of the support bonds change over time.

16. Most CMO PAC structures have more than one class of PAC bonds.

17. A reverse PAC structure is one in which any excess principal payments be made to the longer PAC bonds after all support bonds are paid off.

18. A targeted amortization class (TAC) has a schedule of principal repayment but does not provide protection against extension risk.

19. A reverse TAC has a schedule of principal repayment but does provide protection against extension risk.

20. A very accurately determined maturity (VADM) bond provides protection primarily against extension risk.

21. The key role of support bonds in a CMO structure is to provide prepayment protection for the PAC tranches.

22. Support bonds expose investors to the greatest level of prepayment risk.

23. Support bonds can be partitioned so as to create support bonds with a schedule of principal repayments.

24. While support bonds with a schedule have greater prepayment protection than the support bonds without a schedule of principal repayments, the prepayment protection is less than that provided PAC I bonds.

25. Credit risk exposure is minimal for agency CMOS.

26. A REMIC is a CMO structure that satisfies specific provisions of the tax code, but this distinction is only relevant for other institutional investors and not for credit unions due to their tax-exempt status.

Chapter 7

Prepayment Models and CMO Testing

The objectives of this chapter are to:

1. explain what a prepayment model is;

2. discuss the factors that affect prepayments;

3. explain the high risk securities test for determining whether a CMO is a permissible investment; and,

4. explain the role of prepayment models in the high risk securities test.

A credit union that is considering investing in a collateralized mortgage obligation (CMO) tranche must be aware of a special test that must be performed in order to purchase and retain such a security. Specifically, Part 703 requires that a credit union perform a *high risk security test*. A CMO tranche that is classified as a high risk security based on this test is not a permissible investment. This test is in addition to a *stress test* that is required of all investments to assess the potential price volatility of a security when interest rates change. In this chapter, we focus on the high risk security test for CMOs. In Chapter 11, we explain the stress test required by Part 703. Since both the assessment of the relative value of a CMO tranche and the high risk security test depend on the prepayment model selected, we begin with a discussion of prepayment models.

PREPAYMENT MODELS

A prepayment model is a statistical model that is used to forecast prepayments. It begins by modeling the statistical relationships among the factors that are expected to affect prepayments. We will explain these factors below.

The product of a prepayment forecast is not one prepayment rate but a set of prepayment rates for each month of the remaining term of a mortgage pool. The set of monthly prepayment rates, however, is not reported by Wall Street firms or vendors. Instead, the monthly rates are converted into a single prepayment rate and it is this rate that is reported.

One way to convert a set of monthly prepayment rates into a single prepayment rate is to calculate a simple average of the prepayment rates. The obvious drawback to this approach is that it does not take into consideration the outstanding balance each month. An alternative approach is to use some type of weighted average, selecting the weights to reflect the amount of the monthly cash flow corresponding to a monthly prepayment rate. This is done by first computing the cash flow yield (discussed in Chapter 9) for a passthrough given its market price and the set of monthly prepayment rates. Then a single prepayment rate (CPR or PSA multiple) that gives the same cash flow yield is found.

The factors that affect prepayment behavior are: (1) prevailing mortgage rates, (2) characteristics of the underlying mortgage pool, (3) seasonal factors, and (4) general economic activity. We discuss each factor below.

Prevailing Mortgage Rate

The current mortgage rate affects prepayments in three ways. First, the spread between the prevailing mortgage rate and the contract rate paid by the homeowner affects the incentive to refinance. (By contract rate we mean the rate on the mortgage loan.) Second, the path of mortgage rates since the loan was originated affects prepayments through a phenomenon referred to as *refinancing burnout*. Both the spread and path of mortgage rates affect prepayments that are the product of refinancing. The third way in which the prevailing mortgage rate affects prepayments is through its effect on the affordability of housing and housing turnover.

The single most important factor affecting prepayments because of refinancing is the current level of mortgage rates relative to the borrower's contract rate. The greater the difference between the two, the greater the incentive to refinance the mortgage loan. For refinancing to make economic sense, the interest savings must be greater than the costs associated with refinancing the mortgage. These costs include legal expenses, origination fees, title insurance, and the value of the time associated with obtaining another mortgage loan. Some of these costs — such as title insurance and origination points — will vary proportionately with the amount to be financed. Other costs such as the application fee and legal expenses are typically fixed.

Historically, it has been observed that when mortgage rates fall to more than 200 basis points below the contract rate, prepayment rates increase. However, the creativity of mortgage originators in designing mortgage loans such that the refinancing costs are folded into the amount borrowed has changed the view that mortgage rates must drop dramatically below the contract rate to make refinancing economic. Moreover, mortgage originators now do an effective job of advertising to make homeowners cognizant of the economic benefits of refinancing.

The historical pattern of prepayments and economic theory suggest that it is not only the level of mortgage rates that affects prepayment behavior but also the path that mortgage rates take to get to the current level.

To illustrate why, suppose the underlying contract rate for a pool of mortgage loans is 11% and that, three years after origination, the prevailing mortgage rate declines to 8%. Let's consider two possible paths of the mortgage rate in getting to the 8% level. In the first path, the mortgage rate declines to 8% at the end of the first year, then rises to 13% at the end of the second year, and then falls to 8% at the end of the third year. In the second path, the mortgage rate rises to 12% at the end of the first year, continues its rise to 13% at the end of the second year, and then falls to 8% at the end of the third year.

If the mortgage rate follows the first path, those who can benefit from refinancing will more than likely take advantage of this opportunity when the mortgage rate drops to 8% in the first year. When the mortgage rate drops again to 8% at the end of the third year, the likelihood is that prepayments because of refinancing will not surge; those who can benefit by taking advantage of the refinancing opportunity will have done so already when the mortgage rate declined for the first time. This is the prepayment behavior referred to earlier as refinancing burnout.

In contrast, the expected prepayment behavior when the mortgage rate follows the second path is quite different. Prepayment rates are expected to be low in the first two years. When the mortgage rate declines to 8% in the third year, refinancing activity and therefore, prepayments are expected to surge. Consequently, the burnout phenomenon is related to the path of mortgage rates.

Characteristics of the Underlying Mortgage Loans

The following characteristics of the underlying mortgage loans affect prepayments: (1) the contract rate, (2) whether the loans are FHA/VA-guaranteed or conventional, (3) the amount of seasoning, (4) the type of loan, for example, a 30-year level payment mortgage, 5-year balloon mortgage, etc., and (5) the geographical location of the underlying properties.

Seasonal Factors

There is a well-documented seasonal pattern in prepayments. This pattern is related to activity in the primary housing market, with home buying increasing in the spring, and gradually reaching a peak in the late summer. Home buying declines in the fall and winter. Mirroring this activity are the prepayments that result from the turnover of housing as home buyers sell their existing homes and purchase new ones. Prepayments are low in the winter months and begin to rise in the spring, reaching a peak in the summer months. However, probably because of delays in passing through prepayments, the peak may not be observed until early fall.

Macroeconomic Factors

Economic theory would suggest that general economic activity affects prepayment behavior through its effect on housing turnover. The link is as follows: a growing economy results in a rise in personal income and in opportunities for worker migration; this increases family mobility and as a result increases housing turnover. The opposite holds for a weak economy.

Although some modelers of prepayment behavior may incorporate macroeconomic measures of economic activity such as gross domestic product, industrial production, or housing starts, the trend has been to ignore them or limit their use to specific applications. Macroeconomic variables have been used by some researchers in prepayment models to capture the effect of housing turnover on prepayments by specifying a relationship between interest rates and housing turnover.

CMO TESTING

Part 703 requires that before a credit union can purchase a particular CMO tranche, the portfolio manager must perform a test to determine whether a CMO is a high risk security. The high risk security test is more commonly referred to as the *FFIEC test* and is referred to in Part 703 as the high risk security test (HRST). While prior to the proposed revision to Part 703 a credit union had to apply the HRST to fixed-rate CMO tranches, a significant change in Part 703 was to require the application of the full test to floating-rate CMO tranches.

The FFIEC test was first proposed in 1988 by the Federal Financial Institutions Examination Council (FFIEC). This entity is a government advisory organization consisting of five member agencies: the Board of Governors of the

Federal Reserve System, the Federal Deposit Insurance Corporation, the National Credit Union Administration, the Office of the Comptroller of the Currency, and the Office of Thrift Supervision. In December 1991, the FFIEC approved a policy statement entitled "Supervisory Statement on Securities Activities," which subsequently became effective for depository institutions regulated by these agencies.

The FFIEC supervisory policy statement addresses:

1. how depository institutions should select securities dealers.
2. requirements for establishing prudent strategies for securities transactions.
3. the identification of sales or trading practices viewed by the agencies as unsuitable.
4. the characteristics of loans held for sale or trading.
5. tests for identifying when certain mortgage derivative products are to be classified as high risk securities[1] and thereby held either in a trading account or held-for-sale account.

Our focus here is on the last issue and its application to CMO tranches. The FFIEC test was developed for all depository institutions. Part 703 qualifies these rules for credit unions.

The general principle underlying the FFIEC test is that a CMO tranche that exhibits an average life or price volatility that is greater than a benchmark fixed-rate 30-year passthrough security is to be classified as a high risk security and is not a suitable investment for depository institutions. (The test for classifying a CMO tranche as a high risk security is discussed later.)

The FFIEC supervisory policy statement does not specify that a depository institution cannot acquire a CMO tranche that is classified as a high risk security. Rather, it (1) states how a CMO tranche must be treated for accounting purposes, (2) discusses what the motivation should be for acquiring such a security, and (3) addresses the capacity of a depository institution to accept the risks and understand those risks. However, Part 703 specifies that a credit union may not invest in a CMO tranche classified as a high risk security.

Classification of a CMO Tranche as a High Risk Security

The rule for classifying a CMO tranche as a high risk security has been quantified by the FFIEC supervisory policy statement. A high risk (mortgage) security is defined as any CMO tranche that at the time of purchase, or at a subsequent testing date, meets any one of three tests. The three tests that comprise the FFIEC test or HRST are as follows:

Average life test: The average life of the CMO tranche is greater than 10 years.

---

[1] While Part 703 refers to high risk securities, FFIEC refers to high risk mortgage securities.

Average life sensitivity test: The average life of the CMO tranche either (a) extends by more than four years assuming an immediate and sustained parallel shift in the yield of plus 300 basis points, or (b) shortens by more than six years, assuming an immediate and sustained parallel shift in the yield curve of minus 300 basis points.[2]

Price sensitivity test: The estimated change in the price of the CMO tranche due to an immediate and sustained parallel shift in the yield curve of plus or minus 300 basis points is more than 17%. (The initial price to be used in the price sensitivity test is determined by the offer side of the market and used as the base price.)

As noted at the outset of this chapter, there is a stress test for all investments to assess their price sensitivity to interest rate changes. The HRST includes a price sensitivity test. While a CMO tranche may not fail the price sensitivity test that is part of the HRST, it may fail the stress test.

It should be emphasized that, in general, even if a CMO tranche is not classified as a high risk security, this does not mean that a CMO tranche is an acceptable investment for a credit union. What it means is that examiners will not have a problem with the CMO tranche if it is purchased assuming that it passes the stress test. However, it should be noted that in the wake of the failure of Capital Corporate FCU and the revisions to Part 703, a credit union should be completely prepared for increased regulatory scrutiny concerning the future purchase of CMOs.

There are two critical assumptions in the HRST: (1) the prepayment assumption, and (2) for the price sensitivity test the appropriate rate to discount the cash flows when yields are changed.

Prepayment Assumption

With respect to the prepayment assumption, the same assumption used in the average life test must also be used in the price sensitivity test. There is considerable concern by regulators that credit unions can "play" with the prepayment assumption so as to avoid the classification of a CMO tranche as a high risk security.

To reduce a credit union's flexibility in this matter, the proposed revision to Part 703.4(e) sets forth that the board of directors must make a decision between using a *median* prepayment estimate or the selection of a *minimum* of *two* specific models. Furthermore, the board must state and identify in its policy statement which models it will use. At the time of purchase, a CMO tranche must pass the FFIEC test using each of the prepayment models identified.

As with the case of independent credit valuation, the selection of prepayment models is an instance of credit unions being held to a standard which no other institutional investor must meet. Furthermore, it is doubtful that a credit union director has either the investment experience or acumen to discern which

---

[2] In Chapter 10 we will explain what a parallel shift in the yield curve means.

prepayment model is most appropriate for their institution. Thus, this burden of selecting prepayment models is best left to management with oversight responsibilities of this process resting with the board or asset/liability committee.

Selecting the Appropriate Discount Rate

The appropriate rate to discount the cash flow is specified in the FFIEC supervisory policy statement. As explained in the next chapter, the valuation of a security depends on the interest rate that is used to discount the cash flow. The procedure for determining the discount rate is as follows. First, calculate the yield spread over a comparable average life Treasury. The yield on the Treasury is based on the bid side of the market. "Yield" for the CMO tranche while not specified in the policy statement, means the cash flow yield that we will discuss in Chapter 9. Then the calculated yield spread is added to the Treasury rate when the yield curve is assumed to shift plus and minus 300 basis points.

Applicability of Tests to Certain CMO Tranches

For depository institutions in general, all CMO tranches are subject to the HRST. A CMO tranche such as an interest-only tranche cannot be tested with respect to an average life test or an average life sensitivity test, since there is no principal received. In such cases, the CMO tranche is still subject to the price sensitivity test. This is irrelevant for a credit union since Part 703 prohibits the purchase of an interest-only security.

For depository institutions in general, a floating-rate CMO tranche class is not subject to the average life and average life sensitivity tests if the following three conditions are satisfied at the time of purchase or a subsequent testing date: (1) the rate is below the cap,[3] (2) the rate adjusts at least annually on a one-for-one basis with the index, and (3) the index is a conventional, widely used market interest rate index. The proposed revision to Part 703 overrules this exemption and requires that all three tests that comprise the FFIEC test be applied.

Retesting of a CMO Tranche

The FFIEC test must be conducted prior to executing a trade and at subsequent dates. For all CMO tranches acquired, Part 703 requires that they be retested at least quarterly to determine if any CMO tranche requires reclassification as a high risk security. When this occurs, the CMO tranches reclassified will most likely need to be disposed of by the credit union within the time period established by the proposed divestiture requirement of section 703.7.

The role of the prepayment models identified in the policy statement is different for retesting than for the initial purchase of a CMO tranche. In the latter case, the CMO tranche that is a candidate for purchase must pass the HRST using

---

[3] The cap can be removed by purchasing an interest rate cap. However, a credit union is not permitted to purchase a cap.

all prepayment models identified. For retesting purposes, the CMO tranche held need only pass the HRST for the "majority" of the prepayment models if more than one model is identified. Thus, if three prepayment models are identified, the HRST must be passed using two of the prepayment models. If only two models are identified, then the HRST must be passed using both models. If a median prepayment estimate is identified in the policy statement, then the HRST must be passed using the median prepayment estimate constructed in the same manner.

Part 703 specifies that retesting not only be done on at least a quarterly basis, but that the retesting must be documented. Written notification must be sent to the Board of Directors and the Regional Director if a CMO tranche is reclassified as a high risk security. If a federal credit union does not plan to immediately sell the reclassified security, it must provide the Regional Director with a written divestiture plan. The rule further states that the credit union is not required to sell the investment until a written response to the divestiture plan is received, barring serious safety and soundness concerns.

Other Important Considerations

Managers of credit unions should be aware of two other key aspects of the FFIEC supervisory policy statement when they are contemplating the acquisition of a CMO tranche.

First, an analysis of whether a CMO tranche is a high risk security must be undertaken prior to acquisition. The supporting documentation must be retained and made available to the examiner. Any analysis and supporting documentation performed after an acquisition in order to justify the acquisition is subject to examiner criticism. Reliance on analysis by a dealer firm or other outside party without supporting internal analysis is also subject to examiner criticism.

Second, in undertaking the analysis, a credit union can rely on industry "calculators" used in the mortgage-backed securities marketplace, and considered independent. For newly issued CMO deals whose cash flows are not modeled yet by vendors, the deal must be reverse engineered so that analysis can be performed. Seasoned CMO deals have typically been modeled by the services. Furthermore, it is our understanding that the NCUA, in practice, has discouraged the purchase of unmodeled CMO deals and will continue to do so.

KEY POINTS

1. There are two types of tests required by Part 703 that must be performed by a credit union in connection with a CMO: (1) FFIEC test or high risk security test (HRST) and (2) stress test (required of all investments).

2. Critical to the analysis of mortgage-backed securities is the selection of a prepayment model.

3. A prepayment model is a statistical model used to forecast prepayments.

4. A prepayment model incorporates the four factors that affect prepayments: prevailing mortgage rate, characteristics of the underlying mortgage pool, seasonal factors, and general economic activity.

5. A prepayment forecast is expressed in terms of the PSA prepayment benchmark.

6. The prepayment rates projected by Wall Street firms are reported by financial services.

7. The single most important factor affecting prepayments because of refinancing is the current level of mortgage rates relative to the borrower's contract rate.

8. It is not only the level of mortgage rates that affects prepayment behavior but also the path that mortgage rates take to get to the current level.

9. The following characteristics of the underlying mortgage loans affect prepayments: (1) the contract rate, (2) whether the loans are FHA/VA-guaranteed or conventional, (3) the amount of seasoning, (4) the type of loan, and (5) the geographical location of the underlying properties.

10. There is a well-documented seasonal pattern in prepayments in which prepayments are low in the winter months and begin to rise in the spring, reaching a peak in the summer months.

11. General economic activity affects prepayment behavior through its effect on housing turnover.

12. Part 703 requires that before a credit union can purchase a particular CMO tranche, the portfolio manager must perform a FFIEC test to determine whether a fixed-rate or floating-rate CMO tranche is a high risk security.

13. A CMO tranche that is classified according to the FFIEC test as a high risk security is an ineligible investment and may not be purchased by a credit union.

14. A high risk security is classified as any CMO tranche that at the time of purchase, or at a subsequent testing date, meets any one of three tests: average life test, the average life sensitivity test, and the price sensitivity test.

15. While a CMO tranche may not fail the price sensitivity test which is part of the FFIEC test, it may fail the stress test.

16. In general, passage of the high risk security test does not mean that a CMO tranche is an acceptable investment for a credit union.

17. There is considerable concern by regulators that credit unions can manipulate the prepayment assumption so as to avoid the classification of a CMO tranche as a high risk security.

18. The proposed revision to Part 703.4(e) severely limits the flexibility of a credit union to select a favorable prepayment assumption.

19. The proposed revision to Part 703.4(e) sets forth that the board of directors must make a decision between using a median prepayment estimate or the selection of a minimum of two specific models.

20. The board must state and identify in its policy statement which prepayment models its will use.

21. At the time of purchase, a CMO tranche must pass the high risk security test using each of the prepayment models identified.

22. Part 703 requires that a CMO tranche be retested at least quarterly (more frequently if market conditions warrant) to determine if it requires reclassification as a high risk security and must then be disposed of by the credit union.

23. When retesting a CMO tranche held in a credit union portfolio, that security need only pass the high risk security test for the majority of the prepayment models identified.

Chapter 8

Valuation of Fixed Income Securities

The objectives of this chapter are to:

1. discuss the process involved in valuing a fixed income security;

2. explain the situations in which determination of the cash flow of a fixed income security is complex;

3. explain why a fixed income security should be viewed as a package of zero-coupon securities;

4. demonstrate how the Treasury theoretical spot rate curve can be used to value any Treasury security;

5. explain why the price of a Treasury security will not deviate significantly from its theoretical value based on spot rates;

6. explain how credit risk should be introduced into the term structure;

7. explain what is meant by interest rate volatility and why the volatility assumption is critical in valuing bonds with embedded options.

8. discuss the binomial model for valuing bonds with embedded options;

9. discuss the Monte Carlo simulation model for valuing mortgage-backed securities; and,

10. review the assumptions in each valuation model.

Valuation is the process of determining the fair value of a financial asset. The fundamental principle of valuation is that the value of any financial asset is the present value of the expected cash flow. This principle applies regardless of the financial asset. In this chapter, we will explain the general principles of fixed income valuation and two valuation models. Yields and yield spreads are often cited in the bond market and used as a measure of relative value. We postpone our discussion of yields and yield spread measures until the next chapter where we discuss how they are calculated and their limitations.

ESTIMATING CASH FLOW

Cash flow is simply the cash that is expected to be received each period from an investment. In the case of a fixed income security, it does not make any difference whether the cash flow is interest income or repayment of principal.

The cash flow for only a few types of fixed income securities are simple to project. Noncallable Treasury securities have a known cash flow. For a Treasury coupon security, the cash flow is the coupon interest payments every six months up to the maturity date and the principal payment at the maturity date. So, for example, the cash flow per $100 of par value for a 7%, 10-year Treasury security is the following: $3.5 (7%/2 × $100) every six months for the next 20 6-month periods and $100 20 6-month periods from now. Or, equivalently, the cash flow is $3.5 every six months for the next 19 6-month periods and $103.50 20 6-month periods from now.

In fact, for any fixed income security in which neither the issuer nor the investor can alter the repayment of the principal before its contractual due date, the cash flow can easily be determined assuming that the issuer does not default.

Credit unions will find it difficult to estimate the cash flow when they purchase a fixed income security where (1) either the issuer or the investor has the option to change the contractual due date of the repayment of the principal or (2) the coupon payment is reset periodically based on a formula that depends on some value or values for reference rates, prices or exchange rates. Callable bonds, putable bonds, and mortgage-backed securities are examples of the former; floating rate securities and structured notes are examples of the latter.

As explained in Chapter 2, there are issues that include a provision in the indenture that grants the issuer or the security holder the right to change the scheduled date or dates when the principal repayment is due. Assuming that the issuer does not default, the investor knows that the principal amount will be repaid, but does not know when that principal will be received. Because of this, the cash flow is not known with certainty.

A key factor determining whether either the issuer of the security or the investor would exercise an option is the level of interest rates in the future relative to the security's coupon rate. Specifically, for a callable bond, if the prevailing market rate at which the issuer can call an issue is sufficiently below the issue's coupon rate to justify the costs associated with refunding the issue, the issuer is likely to call the issue. Similarly, for a mortgage loan, if the prevailing refinancing rate available in the mortgage market is sufficiently below the loan's mortgage rate so that there will be savings by refinancing after considering the associated refinancing costs, then the homeowner has an incentive to refinance. For a putable bond, if the rate on comparable securities rises such that the value of the putable bond falls below the value at which it must be repurchased by the issuer, then the investor will put the issue.

What this means is that to properly estimate the cash flow of a fixed income security it is necessary to incorporate into the analysis how interest rates can change in the future and how such changes affect the cash flow. As we will see later, this is done in valuation models by introducing a parameter that reflects the volatility of interest rates.

DISCOUNTING THE CASH FLOW[1]

Once the cash flow for a fixed income security is estimated, the next step is to determine the appropriate interest rate. To determine the appropriate rate, the investor must address the following three questions:

1. What is the minimum interest rate the investor should require?
2. How much more than the minimum interest rate should the investor require?
3. Should the investor use the same interest rate for each estimated cash flow or a unique interest rate for each estimated cash flow?

The minimum interest rate that an investor should require is the yield available in the marketplace on a default-free cash flow. In the U.S., this is the yield on a U.S. Treasury security. The premium over the yield on a Treasury security that the investor should require should reflect the risks associated with realizing the estimated cash flow.

The traditional practice in valuation has been to discount every cash flow of a fixed income security by the same interest rate (or discount rate). For example, consider the three hypothetical 10-year Treasury securities shown in Exhibit 1: a 12% coupon bond, an 8% coupon bond, and a zero-coupon bond. The cash flow for each security is shown in the exhibit. Since the cash flow of all three securities is viewed as default free, the traditional practice is to use the same discount rate to calculate the present value of all three securities and the same discount for the cash flow for each period.

The fundamental flaw of the traditional approach is that it views each security as the same package of cash flows. For example, consider a 10-year U.S. Treasury bond with an 8% coupon rate. The cash flow per $100 of par value

---

[1] For readers unfamiliar with the discounting of cash flows, see the appendix.

would be 19 payments of $4 every six months and at the end of 10 years (20 semi-annual periods) a payment of $104. The traditional practice would discount every cash flow using the same interest rate.

The proper way to view the 10-year 8% coupon bond is as a package of zero-coupon instruments. Each cash flow should be considered a zero-coupon instrument whose maturity value is the amount of the cash flow and whose maturity date is the date of the cash flow. Thus, the 10-year 8% coupon bond should be viewed as 20 zero-coupon instruments. The reason that this is the proper way is because it does not allow a market participant to realize an arbitrage profit. This will be made clearer later in this chapter.

By viewing any financial asset in this way, a consistent valuation framework can be developed. For example, under the traditional approach to the valuation of fixed income securities, a 10-year zero-coupon bond would be viewed as the same financial asset as a 10-year 8% coupon bond. Viewing a financial asset as a package of zero-coupon instruments means that these two bonds would be viewed as different packages of zero-coupon instruments and valued accordingly.

Exhibit 1: Cash Flow for Three 10-Year Hypothetical Treasury Securities Per $1,000 of Par Value
Each period is six months

Period	12% coupon	8% coupon	0 coupon
1	$60	$40	$0
2	60	40	0
3	60	40	0
4	60	40	0
5	60	40	0
6	60	40	0
7	60	40	0
8	60	40	0
9	60	40	0
10	60	40	0
11	60	40	0
12	60	40	0
13	60	40	0
14	60	40	0
15	60	40	0
16	60	40	0
17	60	40	0
18	60	40	0
19	60	40	0
20	1,060	1,040	1,000

Exhibit 2: Comparison of Traditional Approach and Contemporary Approach in Valuing Financial Assets
Each period is six months

	Discount (Interest) Rate		Treasury Security (coupon)		
Period	Traditional Approach	Contemporary Approach	12%	8%	0%
1	10-year Treasury rate	1-period spot rate	$60	$40	$0
2	10-year Treasury rate	2-period spot rate	60	40	0
3	10-year Treasury rate	3-period spot rate	60	40	0
4	10-year Treasury rate	4-period spot rate	60	40	0
5	10-year Treasury rate	5-period spot rate	60	40	0
6	10-year Treasury rate	6-period spot rate	60	40	0
7	10-year Treasury rate	7-period spot rate	60	40	0
8	10-year Treasury rate	8-period spot rate	60	40	0
9	10-year Treasury rate	9-period spot rate	60	40	0
10	10-year Treasury rate	10-period spot rate	60	40	0
11	10-year Treasury rate	11-period spot rate	60	40	0
12	10-year Treasury rate	12-period spot rate	60	40	0
13	10-year Treasury rate	13-period spot rate	60	40	0
14	10-year Treasury rate	14-period spot rate	60	40	0
15	10-year Treasury rate	15-period spot rate	60	40	0
16	10-year Treasury rate	16-period spot rate	60	40	0
17	10-year Treasury rate	17-period spot rate	60	40	0
18	10-year Treasury rate	18-period spot rate	60	40	0
19	10-year Treasury rate	19-period spot rate	60	40	0
20	10-year Treasury rate	20-period spot rate	1,060	1,040	1,000

The difference between the traditional valuation approach and the contemporary approach is depicted in Exhibit 2, which shows how the three bonds whose cash flow is depicted in Exhibit 1 should be valued. With the traditional approach, the minimum interest rate for all three securities is the yield on a 10-year U.S. Treasury security. With the contemporary approach the minimum yield for a cash flow is the theoretical rate that the U.S. Treasury would have to pay if it issued a zero-coupon bond with a maturity date equal to the date the cash flow will be recovered.

Therefore, to implement the contemporary approach it is necessary to determine the theoretical rate that the U.S. Treasury would have to pay to issue a zero-coupon instrument for each maturity. Another name used for the zero-coupon rate is the *spot rate*. As explained later, the spot rate can be estimated from the Treasury yield curve.

SPOT RATES AND THEIR ROLE IN VALUATION

The key to the valuation of any security is the estimation of its cash flow and the discounting of each cash flow by an appropriate rate. The starting point for the determination of the appropriate rate is the theoretical spot rate on default-free securities. Since Treasury securities are viewed as default-free securities, the theoretical spot rates on these securities are the benchmark rates.

The Treasury Yield Curve

The graphical depiction of the relationship between the yield on Treasury securities of different maturities is known as the *yield curve*. The Treasury yield curve is typically constructed from on-the-run Treasury issues. Treasury bills are zero-coupon securities. Treasury notes and bonds are coupon securities. Consequently, the Treasury yield curve is a combination of zero-coupon securities and coupon securities.

In the valuation of securities what is needed is the rate on zero-coupon default-free securities or, equivalently, the rate on zero-coupon Treasury securities. However, there are no zero-coupon Treasury securities issued by the U.S. Department of the Treasury with a maturity greater than one year. Based on arbitrage arguments, it is common for market participants to construct a theoretical rate that the U.S. government would have to offer if it issued zero-coupon securities with a maturity greater than one year.

Exhibit 3 shows a hypothetical yield curve for 20 Treasury securities. The theoretical spot rates are shown in the last column. The procedure for calculating the theoretical spot rates is beyond the scope of this chapter. The theoretical spot rates represent the term structure of default-free spot rate for maturities up to ten years at the particular time to which the bond price quotations refer.

Valuing a Treasury Bond with Spot Rates

Now let's use the theoretical spot rates to price two Treasury securities: an 8% 10-year issue and a 6% 10-year issue. Exhibits 4 and 5 show how this is done. In each exhibit, the cash flow is shown in the third column and the spot rates taken from Exhibit 1 are shown in the fourth column. The present value of each period's cash flow is shown in the last column. The sum of the present values is the theoretical value for the Treasury security. For the 6% 10-year Treasury it is 100. This agrees with the observed price for this security as shown in Exhibit 1. For the 8% 10-year Treasury, the theoretical value is 115.2619.

Why Treasuries Must be Valued Based on Spot Rates

The value of a Treasury security is determined by the spot rates, not the yield-to-maturity of a Treasury coupon security of the same maturity. We will use an illustration to demonstrate the economic forces that will assure that the actual market price of a Treasury coupon security will not depart significantly from its theoretical price.

To demonstrate this, consider the 8% 10-year Treasury security. Suppose that this Treasury security is priced based on the 6% yield to maturity of the 10-year maturity Treasury coupon security in Exhibit 1. Discounting all of the cash flows of the 8% 10-year Treasury security at 6% gives a present value of 114.88.

Exhibit 3: Maturity and Yield to Maturity for 20 Hypothetical Treasury Securities

Period	Years	Yield to maturity	Price	Spot rate
1	0.5	3.00	—	3.0000
2	1.0	3.30	—	3.3000
3	1.5	3.50	100.00	3.5053
4	2.0	3.90	100.00	3.9164
5	2.5	4.40	100.00	4.4376
6	3.0	4.70	100.00	4.7520
7	3.5	4.90	100.00	4.9622
8	4.0	5.00	100.00	5.0650
9	4.5	5.10	100.00	5.1701
10	5.0	5.20	100.00	5.2772
11	5.5	5.30	100.00	5.3864
12	6.0	5.40	100.00	5.4976
13	6.5	5.50	100.00	5.6108
14	7.0	5.55	100.00	5.6643
15	7.5	5.60	100.00	5.7193
16	8.0	5.65	100.00	5.7755
17	8.5	5.70	100.00	5.8331
18	9.0	5.80	100.00	5.9584
19	9.5	5.90	100.00	6.0863
20	10.0	6.00	100.00	6.2169

Exhibit 4: Determination of the Theoretical Price of an 8% 10-Year Treasury

Period	Years	Cash flow	Spot rate	Present Value of $1	Present Value
1	0.5	4.00	3.0000	0.9852	3.9409
2	1.0	4.00	3.3000	0.9678	3.8712
3	1.5	4.00	3.5053	0.9492	3.7968
4	2.0	4.00	3.9164	0.9254	3.7014
5	2.5	4.00	4.4376	0.8961	3.5843
6	3.0	4.00	4.7520	0.8686	3.4743
7	3.5	4.00	4.9622	0.8424	3.3694
8	4.0	4.00	5.0650	0.8187	3.2747
9	4.5	4.00	5.1701	0.7948	3.1791
10	5.0	4.00	5.2772	0.7707	3.0828
11	5.5	4.00	5.3864	0.7465	2.9861
12	6.0	4.00	5.4976	0.7222	2.8889
13	6.5	4.00	5.6108	0.6979	2.7916
14	7.0	4.00	5.6643	0.6764	2.7055
15	7.5	4.00	5.7193	0.6551	2.6205
16	8.0	4.00	5.7755	0.6341	2.5365
17	8.5	4.00	5.8331	0.6134	2.4536
18	9.0	4.00	5.9584	0.5895	2.3581
19	9.5	4.00	6.0863	0.5658	2.2631
20	10.0	104.00	6.2169	0.5421	56.3828
				Total	115.2619

Exhibit 5: Determination of the Theoretical Price of a 6% 10-Year Treasury

Period	Years	Cash flow	Spot rate	Present value of $1	Present value
1	0.5	3.00	3.0000	0.9852	2.9557
2	1.0	3.00	3.3000	0.9678	2.9034
3	1.5	3.00	3.5053	0.9492	2.8476
4	2.0	3.00	3.9164	0.9254	2.7761
5	2.5	3.00	4.4376	0.8961	2.6882
6	3.0	3.00	4.7520	0.8686	2.6057
7	3.5	3.00	4.9622	0.8424	2.5271
8	4.0	3.00	5.0650	0.8187	2.4560
9	4.5	3.00	5.1701	0.7948	2.3843
10	5.0	3.00	5.2772	0.7707	2.3121
11	5.5	3.00	5.3864	0.7465	2.2396
12	6.0	3.00	5.4976	0.7222	2.1667
13	6.5	3.00	5.6108	0.6979	2.0937
14	7.0	3.00	5.6643	0.6764	2.0292
15	7.5	3.00	5.7193	0.6551	1.9654
16	8.0	3.00	5.7755	0.6341	1.9024
17	8.5	3.00	5.8331	0.6134	1.8402
18	9.0	3.00	5.9584	0.5895	1.7686
19	9.5	3.00	6.0863	0.5658	1.6973
20	10.0	103.00	6.2169	0.5421	55.8407
				Total	100.0000

The question is, could this security trade at 114.88 in the market? Let's see what would happen if the 8% 10-year Treasury traded at 114.88. Suppose that a dealer firm buys this issue at 114.88 and strips it. By stripping it, we mean creating zero-coupon instruments. By stripping this issue, the dealer firm creates 20 zero-coupon instruments guaranteed by the U.S. Treasury.

How much can the 20 zero-coupon instruments be sold for by the dealer firm? Expressed equivalently, at what yield can each of the zero-coupon instruments be sold? The answer is in Exhibit 3. The yield at which each zero-coupon instrument can be sold is the spot rate shown in the last column.

The total proceeds received from selling the zero-coupon Treasury securities created would be $115.2619 per $100 of par value of the Treasury issue purchased by the dealer. Since the dealer purchased the issue for $114.88, this would result in an arbitrage profit of $0.3819 per $100 of the 8% 10-year Treasury issue purchased.

To understand why the dealer has the opportunity to realize this arbitrage profit, look at the last column of Exhibit 4 which shows how much the dealer paid for each cash flow by buying the entire package of cash flows (i.e., by buying the issue). For example, consider the $4 coupon payment in 4 years. By buying the 10-year Treasury bond priced to yield 6%, the dealer effectively pays a price based on 6% (3% semiannual) for that coupon payment, or, equivalently, $3.1577. Under the assumptions of this illustration, however, investors were willing to accept a lower yield to maturity (the 4-year spot rate), 5.065% (2.5325% semiannual), to purchase a zero-coupon Treasury security with 4 years to maturity. Thus investors were willing to pay $3.2747. On this one coupon payment, the dealer realizes a profit equal to the difference between $3.2747 and $3.1577 (or $0.117). From all the cash flows, the total profit is $0.3819.

Suppose that instead of the observed yield to maturity from Exhibit 1, the yields that investors want are the same as the theoretical spot rates that are shown in the exhibit. As can be seen in Exhibit 4, if we use these spot rates to discount the cash flows, the total proceeds from the sale of the zero-coupon Treasury securities would be equal to $115.2619, making coupon stripping uneconomic since the proceeds from stripping would be the same as the cost of purchasing the issue.

It is the process of coupon stripping that will prevent the market price of Treasury securities from departing significantly from their theoretical price.

THE TERM STRUCTURE OF CREDIT SPREADS

The Treasury spot rates can then be used to value any default-free security. As we illustrated earlier, failure of Treasury securities to be priced according to the Treasury spot rates creates the opportunity for arbitrage profits.

For a non-Treasury bond, the theoretical value is not as easy to determine. The value of a non-Treasury bond must reflect not only the spot rate for default-free bonds but also a risk premium to reflect default risk and any options embedded in the issue.

In practice, the spot rate that has been used to discount the cash flow of a non-Treasury bond is the Treasury spot rate plus a constant credit spread. For example, if the 6-month Treasury spot rate is 3%, and the 10-year Treasury spot rate is 6%, and a suitable credit spread is deemed to be 100 basis points, then a 4% spot rate is used to discount a 6-month cash flow of a non-Treasury bond and a 7% discount rate to discount a 10-year cash flow.

The drawback of this approach is that there is no reason to expect the credit spread to be the same regardless of when the cash flow is expected to be received. Instead, it might be expected that the credit spread increases with the maturity of the bond. That is, there is a term structure for credit spreads.

In practice, the difficulty in estimating a term structure for credit spreads is that unlike Treasury securities in which there is a wide-range of maturities from which to construct a Treasury spot rate curve, there are no issuers that offer a sufficiently wide range of non-Treasury zero-coupon securities to construct a zero-coupon spread curve.

Dealer firms typically construct a term structure for credit spreads for a particular rating based on the input of traders. Generally, the credit spread increases with maturity. This is a typical shape for the term structure of credit spreads. In addition, the shape of the term structure is not the same for all credit ratings. The lower the credit rating, the steeper the term structure.

Benchmark Spot Rate Curve

When the generic zero spreads for a given issuer are added to the default-free spot rates, the resulting term structure is used to value bonds of issuers of the same credit quality. This term structure is referred to as the *benchmark spot rate curve* or *benchmark zero coupon rate curve*.

For example, Exhibit 6 reproduces the default-free spot rate curve in Exhibit 4. Also shown in the exhibit is a hypothetical generic zero spread for an agency. The resulting benchmark spot rate curve is in the next-to-the-last column. It is this spot rate curve that is used to value the securities of this agency. This is done in Exhibit 6 for a hypothetical 8% 10-year issue for this agency. The theoretical price is 108.4615.

Exhibit 6: Calculation of Value of a Hypothetical 8% 10-Year Agency Issue Using Generic Zero Spread

Period	Years	Cash flow	Spot rate	Generic zero spread	Benchmark spot rate	Present value
1	0.5	4.00	3.0000	0.20	3.2000	3.9370
2	1.0	4.00	3.3000	0.20	3.5000	3.8636
3	1.5	4.00	3.5053	0.25	3.7553	3.7829
4	2.0	4.00	3.9164	0.30	4.2164	3.6797
5	2.5	4.00	4.4376	0.35	4.7876	3.5538
6	3.0	4.00	4.7520	0.35	5.1020	3.4389
7	3.5	4.00	4.9622	0.40	5.3622	3.3237
8	4.0	4.00	5.0650	0.45	5.5150	3.2177
9	4.5	4.00	5.1701	0.45	5.6201	3.1170
10	5.0	4.00	5.2772	0.50	5.7772	3.0088
11	5.5	4.00	5.3864	0.55	5.9364	2.8995
12	6.0	4.00	5.4976	0.60	6.0976	2.7896
13	6.5	4.00	5.6108	0.65	6.2608	2.6794
14	7.0	4.00	5.6643	0.70	6.3643	2.5799
15	7.5	4.00	5.7193	0.75	6.4693	2.4813
16	8.0	4.00	5.7755	0.80	6.5755	2.3838
17	8.5	4.00	5.8331	0.85	6.6831	2.2876
18	9.0	4.00	5.9584	0.90	6.8584	2.1801
19	9.5	4.00	6.0863	0.95	7.0363	2.0737
20	10.0	104.00	6.2169	1.00	7.2169	51.1833
					Total	108.4615

VALUATION MODELS

A valuation model provides the fair value of a security. In the fixed income area, there are two valuation models that are commonly used — the binomial model and the Monte Carlo simulation model. The former model is used to value callable bonds, putable bonds, floating-rate notes, and structured notes in which the coupon formula is based on an interest rate. The Monte Carlo simulation model is used to value mortgage-backed securities.

Both valuation models use the principles of valuation described earlier in this chapter. There are four things that are common to both models. First, each model begins with the on-the-run issues for Treasury securities. Second, each model makes an assumption about the volatility of short-term interest rates. This is a critical assumption in each model since it can significantly affect the fair value estimated. Third, based on the volatility assumption, different paths that the short-term interest rate can take are generated. Fourth, the model is calibrated to the Treasury market. This means that if an on-the-run Treasury issue is valued using the model, the model will produce the observed market price.

While it is beyond the scope of this chapter to go into the details of the two models, we will give an overview of each.[2] The purpose in this overview is to introduce the critical assumptions that are made. We begin with an intuitive idea of what is meant by interest rate volatility since an assumption about this value is used in both valuation models.

Interest Rate Volatility

Interest rate volatility is a measure of how much interest rates can vary around an average value. The standard deviation is a measure of this volatility. Volatility is typically measured relative to the current level of rates. For example, suppose a volatility of short-term interest rates of 15% is assumed and that the short-term rate is 6%. Then the volatility of short-term interest rates can be translated into basis points by multiplying the volatility by the level of short-term rates. In our example it is 0.15 times 0.06 which equals 0.0090 or 90 basis points. The greater the standard deviation the greater the expected volatility of short-term interest rates. For example, a volatility of 20% means a standard deviation of 120 basis points if the short-term rate is 6%.

What does a standard deviation measured in basis points tell us? For those who have had a course in elementary statistics, a normal probability distribution was discussed. The normal probability distribution has the following properties: (1) there is a 66% probability that the outcome will be between one standard deviation below and above the mean; (2) there is a 95% probability that the outcome will between two standard deviations below and above the mean; and, (3) there is a 99.7% probability that the outcome will be between three standard deviations below and above the mean.

---

[2] The details are provided in Frank J. Fabozzi, *Valuation of Fixed Income Securities and Derivatives* (New Hope, PA: Frank J. Fabozzi Associates, 1995).

For example, suppose that the current value of the short-term rate is 6% and the standard deviation is 90 basis points. This means that there is a 66% probability that the short-term rate one year from now will be between 5.1% (= 6% − 90 basis points) and 6.9% (= 6% + 90 basis points). There is a 95% probability that the short-term rate one year from now will be between 4.2% (= 6% − 180 basis points) and 7.8% (= 6% + 180 basis points). There is a 99.7% probability that the short-term rate one year from now will be between 3.3% (= 6% − 270 basis points) and 8.7% (= 6% + 270 basis points).

Notice that the larger the volatility assumed (i.e., the larger the standard deviation), the wider the interval for the possible outcome of the short-term rate for a given probability.

Binomial Model

The binomial model, as with the Monte Carlo simulation model, begins with the generation of possible interest rate scenarios in the future. In the case of the binomial model, an interest rate tree which considers the different paths that interest rates can take over the bond's life is constructed. The key is that it is constructed so as to ensure that the tree is consistent with the on-the-run yield curve and volatility of rates. An example of an interest rate tree for a 3-year bond is shown in Exhibit 7. At each node (i.e., each point), a 1-year rate is shown. Also, the 1-year rate for the next year is assumed to take on two possible values, each with an equal probability of occurring. The model is called a binomial model because it allows the rate to take on two possible values in the next period (i.e., year in our example). The binomial interest rate tree shown in Exhibit 7 is based on an assumed short-term rate volatility of 10%.

Exhibit 7: 3-Year Binomial Interest Rate Tree

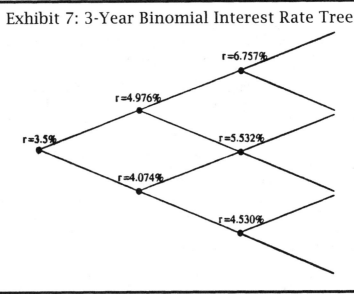

Exhibit 8: Coupon and Par Value at Each Interest Rate Node for a 3-Year Bond

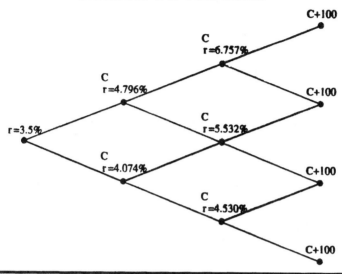

The objective in the valuation process is to obtain an interest rate tree such that when any on-the-run issue is valued, it will always correctly value that bond; that is, it will produce the observed market price. An explanation of the methodology for deriving the interest rate tree is beyond the scope of this chapter.

Valuing an Option-Free Bond Using the Interest Rate Tree Let's look at how the interest rate tree in Exhibit 7 is used to value a bond. Exhibit 8 shows the cash flow of the bond at each node. This is the coupon interest for years prior to maturity and coupon interest plus par at maturity. The procedure is straightforward. At each node, the value of the bond is found using the following steps:

Step 1: For a given year, determine the cash flow for the two possible interest rates 1-year from this node. The cash flow is the value of the bond 1-year from this point plus the coupon payment. Hold aside for now how we get these two values because, as we will see, the process involves starting from the last year in the tree and working backwards to get the bond's theoretical value today.

Step 2: Calculate the present value of the cash flows for each of the two possible interest rates one-year from now. The discount rate is the one-year rate at the node. This is illustrated in Exhibit 9 for any node assuming that the one-year rate is r_* at the node where the valuation is sought and letting:

V_H = bond's value for the higher 1-year rate
V_L = bond's value for the lower 1-year rate
C = coupon payment

Exhibit 9: Calculating Value at a Node

V_H = Bond's value in higher-rate state 1-year forward
V_L = Bond's value in lower-rate state 1-year forward
C = Coupon on the bond

Using our notation, the cash flow at a node is either:

$V_H + C$ for the higher 1-year rate

or

$V_L + C$ for the lower 1-year rate

The present value of these two cash flows using the 1-year rate at the node, r_*, is:

$$\frac{V_H + C}{(1 + r_*)} = \text{Present value for the higher 1-year rate}$$

$$\frac{V_L + C}{(1 + r_*)} = \text{Present value for the lower 1-year rate}$$

Step 3: Calculate the average of the two values computed in the previous step. Then, the value of the bond at the node is found as follows:

$$\text{Value [at a node]} = \frac{1}{2}\left(\frac{V_H + C}{(1 + r_*)} + \frac{V_L + C}{(1 + r_*)}\right)$$

The same process continues for each node on the interest rate tree. The process begins by starting in the last period and working backwards.

To illustrate these three steps, suppose that the binomial interest tree is that shown in Exhibit 7. Consider a 3-year, 4.5% option-free issue. Step 2 requires the determination of the cash flow along the interest rate tree. Exhibit 10 shows the interest rate tree and the cash flow at each node. The only known cash flows are the coupon payments, and, in year 3, the maturity value ($100) plus the coupon interest of $4.5. To see how to use steps 2 and 3 outlined above to get the value of the bond at the top node in the second year, we will use Exhibit 11 which has labeled by letter three of the nodes on the interest rate tree. The interest rate tree in Exhibit 11 is identical to that in Exhibit 10, but the labeling of the nodes will make it easier to follow the explanation. In addition, bond values at each node, which we explain how to derive below, are also displayed.

In terms of Exhibit 11, a value for the bond in year 2 is the node marked with the label W. The value of this bond at node W is the present value of the cash flows for the two nodes to the right of the node (i.e., for the two nodes in year three that are to the right of node W).

Exhibit 10: Cash Flows for a 3-Year 4.5% Bond

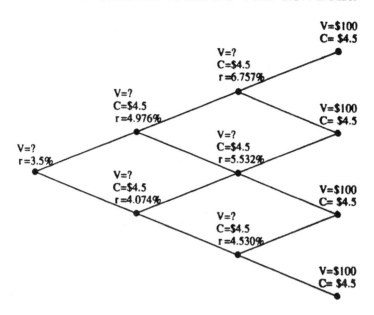

Exhibit 11: Cash Flows of a 3-Year 4.5% Bond with Labels

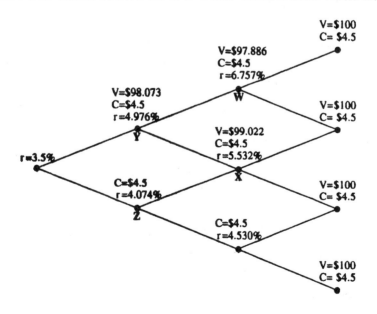

Step 2 above indicates how this present value should be calculated at node W to get the bond value at node W. To get the present value, the rate at node W, 6.757%, is used. Using the notation V_H for the upper node to the right of node W, then the present value of the cash flow for the higher 1-year rate is

$$\frac{100 + 4.5}{1.06757} = 97.886$$

Since the cash flows at the lower node to the right of node W are identical to the upper node, the present value of the cash flow for the lower 1-year rate is also 97.886.

Step 3 states that the present value for the two cash flows should be averaged (assuming an equal probability of each outcome) to get the value of the bond at node W. Since the two present values are the same, the average value equals 97.886. This is the bond value shown in Exhibit 11 at node W.

The value of the bond at node X, and all other nodes in year two, would be determined similarly. At this node, the 1-year rate that would be used to calculate the present value of the cash flows for the two nodes to the right of node X would be 5.532%. In step 2, since V_H and V_L to the right of node X are both 100 and the coupon is 4.50, the cash flow is identical. The present value of the cash flow at both nodes to the right of node X is then:

$$\frac{100 + 4.5}{1.05532} = 99.022$$

The average of the two present values is then 99.022 and is therefore the value of the bond at node X.

As you can see, getting the bond value for the two nodes for the year just before the maturity date is easy. Now let's look at how to get the value of the bond at a node in year 1. We will use node Y in Exhibit 11. At node Y, the two nodes to the right are node W (the upper node reflecting a higher 1-year rate) and node X (the lower node reflecting a lower 1-year rate). Now to get the bond value at node Y, we need the cash flow at node W and node X. The cash flow is the bond's value at these two nodes plus the coupon. The cash flow at nodes W and X will then be discounted at the 1-year rate at node Y which is 4.976% and then averaged to get the bond's value at node Y. But where do we get the bond's value at nodes W and X? We calculated it above, it is 97.886 and 99.022, respectively. This is why the procedure we are using is called *backward induction*: we work our way backward in the interest rate tree from the maturity date to the root of the tree (today). The bond values at each node were in turn used to get the bond value at an earlier period.

Thus the value of the bond at node Y is determined from the values calculated at nodes W and X. In this case V_H is the value at node W which is 97.886 and V_L is the value at node X which is 99.022. Then:

Present value of cash flow for the higher 1-year rate =

$$\frac{97.886 + 4.5}{1.04976} = 97.533$$

Exhibit 12: Cash Flows of a 3-Year 4.5% Bond

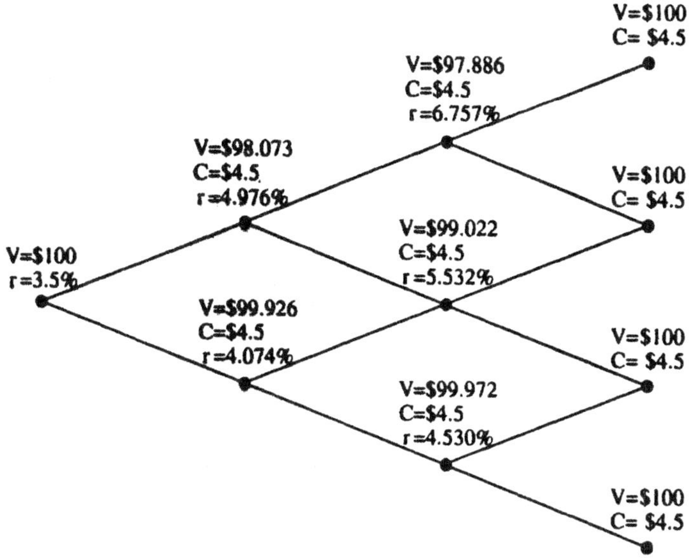

Present value of cash flow for the lower 1-year rate =

$$\frac{99.022 + 4.5}{1.04976} = 98.615$$

The average present value is then 98.073 [(97.533 + 98.615)/2]. This is the bond's value shown in Exhibit 11 at node Y.

The value of the bond at node Z would be similarly determined. The value of the bond today (node 0) would be determined from the values of the cash flow at nodes Y and Z.

Exhibit 12 shows the completed interest rate tree with the values shown at each node. Notice that the value at the root (i.e., the value today) is 100, which agrees with the observed market price.

Valuing a Callable Bond Using the Interest Rate Tree If a bond is callable, the valuation must take into account the possibility that the bond will be called when interest rates decline below the coupon rate. To do this, the cash flow at each node is adjusted to reflect a possible call at that node. Here the bond's price at each node is equal to the lower of the calculated price and the call price.

For example, assume an issue with a 6% coupon with two years to maturity is callable in one year and thereafter at par. The value in each year is the lower of the price assuming no call and the call price of 100. The value of the bond is then found using the three steps given earlier using the interest rate tree.

Exhibit 13: Value of a 3-Year 6% Callable Bond Callable at Par in One Year

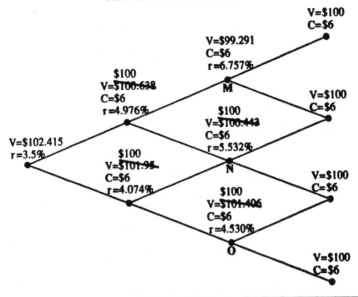

This is illustrated in Exhibit 13. It is assumed that the interest rate tree in Exhibit 7 is the proper tree for valuing the callable bond for this issue. That is, the tree reflects the credit risk.

The value at node M in Exhibit 13 equals the expected value of the bond given the two possible interest rate scenarios, 99.291. The value at node N, calculated from the two possible outcomes (i.e., the two nodes to the right of node N), would be 100.443. However, since interest rates have fallen below the coupon rate (6%), we assume that the issuer would call the bond at point N, resulting instead in a value of 100, not the 100.443 calculated value. The value at point 0 is the call price of 100 rather than the calculated price of 101.406 since the issuer would call the bond at this point.

The value at each point of an interest rate tree for a callable bond is the minimum of (1) the calculated value or (2) the call price (plus issuance costs). The same procedure is repeated until we reach the beginning of the interest rate tree, which will be the value of the bond today. Thus, another important assumption that has been added to the valuation process is a rule as to when the issuer will call the issue.

Valuing Putable Bonds Putable bonds can be analyzed within the framework outlined above. However, for the interest rate tree, on the upper branches, the maximum of the put price or the calculated bond price will be used. This is because as rates in the market rise above the coupon rate on the putable bond, the investor would prefer to put the bond and reinvest the proceeds in a higher coupon rate bond. If interest rates fall below the coupon rate of the issue, investors will prefer to retain the bond. For example, assume that a putable bond with a 3-year 5.5% coupon is putable in one year and each subsequent year at 100. Using the interest rate tree in Exhibit 7, the bond value at each node is shown in Exhibit 14. Therefore the calculated bond value is 102.958.

Valuing Floating-Rate Securities and Structured Notes The same procedure is used to value floating-rate notes that have a cap and/or floor and a structured note whose coupon reset formula is based on a reference rate.

Remember the Assumptions It is worthwhile to review the assumptions of the binomial model. First, it is assumed that the on-the-run yield curve for the issuer that is used to obtain the interest rate tree is properly created. Second, a short-term interest rate volatility is assumed. Third, the rule for when the issuer or investor will exercise the embedded option is assumed.

As mentioned earlier, the volatility assumption is crucial. For a bond with an embedded option that is beneficial to the issuer (e.g., a callable bond), the smaller the volatility assumed, the higher the theoretical value obtained for the bond. For a bond with an embedded option that is beneficial to the investor (e.g., a putable bond), the larger the volatility assumed, the higher the theoretical value obtained for the bond. Consequently, relying on a dealer or vendor valuation model without knowing the volatility assumption can be expensive.

Exhibit 14: Value of a 3-Year 5.5% Putable Bond Putable at Par in Year 1

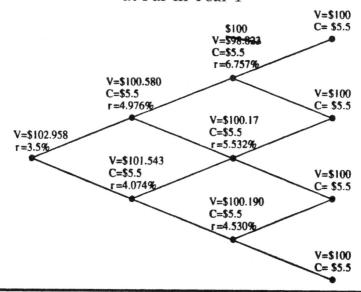

Monte Carlo Simulation Model

The Monte Carlo simulation model, or simply, the Monte Carlo model, involves simulating a sufficiently large number of potential interest rate paths in order to assess the value of a security along these different paths. This model can accommodate fixed income securities whose cash flows are path-dependent. This means that the cash flow received in one period is determined not only by the current and future interest rate levels, but also by the path that interest rates took to get to the current level.

In the case of mortgage passthrough securities, prepayments are path-dependent because this month's prepayment rate depends on whether there have been prior opportunities to refinance since the underlying mortgages were originated. Unlike passthroughs, the decision as to whether a corporate issuer will elect to refund an issue when the current rate is below the issue's coupon rate is not dependent on how rates evolved over time to the current level.

For collateralized mortgage obligations (CMOs), there are typically two sources of path dependency in a tranche's cash flows. First, the collateral prepayments are path-dependent as discussed above. Second, the cash flow to be received in the current month by a CMO tranche depends on the outstanding balances of the other tranches in the deal. Thus, we need the history of prepayments to calculate these balances.

Using Simulation to Generate Interest Rate Paths and Cash Flows The typical model that Wall Street firms and commercial vendors use to generate these random interest rate paths takes as input today's term structure of interest rates and a volatility assumption. Each model has its own model of the evolution of future interest rates and its own volatility assumptions. Typically, there are no significant differences in the interest rate models of dealer firms and vendors, although their volatility assumptions can be significantly different.

The simulation works by generating many scenarios of future interest rate paths. In each month of the scenario, a monthly interest rate and a mortgage refinancing rate are generated. The monthly interest rates are used to discount the projected cash flows in the scenario. The mortgage refinancing rate is needed to determine the cash flow because it represents the opportunity cost the mortgagor is facing at that time.

If the refinancing rates are high relative to the mortgagor's original rate, the mortgagor will have less incentive to refinance, or even a positive disincentive (i.e., the homeowner will avoid moving in order to avoid refinancing). If the refinancing rate is low relative to the mortgagor's coupon rate, the mortgagor has an incentive to refinance.

Prepayments are projected by feeding the refinancing rate and loan characteristics, such as age, into a prepayment model. Given the projected prepayments, the cash flow along an interest rate path can be determined.

To make this more concrete, consider a newly issued mortgage passthrough security with a maturity of 360 months. Exhibit 15 shows N simulated interest rate path scenarios. Each scenario consists of a path of 360 simulated 1-month future interest rates. Exhibit 16 shows the paths of simulated mortgage refinancing rates corresponding to the scenarios shown in Exhibit 15. Going from the rates in Exhibit 15 to those on Exhibit 16 requires an assumption about the relationship between short-term rates and refinancing rates. Then, assuming the mortgage refinancing rates in Exhibit 16, the cash flow for each scenario path is shown in Exhibit 17.

Determining the Theoretical Value Given the cash flow on an interest rate path, its present value can be calculated. The discount rate for determining the present value is the simulated spot rate for each month on the interest rate path plus an appropriate spread. The spot rate on a path can be determined from the simulated future monthly rates.

The present value of a given interest rate path can be thought of as the theoretical value of a passthrough if that path was actually realized. The theoretical value of the passthrough can be determined by calculating the average of the theoretical values of all the interest rate paths.

This procedure for valuing a passthrough is also followed for a CMO tranche. The cash flow for each month on each interest rate path is found according to the principal repayment and interest distribution rules of the deal. In order to do this, a CMO structuring model is needed. In any analysis of CMOs, one of the major stumbling blocks is getting a good CMO structuring model.

Distribution of Path Present Values The Monte Carlo simulation model is a commonly used management science tool in business. It is employed when the outcome of a business decision depends on the outcome of several random variables. The product of the simulation is the average value and the probability distribution of the possible outcomes.

Exhibit 15: Simulated Paths of
1-Month Future Interest Rates

	Interest Rate Path Number						
Month	1	2	3	...	n	...	N
1	$f_1(1)$	$f_1(2)$	$f_1(3)$	...	$f_1(n)$	...	$f_1(N)$
2	$f_2(1)$	$f_2(2)$	$f_2(3)$	...	$f_2(n)$	...	$f_2(N)$
3	$f_3(1)$	$f_3(2)$	$f_3(3)$	...	$f_3(n)$	...	$f_3(N)$
t	$f_t(1)$	$f_t(2)$	$f_t(3)$	...	$f_t(n)$	...	$f_t(N)$
358	$f_{358}(1)$	$f_{358}(2)$	$f_{358}(3)$	...	$f_{358}(n)$	...	$f_{358}(N)$
359	$f_{359}(1)$	$f_{359}(2)$	$f_{359}(3)$	...	$f_{359}(n)$	...	$f_{359}(N)$
360	$f_{360}(1)$	$f_{360}(2)$	$f_{360}(3)$	...	$f_{360}(n)$	...	$f_{360}(N)$

Notation:

$f_t(n)$ = 1-month future interest rate for month t on path n

N = total number of interest rate paths

Exhibit 16: Simulated Paths of Mortgage Refinancing Rates

Month	Interest Rate Path Number						
	1	2	3	...	n	...	N
1	$r_1(1)$	$r_1(2)$	$r_1(3)$	...	$r_1(n)$	...	$r_1(N)$
2	$r_2(1)$	$r_2(2)$	$r_2(3)$	...	$r_2(n)$	...	$r_2(N)$
3	$r_3(1)$	$r_3(2)$	$r_3(3)$	...	$r_3(n)$	...	$r_3(N)$
t	$r_t(1)$	$r_t(2)$	$r_t(3)$	...	$r_t(n)$	...	$r_t(N)$
358	$r_{358}(1)$	$r_{358}(2)$	$r_{358}(3)$	...	$r_{358}(n)$	...	$r_{358}(N)$
359	$r_{359}(1)$	$r_{359}(2)$	$r_{359}(3)$	...	$r_{359}(n)$	...	$r_{359}(N)$
360	$r_{360}(1)$	$r_{360}(2)$	$r_{360}(3)$	...	$r_{360}(n)$	...	$r_{360}(N)$

Notation:
$r_t(n)$ = mortgage refinancing rate for month t on path n
N = total number of interest rate paths

Exhibit 17: Simulated Cash Flow on Each of the Interest Rate Paths

Month	Interest Rate Path Number						
	1	2	3	...	n	...	N
1	$C_1(1)$	$C_1(2)$	$C_1(3)$	...	$C_1(n)$	...	$C_1(N)$
2	$C_2(1)$	$C_2(2)$	$C_2(3)$	...	$C_2(n)$	...	$C_2(N)$
3	$C_3(1)$	$C_3(2)$	$C_3(3)$	...	$C_3(n)$	...	$C_3(N)$
t	$C_t(1)$	$C_t(2)$	$C_t(3)$	...	$C_t(n)$	...	$C_t(N)$
358	$C_{358}(1)$	$C_{358}(2)$	$C_{358}(3)$	...	$C_{358}(n)$	...	$C_{358}(N)$
359	$C_{359}(1)$	$C_{359}(2)$	$C_{359}(3)$	...	$C_{359}(n)$	...	$C_{359}(N)$
360	$C_{360}(1)$	$C_{360}(2)$	$C_{360}(3)$	...	$C_{360}(n)$	...	$C_{360}(N)$

Notation:
$C_t(n)$ = cash flow for month t on path n
N = total number of interest rate paths

Unfortunately, the use of Monte Carlo simulation to value mortgage-backed securities has been limited to just the reporting of the average value, which is referred to as the theoretical value of the security. This means that all of the information about the distribution of the path present values is ignored. Yet, this information is quite valuable.

For example, consider a well protected PAC bond. The distribution of the present value for the paths should be concentrated around the theoretical value. That is, the standard deviation should be small. In contrast, for a support tranche, the distribution of the present value for the paths could be wide, or equivalently, the standard deviation could be large.

Therefore, before using the theoretical value for a mortgage-backed security generated from the Monte Carlo model, a credit union should ask for information about the distribution of the path present values.

Simulated Average Life In Chapter 5, we described the average life measure for a mortgage-backed security. The average life reported in a Monte Carlo model is the average of the average lives along the interest rate paths. That is, for each interest rate path, there is an average life. The average of these average lives is the average life reported. Additional information is conveyed by the distribution of the average life. The greater the range and standard deviation of the average life, the more uncertainty there is about the tranche's average life.

Remember the Assumptions Once again, it is worthwhile to review the assumptions of the Monte Carlo model for valuing mortgage-backed securities. First, a short-term interest rate volatility is assumed. Second, a relationship is assumed between short-term interest rates and refinancing rates. Finally, a prepayment model is assumed.

Modeling Risk

The user of any valuation model is exposed to *modeling risk*. This is the risk that the output of the model is incorrect because the assumptions upon which it is based are incorrect. Consequently, it is imperative that the results of a valuation model be stress tested for modeling risk by altering the assumptions.

KEY POINTS

1. Valuation is the process of determining the fair value of a financial asset.

2. The fundamental principle of valuation is that the value of any financial asset is the present value of the expected cash flow, where the cash flow is the cash that is expected to be received each period from an investment.

3. For any fixed income security in which neither the issuer nor the investor can alter the repayment of the principal before its contractual due date, the cash flow can easily be determined assuming that the issuer does not default.

4. The difficulty in determining the cash flow arises for securities where either the issuer or the investor can alter the cash flow or the coupon rate is reset by a formula that depends on the future value of some reference rate, price or exchange rate.

5. The base interest rate in valuing fixed income securities is the rate on default-free securities and U.S. Treasury securities are viewed as default-free securities.

6. The traditional valuation methodology is to discount every cash flow of a fixed income security by the same interest rate (or discount rate), thereby incorrectly viewing each security as the same package of cash flows.

7. The contemporary approach values a bond as a package of cash flows, with each cash flow viewed as a zero-coupon instrument and each cash flow discounted at its own unique discount rate.

8. To properly value fixed-income securities, the rate on zero-coupon Treasury securities should be used.

9. The Treasury yield curve indicates the relationship between the yield on Treasury securities and maturity.

10. From a Treasury spot rate curve, the value of any default-free security can be determined.

11. The economic force that assures that securities will be priced based on spot rates creates the opportunity for government dealers to strip Treasury securities.

12. To value a security with credit risk, it is necessary to determine a term structure of credit risk.

13. Adding the zero-coupon credit spread for a particular issue to the Treasury spot rate curve gives the benchmark spot rate curve that should be used to value that issuer's security.

14. There are two valuation models that are being used today to value bonds with embedded options: the binomial model and the Monte Carlo simulation model.

15. Valuation models seek to estimate the fair or theoretical value of the bond.

16. The uncertainty of interest rates is captured in a valuation model by introducing the volatility of interest rates.

17. The standard deviation is a statistical measure of volatility and the assumed value has an important impact on the theoretical value of a bond with an embedded option.

18. The binomial model involves generating a binomial interest rate tree based on an issuer's on-the-run yield curve and an assumed interest rate volatility.

19. The binomial interest rate tree provides the appropriate rates that should be used to discount the expected cash flows of a bond.

20. In valuing a bond using the binomial interest rate tree, the cash flows at a node are modified to take into account any embedded options.

21. A path-dependent cash flow is one in which the cash flow received in one period is determined not only by the current and future interest rate levels, but also by the path that interest rates took to get to the current level.

22. The cash flow of mortgage-backed securities is path dependent and consequently the Monte Carlo model is commonly used to value these securities.

23. The Monte Carlo model involves randomly generating many scenarios of future interest rate paths based on some volatility assumption for short-term interest rates.

23. The Monte Carlo model applied to mortgage-backed securities involves randomly generating a set of cash flows based on simulated future mortgage refinancing rates.

24. The theoretical value of a security on any interest rate path is the present value of the cash flow on that path where the spot rates are those on the corresponding interest rate path.

25. The theoretical value of a security is the average of the theoretical values over all the interest rate paths.

26. Information about the distribution of the present value for the interest rate paths provides guidance as to the degree of uncertainty associated with the theoretical value derived from the Monte Carlo model.

27. The user of a valuation model is exposed to modeling risk and should test the sensitivity of the model to alternative assumptions.

Chapter 9

Yield Measures and their Limitations

The objectives of this chapter are to:

1. discuss the sources of return from holding a bond to maturity;

2. explain the various yield measures (current yield, yield to maturity, yield to call, yield to worst, cash flow yield, and discounted margin) and their limitations as a measure of relative value;

3. explain what the nominal spread is and its limitations;

4. describe a measure called the static spread that is superior to the nominal spread measure, and describe the circumstances under which the two spread measures will deviate;

5. explain what is meant by the option-adjusted spread;

6. explain why the option-adjusted spread is a byproduct of a valuation model; and,

7. demonstrate why relying on the nominal spread may hide the option risk associated with a bond with an embedded option.

In the previous chapter we focused on the principles for valuing a fixed income security and two valuation models. Frequently, investors assess the relative value of a security by some yield or yield spread measure. There are various yield measures that are quoted in the market. These measures are based on assumptions that limit their use to gauge relative value. This chapter explains the various yield and spread measures and their limitations. In Chapter 11 we provide a better framework for assessing the potential performance of a security.

SOURCES OF RETURN

When a credit union purchases a bond, it can expect to receive a dollar return from one or more of the following sources:[1]

1. the coupon interest payments made by the issuer,
2. any capital gain (or capital loss — negative dollar return) when the bond matures, is called or is sold, and
3. income from reinvestment of the interim cash flow.

Any yield measure that purports to measure the potential return from a bond should consider all three sources of return described above.

Coupon Interest Payments

The most obvious source of return is the periodic coupon interest payments. For zero coupon instruments, the return from this source is zero, despite the fact that the investor is effectively receiving interest by purchasing an instrument below its par value and realizing interest at the maturity date when the investor receives the par value.

Capital Gain or Loss

When the proceeds received when a bond matures, is called or is sold are greater than the purchase price, a capital gain results. For a bond held to maturity, there will be a capital gain if the bond is purchased below its par value. A bond purchased below its par value is said to be purchased at a discount. For example, a bond purchased for $94.17 with a par value of $100 will generate a capital gain of $5.83 ($100 − $94.17) if held to maturity. For a callable bond, a capital gain results if the price at which the

---

[1] The classification of the sources of return in our discussion in this chapter is different from the treatment in the U.S. tax code. For example, for zero coupon instruments purchased at issuance, the tax code treats the difference between the par value and the purchase price as interest income. More specifically, the discount from par value is called an *original interest discount*. In our discussion below, it would be classified as a capital gain. As a second example, the tax code has rules for the treatment of what it defines as a bond purchased below par value because of changes in market interest rates. The difference between the par value and market price is called a *market discount* and is treated as interest income under the tax code. In our discussion we would define the difference as a capital gain.

bond is called (i.e., the call price) is greater than the purchase price. For example, if the bond in our previous example is callable and subsequently called at $100.5, a capital gain of $6.33 ($100.5 − $94.17) will be realized. If the same bond is sold prior to its maturity or before it is called, a capital gain will result if the proceeds exceed the purchase price. So, if our hypothetical bond is sold prior to the maturity date for $103, the capital gain would be $8.83 ($103 − $94.17).

A capital loss is generated when the proceeds received when a bond matures, is called or is sold are less then the purchase price. For a bond held to maturity, there will be a capital loss if the bond is purchased for more than its par value. A bond purchased for more than its par value is said to be purchased at a premium. For example, a bond purchased for $102.5 with a par value of $100 will generate a capital loss of $2.5 ($102.5 − $100) if held to maturity. For a callable bond, a capital loss results if the price at which the bond is called is less than the purchase price. For example, if the bond in our previous example is callable and subsequently called at $100.5, a capital loss of $2.0 ($102.5 − $100.5) will be realized. If the same bond is sold prior to its maturity or before it is called, a capital loss will result if the sale price is lower than the purchase price. So, if our hypothetical bond is sold prior to the maturity date for $98.5, the capital loss would be $4.0 ($102.5 − $98.5).

Reinvestment Income

With the exception of zero coupon instruments and accrued interest instruments, bonds make periodic payments of interest that can be reinvested until the bond is removed from the portfolio. There are also instruments in which there are periodic principal payments which can be reinvested until the bond is removed from the portfolio. As explained in Chapter 2, repayment of principal prior to the maturity date occurs for amortizing instruments such as mortgage-backed securities and asset-backed securities. The interest earned from reinvesting the interim cash flow (interest or principal) until the bond is removed from the portfolio is called *reinvestment income*.

YIELD MEASURES

There are several yield measures cited in the bond market. These include current yield, yield to maturity, yield to call (for callable bonds), yield to worst (for callable bonds), and cash flow yield (for mortgage-backed securities). For floating-rate securities, a measure called discounted margin is computed. These yield measures are expressed as a percent return rather than a dollar return. Below we explain how each measure is calculated and its limitations.

Current Yield

The current yield relates the *annual* coupon interest to the market price. The formula for the current yield is:

$$\text{Current yield} = \frac{\text{Annual dollar coupon interest}}{\text{Price}}$$

For example, the current yield for a 7% 8-year bond whose price is 94.17 is 7.43% as shown below:

Annual dollar coupon interest $= 0.07 \times \$100 = \$7$

Price $= \$94.17$

$$\text{Current yield} = \frac{\$7}{\$94.17} = 0.0743 \text{ or } 7.43\%$$

The current yield will be greater than the coupon rate when the bond sells at a discount; the reverse is true for a bond selling at a premium. For a bond selling at par, the current yield will be equal to the coupon rate.

The drawback of the current yield is that it considers only the coupon interest and no other source that will impact an investor's return. No consideration is given to the capital gain that the investor will realize when a bond is purchased at a discount and held to maturity; nor is there any recognition of the capital loss that the investor will realize if a bond purchased at a premium is held to maturity.

Yield to Maturity

The most popular measure of yield in the bond market is the yield to maturity. The yield to maturity is the interest rate that will make the present value of the cash flows from a bond equal to its market price plus accrued interest. Calculation of the yield to maturity of a bond is the reverse process of calculating the price of a bond. As explained in the previous chapter, to find the price of a bond we determined the cash flows and the required yield, then we calculated the present value of the cash flows to obtain the price. To find the yield to maturity, we first determine the cash flows. Then we search by trial and error for the interest rate that will make the present value of the cash flows equal to the market price plus accrued interest. In the illustrations presented in this chapter, we assume that the next coupon payment will be six months from now so that accrued interest is ignored.

To illustrate, consider a 7% 8-year bond selling for 94.17. The cash flows for this bond are (1) 16 payments every 6-months of $3.50 and (2) a payment 16 6-month periods from now of $100. The present value using various discount (interest) rates is:

Interest rate	3.5%	3.6%	3.7%	3.8%	3.9%	4.0%
Present value	100.00	98.80	97.62	96.45	95.30	94.17

When a 4.0% interest rate is used, the present value of the cash flows is equal to 94.17, which is the price of the bond. Hence, 4.0% is the semiannual yield to maturity.

The market convention adopted is to double the semiannual interest rate and call that interest rate the yield to maturity. Thus, the yield to maturity for the above bond is 8% (2 times 4.0%). The yield to maturity computed using this convention — doubling the semiannual yield — is called a *bond equivalent yield* or *coupon equivalent yield*.

The following relationship between the price of a bond, coupon rate, current yield, and yield to maturity holds:

Bond selling at a	Relationship
par	coupon rate = current yield = yield to maturity
discount	coupon rate < current yield < yield to maturity
premium	coupon rate > current yield > yield to maturity

The yield to maturity considers not only the coupon income but any capital gain or loss that the investor will realize by *holding the bond to maturity*. The yield to maturity also considers the timing of the cash flows. It does consider interest on interest; *however, it assumes that the coupon payments can be reinvested at an interest rate equal to the yield to maturity*. So, if the yield to maturity for a bond is 8%, for example, to earn that yield the coupon payments must be reinvested at an interest rate equal to 8%. The following illustration clearly demonstrates this.

Suppose an investor has $94.17 and places the funds in a certificate of deposit that pays 4% every six months for 8 years or 8% per year (on a bond equivalent basis). At the end of 8 years, the $94.17 investment will grow to $176.38. Instead, suppose an investor buys the following bond: a 7% 8-year bond selling for $94.17. The yield to maturity for this bond is 8%. The investor would expect that at the end of 8 years, the total dollars from the investment will be $176.38.

Let's look at what the investor will receive. There will be 16 semiannual interest payments of $3.50 which will total $56. When the bond matures, the investor will receive $100. Thus, the total dollars that the investor will receive is $156 by holding the bond to maturity. But this is less than the $176.38 necessary to produce a yield of 8% on a bond equivalent basis by $20.38 ($176.38 minus $156). How is this deficiency supposed to be made up? If the investor reinvests the coupon payments at a semiannual interest rate of 4% (or 8% annual rate on a bond equivalent basis), then the interest earned on the coupon payments will be $20.38. Consequently, of the $82.21 total dollar return ($176.38 minus $94.17) necessary to produce a yield of 8%, about 25% ($20.38 divided by $82.21) must be generated by reinvesting the coupon payments.

Clearly, the investor will only realize the yield to maturity that is stated at the time of purchase if (1) the coupon payments can be reinvested at the yield to maturity, and (2) if the bond is held to maturity. With respect to the first assumption, the risk that an investor faces is that future reinvestment rates will be less than the yield to maturity at the time the bond is purchased. This risk is referred to as *reinvestment risk*. If the bond is not held to maturity, the price of the bond may have to be sold for less than its purchase price, resulting in a return that is less than the yield to maturity. The risk that a bond will have to be sold at a loss is referred to as *interest rate risk* or *price risk*.

There are two characteristics of a bond that determine the degree of reinvestment risk. First, for a given yield to maturity and a given coupon rate, the longer the maturity the more the bond's total dollar return is dependent on reinvestment income to realize the yield to maturity at the time of purchase. That is, the greater the reinvestment risk. The implication is that the yield to maturity measure for long-term coupon bonds tells little about the potential yield that an investor may realize if the bond is held to maturity. For long-term bonds, in high interest rate environments the interest on interest component may be as high as 70% of the bond's potential total dollar return.

The second characteristic that determines the degree of reinvestment risk is the coupon rate. For a given maturity and a given yield to maturity, the higher the coupon rate, the more dependent the bond's total dollar return will be on the reinvestment of the coupon payments in order to produce the yield to maturity at the time of purchase. This means that holding maturity and yield to maturity constant, premium bonds will be more dependent on reinvestment income than bonds selling at par. In contrast, discount bonds will be less dependent on reinvestment income than bonds selling at par. For zero coupons bonds, none of the bond's total dollar return is dependent on reinvestment income. So, a zero coupon bond has no reinvestment risk if held to maturity.

The dependence of the total dollar return on reinvestment income for bonds with different coupon rates and maturities is shown in Exhibit 1.

Exhibit 1: Percentage of Total Dollar Return from Reinvestment Income

	Years to maturity				
	1	3	5	8	15
7% coupon					
Price ($)	98.19	97.38	95.94	94.17	91.35
Percent of total	5.2%	8.6%	15.2%	24.8%	44.5%
8% coupon					
Price ($)	100.00	100.00	100.00	100.00	100.00
Percent of total	5.8%	9.5%	16.7%	26.7%	46.5%
12% coupon					
Price ($)	107.26	110.48	116.22	122.30	134.58
Percent of total	8.1%	12.9%	21.6%	31.0%	51.8%

A bond's price moves in the opposite direction of the change in interest rates. As interest rates rise (fall), the price of a bond will fall (rise). For a portfolio manager who plans to hold a bond to maturity and therefore includes it in the held-to-maturity account, the change in the bond's price prior to maturity will not realize a loss. However, revised Part 703 will require disclosure of portfolio price movements without regard to FAS 115 classification. For bonds included in the available-for-sale and trading accounts, an increase in interest rates subsequent to the time the bond was purchased will mean the realization of a capital loss. As explained in the next chapter, not all bonds have the same degree of interest-rate risk.

Yield to Call

When a bond is callable, the practice has been to calculate a yield to call as well as a yield to maturity. As explained in Chapter 2, a callable bond may have a call schedule. The yield to call assumes that the issuer will call the bond at some assumed call date and the call price is then the call price specified in the call schedule. Typically, investors calculate a *yield to first call* and a *yield to par call*.

The procedure for calculating the yield to call is the same as for any yield calculation: determine the interest rate that will make the present value of the expected cash flows equal to the price. In the case of yield to first call, the expected cash flows are the coupon payments to the first call date and the call price. For the yield to par call, the expected cash flows are the coupon payments to the first date at which the issuer can call the bond at par.

To illustrate the computation, consider a 7% 8-year bond with a maturity value of $100 selling for $106.36. Suppose that the first call date is three years from now and the call price is $103. The cash flows for this bond if it is called in three years are (1) 6 coupon payments of $3.50 every six months and (2) $103 in six 6-month periods from now.

The process for finding the yield to first call is the same as for finding the yield to maturity. The present value for several semiannual interest rates is shown in Exhibit 2. Since a semiannual interest rate of 2.8% makes the present value of the cash flows equal to the price, 2.8% is the yield to first call. Therefore, the yield to first call on a bond equivalent basis is 5.6%.

Exhibit 2: Yield to Call for a 7% 8-Year Bond with a Maturity Value of $100, First Call Date is the End of Year 3 and Call Price of $103

Annual interest rate (%)	Semiannual rate (%)	Present value of 6 payments of $3.5	Present value of $103 6 periods from now	Present value of cash flows
5.0	2.5	16.27	91.83	108.10
5.2	2.6	16.21	91.30	107.51
5.4	2.7	16.16	90.77	106.93
5.6	2.8	16.12	90.24	106.36

Let's take a closer look at the yield to call as a measure of the potential return of a security. The yield to call does consider all three sources of potential return from owning a bond. However, as in the case of the yield to maturity, it assumes that all cash flows can be reinvested at the yield to call until the assumed call date. As we just demonstrated, this assumption may be inappropriate. Moreover, the yield to call assumes that (1) the investor will hold the bond to the assumed call date and (2) the issuer will call the bond on that date.

These assumptions underlying the yield to call are oftentimes unrealistic. They do not take into account how an investor will reinvest the proceeds if the issue is called. For example, consider two bonds, M and N. Suppose that the yield to maturity for bond M, a 5-year noncallable bond, is 7.5% while for bond N the yield to call assuming the bond will be called in three years is 7.8%. Which bond is better for an investor with a 5-year investment horizon? It's not possible to tell for the yields cited. If the investor intends to hold the bond for five years and the issuer calls in the bond after three years, the total dollars that will be available at the end of five years will depend on the interest rate that can be earned from investing funds from the call date to the end of the investment horizon.

Yield to Worst

The yield to first call is only the yield to the first call date. Since most bonds can be called at any time after the first call date, a yield to every coupon anniversary date following the first call date can be calculated. Then, all yield to calls calculated and the yield to maturity are compared. The lowest of these yields is called the *yield to worst*. For example, suppose that there are only four possible call dates for a callable bond and that a yield to call assuming each possible call date is 6%, 6.2%, 5.8% and 5.7%, and that the yield to maturity is 7.5%. Then the yield to worst is the minimum of these values, 5.7% in our example.

The yield to worst measure holds little meaning because of its underlying assumptions.

Cash Flow Yield

For mortgage-backed securities, the yield calculated is the *cash flow yield*. It is the interest rate that equates the present value of the cash flow to the market price plus accrued interest of the security. As explained in Chapter 5, the only way to calculate a cash flow yield is to assume a prepayment rate.

The interest rate that will make the present value of the projected principal and interest payments equal to the price plus accrued interest is a monthly rate. The bond equivalent yield is found by calculating the effective 6-month interest rate and then doubling it. That is:

$$\text{Cash flow yield on a bond equivalent basis} = 2[(1 + \text{Monthly interest rate})^6 - 1]$$

As we have noted, the yield to maturity has two shortcomings as a measure of a bond's potential return: (1) it is assumed that the coupon payments can be reinvested at a rate equal to the yield to maturity and (2) it is assumed that the bond is held to maturity. These shortcomings are equally present in application of the cash flow yield measure: (1) the projected cash flows are assumed to be reinvested at the cash flow yield and (2) the mortgage-backed security is assumed to be held until the final payout based on some prepayment assumption. The importance of reinvestment risk, the risk that the cash flow will be reinvested at a rate less than the cash flow yield, is particularly important for mortgage-backed securities since payments are monthly. Moreover, the cash flow yield is dependent on realization of the projected cash flow according to some prepayment rate. If actual prepayments vary from the prepayment rate assumed, the cash flow yield will not be realized.

Yield Measure for Floating-Rate Securities

The coupon rate for a floating-rate security changes periodically according to a designated reference rate (such as LIBOR or a Treasury rate). Since the future value for the reference rate is unknown, it is not possible to determine the cash flows. This means that a yield to maturity cannot be calculated.

A conventional measure used to estimate the potential return for a floating-rate security is the security's *discounted margin* (also called *effective margin*). This measure estimates the average spread or margin over the reference rate that the investor can expect to earn over the life of the security. The procedure for calculating the discounted margin is as follows:

Step 1. Determine the cash flows assuming that the reference rate does not change over the life of the security.

Step 2. Select a margin (spread).

Step 3. Discount the cash flows found in Step 1 by the current value of the reference rate plus the margin selected in Step 2.

Step 4. Compare the present value of the cash flows as calculated in Step 3 to the price. If the present value is equal to the security's price, the discounted margin is the margin assumed in Step 2. If the present value is not equal to the security's price, go back to Step 2 and try a different margin.

For a security selling at par, the discounted margin is simply the spread over the reference rate.

To illustrate the calculation, suppose that a 6-year floating-rate security selling for $99.3098 pays a rate based on 6-month LIBOR plus 80 basis points. The coupon rate is reset every six months. Assume that the current interest rate for the index is 10%.

Exhibit 3 shows the calculation of the discounted margin for this security. The second column shows the current value for 6-month LIBOR. The third column sets forth the cash flows for the security. The cash flow for the first 11 periods is equal to one-half the current 6-month LIBOR (5%) plus the semiannual spread of 40 basis points multiplied by $100. At the maturity date (i.e., period 12), the cash flow is $5.4 plus the maturity value of $100. The top row of the last five columns shows the assumed margin. The rows below the assumed margin show the present value of each cash flow. The last row gives the total present value of the cash flows.

For the five assumed yield spreads, the present value is equal to the price of the floating-rate security ($99.3098) when the assumed margin is 96 basis points. Therefore, the discounted margin is 96 basis points. Notice that the discounted margin is 80 basis points, the same as the spread over the reference rate, when the security is selling at par.

There are two drawbacks of the discounted margin as a measure of the potential return from investing in a floating-rate security. First, the measure assumes that the reference rate will not change over the life of the security. Second, if the floating-rate security has a cap or floor, this is not taken into consideration.

Exhibit 3: Calculation of the Discounted Margin for a Floating-Rate Security

Maturity = 6 years
Coupon rate = LIBOR + 80 basis points
Reset every six months

Period	LIBOR (%)	Cash flow ($)*	Present value ($) at assumed margin of				
			80 bp	84 bp	88 bp	96 bp	100 bp
1	10	5.4	5.1233	5.1224	5.1214	5.1195	5.1185
2	10	5.4	4.8609	4.8590	4.8572	4.8535	4.8516
3	10	5.4	4.6118	4.6092	4.6066	4.6013	4.5987
4	10	5.4	4.3755	4.3722	4.3689	4.3623	4.3590
5	10	5.4	4.1514	4.1474	4.1435	4.1356	4.1317
6	10	5.4	3.9387	3.9342	3.9297	3.9208	3.9163
7	10	5.4	3.7369	3.7319	3.7270	3.7171	3.7122
8	10	5.4	3.5454	3.5401	3.5347	3.5240	3.5186
9	10	5.4	3.3638	3.3580	3.3523	3.3409	3.3352
10	10	5.4	3.1914	3.1854	3.1794	3.1673	3.1613
11	10	5.4	3.0279	3.0216	3.0153	3.0028	2.9965
12	10	105.4	56.0729	55.9454	55.8182	55.5647	55.4385
		Present value	100.0000	99.8269	99.6541	99.3098	99.1381

* For periods 1-11: Cash flow = $100 (0.5) (LIBOR + Assumed margin)
   For period 12: Cash flow = $100 (0.5) (LIBOR + Assumed margin) + $100

YIELD SPREAD MEASURES

Traditional analysis of the yield premium for a non-Treasury bond involves calculating the difference between the bond's yield and the yield to maturity of a comparable maturity Treasury coupon security. The latter is obtained from the Treasury yield curve. For example, consider the following 10-year bonds:

Issue	Coupon	Price	Yield to maturity
Treasury	6%	100.00	6.00%
Non-Treasury	8%	104.19	7.40%

The yield spread for these two bonds as traditionally computed is 140 basis points (7.4% minus 6%). We refer to this traditional yield spread as the *nominal spread*.

The drawbacks of this convention, however, are (1) for both bonds, the yield fails to take into consideration the term structure of the spot rates[2]; and (2) in the case of callable and/or putable bonds, expected interest rate volatility may alter the cash flow of the non-Treasury bond. Let's focus on the first problem.

Static Spread

The *static spread* is a measure of the spread that the investor would realize over the entire Treasury spot rate curve if the bond is held to maturity. It is not a spread off one point on the Treasury yield curve, as is the nominal spread. The static spread, also called the *zero-volatility spread* or *Z-spread*, is calculated as the spread that will make the present value of the cash flows from the non-Treasury bond, when discounted at the Treasury spot rate plus the spread, equal to the non-Treasury bond's price. A trial-and-error procedure is required to determine the static spread.

To illustrate how this is done, let's use the non-Treasury bond in our previous illustration and the Treasury yield curve in Exhibit 1 of the previous chapter. The Treasury spot rates are reproduced in the fourth column of Exhibit 4. The third column in the exhibit is the cash flow for the 8% 10-year non-Treasury issue. The goal is to determine the spread that when added to all the Treasury spot rates that will produce a present value for the cash flows of the non-Treasury bond equal to its market price of $104.19.

Suppose we select a spread of 100 basis points. To each Treasury spot rate shown in the fourth column 100 basis points is added. So, for example, the 5-year (period 10) spot rate is 6.2772% (5.2772% plus 1%). The spot rate plus 100 basis points is then used to calculate the present value of 107.5414. Because the present value is not equal to the non-Treasury issue's price (104.19), the static spread is not 100 basis points. If a spread of 125 basis points is tried, it can be seen from the next-to-the-last column of Exhibit 4 that the present value is 105.7165; again, because this is not equal to the non-Treasury issue's price, 125 basis points is not the static spread. The last column of Exhibit 4 shows the present value when a 146 basis point spread is tried. The present value is equal to the non-Treasury issue's price. Therefore 146 basis points is the static spread, compared to the nominal spread of 140 basis points.

---

[2] Spot rates are explained in the previous chapter.

Exhibit 4: Determination of the Static Spread for an 8%, 10-Year Non-Treasury Issue Selling at 104.19 to Yield 7.4%

Period	Years	Cash flow ($)	Spot rate (%)	Present value ($) assuming a spread of		
				100 bp	125 bp	146 bp
1	0.5	4.00	3.0000	3.9216	3.9168	3.9127
2	1.0	4.00	3.3000	3.8334	3.8240	3.8162
3	1.5	4.00	3.5053	3.7414	3.7277	3.7163
4	2.0	4.00	3.9164	3.6297	3.6121	3.5973
5	2.5	4.00	4.4376	3.4979	3.4767	3.4590
6	3.0	4.00	4.7520	3.3742	3.3497	3.3293
7	3.5	4.00	4.9622	3.2565	3.2290	3.2061
8	4.0	4.00	5.0650	3.1497	3.1193	3.0940
9	4.5	4.00	5.1701	3.0430	3.0100	2.9826
10	5.0	4.00	5.2772	2.9366	2.9013	2.8719
11	5.5	4.00	5.3864	2.8307	2.7933	2.7622
12	6.0	4.00	5.4976	2.7255	2.6862	2.6537
13	6.5	4.00	5.6108	2.6210	2.5801	2.5463
14	7.0	4.00	5.6643	2.5279	2.4855	2.4504
15	7.5	4.00	5.7193	2.4367	2.3929	2.3568
16	8.0	4.00	5.7755	2.3472	2.3023	2.2652
17	8.5	4.00	5.8331	2.2596	2.2137	2.1758
18	9.0	4.00	5.9584	2.1612	2.1148	2.0766
19	9.5	4.00	6.0863	2.0642	2.0174	1.9790
20	10.0	104.00	6.2169	51.1833	49.9638	48.9630
			Total	107.5414	105.7165	104.2145

Notice that the procedure for calculating the static spread is the same as for calculating the discounted margin for a floating-rate security.

Typically, for standard coupon paying bonds with a bullet maturity (i.e., a single payment of principal) the static spread and the nominal spread will not differ significantly. In our example it is only 6 basis points.

For short-term issues, there is little divergence. The main factor causing any difference is the shape of the yield curve. The steeper the yield curve, the greater the difference. To illustrate this, consider the two yield curves shown in Exhibit 5. The yield for the longest maturity of both yield curves is 6%. The first yield curve is steeper than the one used in Exhibit 5; the second yield curve is flat, with the yield for all maturities equal to 6%. It can be shown that for the first yield curve the static spread is 154. Thus, with this steeper yield curve, the difference between the static spread and the nominal yield spread is 14 basis points. For the flat yield curve the static spread is 140 basis points, the same as the nominal spread. This will always be the case.

Exhibit 5: Two Hypothetical Yield Curves

Period	Years	Steep curve (%)	Flat curve (%)
1	0.5	2.00	6.00
2	1.0	2.40	6.00
3	1.5	2.80	6.00
4	2.0	2.90	6.00
5	2.5	3.00	6.00
6	3.0	3.10	6.00
7	3.5	3.30	6.00
8	4.0	3.80	6.00
9	4.5	3.90	6.00
10	5.0	4.20	6.00
11	5.5	4.40	6.00
12	6.0	4.50	6.00
13	6.5	4.60	6.00
14	7.0	4.70	6.00
15	7.5	4.90	6.00
16	8.0	5.00	6.00
17	8.5	5.30	6.00
18	9.0	5.70	6.00
19	9.5	5.80	6.00
20	10.0	6.00	6.00

The difference between the static spread and the nominal spread is greater for issues in which the principal is repaid over time rather than only at maturity. Thus the difference between the nominal spread and the static spread will be considerably greater for mortgage-backed securities and asset-backed securities in a steep yield curve environment.

Static Spread Relative to any Benchmark

In the same way that a static spread relative to a default-free spot rate curve can be calculated, a static spread to any benchmark spot rate curve can be calculated. To illustrate, suppose that a hypothetical agency issue with a coupon rate of 8% and a 10-year maturity is trading at 105.5423. Assume that the benchmark spot rate curve for this issuer is the one given in Exhibit 4 of the previous chapter. The static spread relative to that agency's benchmark spot rate curve is the spread that must be added to the rates shown in the next-to-last column of that exhibit that will make the present value of the cash flows equal to the market price. In our illustration, the static spread relative to this benchmark is 40 basis points.

Thus, when a static spread is cited, it must be cited relative to some benchmark spot rate curve. This is necessary because it indicates the credit and sector risks that are being considered when the static spread was calculated. In the case of agency mortgage-backed securities, the benchmark is the Treasury spot rates.

Option-Adjusted Spread

The static spread seeks to measure the spread over the spot rate curve. This over-comes the first problem of the traditional spread measure — the nominal spread —that we cited earlier. Now let's look at the second shortcoming — failure to take future interest rate volatility into account which could change the cash flow.

What an investor seeks to do is to buy securities whose value is greater than their price. A valuation model such as the two described in the previous chapter allows an investor to estimate the value of a security, which at this point would be sufficient to determine the fairness of the security's price. That is, the investor can say that this bond is 1 point cheap or 2 points cheap, and so on.

A valuation model need not stop here, however. Instead, it can convert the divergence between the market price for the security and the value derived from the model into a yield spread measure. This step is necessary since most market participants find it more convenient to think about yield spread than about price differences.

The *option-adjusted spread* (OAS) was developed as a measure of the yield spread that can be used to convert dollar differences between value and market price. Thus, basically, the OAS is used to reconcile value with market price. But what is it a "spread" over? The OAS is a spread over the issuer's spot rate curve or benchmark. The spot rate curve itself is not a single curve, but a series of spot rate curves that allow for changes in rates.

The reason that the resulting spread is referred to as "option-adjusted" is because the cash flows of the security whose value we seek are adjusted to reflect the embedded option. In contrast, the static spread does not consider how the cash flows will change when interest rates change in the future. That is, the static spread assumes that interest rate volatility is zero. This is why the static spread is also referred to as the zero volatility OAS.

Thus, the OAS is only as good as the valuation model.[3] In the case of the binomial model, the OAS is the constant spread that when added to the binomial interest rate tree and then used to value the security will produce the security's market price. In the Monte Carlo simulation model, the OAS is the constant spread that when added to all of the rates on the interest rate paths will produce a theoretical value equal to the market price.

As we explained in the previous chapter, there are assumptions that underlie a valuation model. Consequently, these assumptions affect the calculated OAS. One critical assumption is interest rate volatility. Specifically, the larger the interest rate volatility assumed, the lower the OAS.

In comparing the OAS of dealer firms, it is critical to check on the volatility assumption made. Moreover, it is important to inquire as to the benchmark on-the-run yield curve used in generating the binomial tree. Some dealers use the Treasury on-the-run issues. As a result, the OAS is capturing the credit spread. In

---

[3] Valuation models are explained in the previous chapter.

contrast, some vendors and dealers use the issuer's on-the-run issue which reflects the issuer's credit risk. In the case of agency mortgage-backed securities, the benchmark is the Treasury on-the-run issues.

Option Cost The implied cost of the option embedded in any security can be obtained by calculating the difference between the OAS at the assumed volatility of interest rates and the static spread. That is,

Option cost = Static spread – OAS

The reason that the option cost is measured in this way is as follows. In an environment of *no* interest rate changes, the investor *would earn the static spread*. When future interest rates are uncertain, the spread is different because of the embedded option; the OAS reflects the spread after adjusting for this option. Therefore, the option cost is the difference between the spread that would be earned in a static interest rate environment (the static spread, or equivalently, the zero volatility OAS) and the spread after adjusting for the option (the OAS).

For callable bonds and mortgage passthrough securities, the option cost is positive. This is because the borrower's ability to alter the cash flow will result in an OAS that is less than the static spread. In the case of a putable bond, the OAS is greater than the static spread so that the option cost is negative. This occurs because of the investor's ability to alter the cash flow.

In general, when the option cost is positive, this means that the investor has sold or is short an option. This is true for callable bonds and mortgage-passthrough securities. A negative value for the option cost means that the investor has purchased or is long an option. A putable bond is an example of this negative option cost. There are certain securities in the mortgage-backed securities market that also have an option cost that is negative.

Highlighting the Pitfalls of the Nominal Spread We can use the concepts presented in this chapter to highlight the pitfalls of the nominal spread. First, we can recast the relationship between the options cost, static spread, and OAS as follows:

Static spread = OAS + Option cost

Next, recall that the nominal spread and the static spread may not diverge significantly. Suppose that the nominal spread is approximately equal to the static spread, then we can substitute nominal spread for static spread in the previous relationship giving:

Nominal spread = OAS + Option cost

This relationship tells us that a high nominal spread could be hiding a high option cost. That is, an investor is only compensated for the OAS. The option cost represents the portion of the spread that the investor has given to the borrower. Thus, while the nominal spread for an agency security that is callable or a mortgage-backed security might be, say 200 basis points, the option cost may be 170 and the OAS only 30 basis points. A credit union that relies on the nominal spread may not be adequately compensated for taking on the option risk associated with a bond with an embedded option.

KEY POINTS

1. The sources of return from holding a bond to maturity are the coupon interest payments, any capital gain or loss, and reinvestment income.

2. Reinvestment income is the interest income generated by reinvesting coupon interest payments and any principal repayments from the time of receipt to the bond's maturity.

3. The current yield relates the annual coupon interest to the market price and fails to recognize any capital gain or loss and reinvestment income.

4. The yield to maturity is the interest rate that will make the present value of the cash flows from a bond equal to the price plus accrued interest.

5. The market convention to annualize a semiannual yield is to double it and the resulting annual yield is referred to as a bond equivalent yield.

6. The yield to maturity takes into account all three sources of return but assumes that the coupon payments and any principal repayments can be reinvested at an interest rate equal to the yield to maturity.

7. The yield to maturity will only be realized if the interim cash flows can be reinvested at the yield to maturity and the bond is held to maturity.

8. The risk an investor faces that future reinvestment rates will be less than the yield to maturity at the time a bond is purchased is called reinvestment risk.

9. Price or interest rate risk is the risk that if a bond is not held to maturity, an investor may have to sell it for less than the purchase price.

10. The longer the maturity and the higher the coupon rate, the more a bond's return is dependent on reinvestment income to realize the yield to maturity at the time of purchase.

11. The yield to call is the interest rate that will make the present value of the expected cash flows to the assumed call date equal to the price.

12. The yield to call does consider all three sources of potential return but assumes that all cash flows can be reinvested at the yield to call until the assumed call date, the investor will hold the bond to the assumed call date, and the issuer will call the bond on the assumed call date.

13. The yield to worst is the lowest yield from among all possible yield to calls and the yield to maturity.

14. For mortgage-backed securities, cash flow yield based on some prepayment rate is the interest rate that equates the present value of the projected principal and interest payments to the market price plus accrued interest.

15. The cash flow yield assumes that all cash flows (principal payments and interest payments) can be reinvested at the calculated yield and that the prepayment rate will be realized over the security's life.

16. For a floating-rate security the discounted margin is the conventional measure that estimates the average spread or margin over the reference rate that the investor can expect to earn over the life of the security.

17. The discounted margin assumes that the reference rate will not change over the life of the security and that there is no cap or floor restriction on the coupon rate.

18. The nominal spread is the difference between the yield for a non-Treasury bond and a comparable maturity Treasury coupon security.

19. The nominal spread fails to consider the term structure of the spot rates and the fact that for bonds with embedded options future interest rate volatility may alter the cash flow.

21. The static spread is a measure of the spread that the investor would realize over the entire Treasury spot rate curve if the bond is held to maturity, thereby recognizing the term structure of interest rates.

22. Unlike the nominal spread, the static spread is not a spread off one point on the Treasury yield curve but is a spread over the entire spot rate curve.

23. For bullet bonds, unless the yield curve is very steep, the nominal spread will not differ significantly from the static spread; for securities where principal is repaid over time rather than just at maturity there can be a significant difference, particularly in a steep yield curve environment.

24. The option-adjusted spread (OAS) converts the cheapness or richness of a bond into a spread over the future possible spot rate curves.

25. An OAS is said to be option adjusted because it allows for future interest rate volatility to affect the cash flows.

26. The OAS is a product of a valuation model and when comparing the OAS of dealer firms, it is critical to check on the volatility assumption employed in the valuation model.

27. The cost of the embedded option is measured as the difference between the static spread and the option-adjusted spread.

28. Credit unions should not rely on the nominal spread for bonds with embedded options since it hides how the spread is split between the OAS and the option cost.

Chapter 10

Measuring Interest Rate Risk

The objectives of this chapter are to:

1. illustrate the price volatility properties of an option-free bond;

2. provide a general formula that can be used to calculate the duration of any security;

3. explain why the traditional duration measure, modified duration, is of limited value in determining the duration of a security with an embedded option;

4. distinguish between modified duration and effective duration;

5. explain what is meant by negative convexity for a callable bond and a mortgage passthrough security;

6. explain what the convexity measure of a bond is and the distinction between modified convexity and effective convexity;

7. describe the relationship between Macaulay duration and modified duration; and,

8. illustrate the limitations of using duration and convexity in assessing the potential performance of a portfolio to nonparallel yield curve shifts.

A major risk faced by a credit union is interest rate risk. To effectively control a portfolio's exposure to interest rate risk, it is necessary to quantify this risk. In this chapter we explain how this is done. The most popular measure of interest rate risk is duration. We will explain this measure and demonstrate its limitations. We will then look at other measures that provide additional information about the interest rate risk exposure of a portfolio.

PRICE VOLATILITY CHARACTERISTICS OF OPTION-FREE BONDS

A fundamental principle of an option-free bond (that is, a bond that does not have any embedded options) is that the price of the bond changes in the opposite direction from a change in the bond's yield. Exhibit 1 illustrates this property for four hypothetical bonds, where the bond prices are shown assuming a par value of 100.

When the price/yield relationship for any option-free bond is graphed, it exhibits the shape shown in Exhibit 2. Notice that as the yield rises, the price of the option-free bond declines. However, this relationship is not linear (that is, it is not a straight line). The shape of the price/yield relationship for any option-free bond is referred to as *convex*. The price/yield relationship that we have discussed refers to an instantaneous change in yield.

Properties of Option-Free Bonds

Exhibit 3 uses the four hypothetical bonds in Exhibit 1 to show the percentage change in each bond's price for various changes in the yield, assuming that the initial yield for all four bonds is 6%. An examination of Exhibit 3 reveals several properties concerning the price volatility of an option-free bond.

Exhibit 1: Price/Yield Relationship for Four Hypothetical Bonds

Yield (%)	Price ($)			
	6%/5 year	6%/20 year	9%/5 year	9%/20 year
4.00	108.9826	127.3555	122.4565	168.3887
5.00	104.3760	112.5514	117.5041	150.2056
5.50	102.1600	106.0195	115.1201	142.1367
5.90	100.4276	101.1651	113.2556	136.1193
5.99	100.0427	100.1157	112.8412	134.8159
6.00	100.0000	100.0000	112.7953	134.6722
6.01	99.9574	99.8845	112.7494	134.5287
6.10	99.5746	98.8535	112.3373	133.2472
6.50	97.8944	94.4479	110.5280	127.7605
7.00	95.8417	89.3225	108.3166	121.3551
8.00	91.8891	80.2072	104.0554	109.8964

Exhibit 2: Price/Yield Relationship for an Option-Free Bond

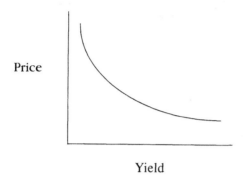

Exhibit 3: Instantaneous Percentage Price Change
for Four Hypothetical Bonds
(Initial yield for all four bonds is 6%)

New Yield (%)	Percent Price Change			
	6%/5 year	6%/20 year	9%/5 year	9%/20 year
4.00	8.98	27.36	8.57	25.04
5.00	4.38	12.55	4.17	11.53
5.50	2.16	6.02	2.06	5.54
5.90	0.43	1.17	0.41	1.07
5.99	0.04	0.12	0.04	0.11
6.01	−0.04	−0.12	−0.04	−0.11
6.10	−0.43	−1.15	−0.41	−1.06
6.50	−2.11	−5.55	−2.01	−5.13
7.00	−4.16	−10.68	−3.97	−9.89
8.00	−8.11	−19.79	−7.75	−18.40

Property 1: Although the prices of all option-free bonds move in the opposite direction from the change in yield, the percentage price change is not the same for all bonds.

Property 2: For small changes in yield, the percentage price change for a given bond is roughly the same, whether the yield increases or decreases.

Property 3: For large changes in yield, the percentage price change is not the same for an increase in yield as it is for a decrease in yield.

Property 4: For a given large change in basis points, the percentage price increase is greater than the percentage price decrease.

The implication of Property 4 is that if a credit union owns a bond, the price appreciation that will be realized if the yield decreases is greater than the capital loss that will be realized if the yield rises by the same number of basis points.

An explanation for these four properties of bond price volatility lies in the convex shape of the price/yield relationship.

Characteristics of a Bond that Affect its Price Volatility

There are two characteristics of an option-free bond that affect its price volatility: coupon and term to maturity.

Characteristic 1: For a given term to maturity and initial yield, the lower the coupon rate, the greater the price volatility of a bond.

Characteristic 2: For a given coupon rate and initial yield, the longer the term to maturity, the greater the price volatility.

These properties can be verified by examining Exhibit 3.

An implication of the second characteristic is that credit unions who want to increase a portfolio's price volatility because they expect interest rates to fall, all other factors being constant, should hold bonds with long maturities in the portfolio. To reduce a portfolio's price volatility in anticipation of a rise in interest rates, bonds with shorter-term maturities should be held in the portfolio.

The Effect of Yield to Maturity

Credit considerations cause different bonds to trade at different yields, even if they have the same coupon and maturity. How, then, holding other factors constant, does the yield to maturity affect a bond's price volatility? As it turns out, the higher the yield to maturity that a bond trades at, the lower the price volatility.

To see this, we can compare a 6% 20-year bond initially selling at a yield of 6%, and a 6% 20-year bond initially selling at a yield of 10%. The former is initially at a price of 100, and the latter carries a price of 65.68. Now, if the yield on both bonds increase by 100 basis points, the first bond trades down by 10.68 points (10.68%). After the assumed increase in yield, the second bond will trade at a price of 59.88, for a price decline of only 5.80 points (or 8.83%). Thus, we see that the bond that trades at a lower yield is more volatile in both percentage price change and absolute price change, as long as the other bond characteristics are the same.

An implication of this is that, for a given change in yields, price volatility is lower when the yield level in the market is high, and price volatility is higher when the yield level is low.

DURATION AS A MEASURE OF INTEREST RATE RISK

The most obvious way to measure the price sensitivity as a percentage of the security's current price to changes in interest rates is to change rates by a small number of basis points and calculate how the price or value of the security will change.

Now let's focus on the measure of interest. We are interested in the percentage change in the price of a security when interest rates change. The name popularly used to refer to the approximate percentage price change is *duration*. It can be demonstrated that the following formula gives the approximate percentage price change for a 100 basis point change in yield:

$$\text{Duration} = \frac{\text{Value if rates fall} - \text{Value if rates rise}}{2(\text{Initial value})(\text{Change in yield in decimal})}$$

where "value if rates fall" is the estimated value of the security if the yield falls by a small number of basis points, "value if rates rise" is the estimated value of the security if the yield rises by a small number of basis points, "initial value" is the current price, and "change in yield in decimal" is the number of basis points by which the yield is changed to obtain the values in the numerator.

The two values in the numerator are obtained from a valuation model. Consequently, *the duration of a security is only as good as the valuation model employed.*

To illustrate the duration calculation, consider the following option-free bond: a 6% coupon 5-year bond trading at par to yield 6%. The initial value is 100. Suppose the yield is changed by 50 basis points. Thus, the change in yield in decimal points is 0.005. If the yield is decreased to 5.5%, the value of this bond would be 102.1600 (see Exhibit 1). If the yield is increased to 6.5%, the value of this bond would be 97.8944 (see Exhibit 1). Substituting these values into the duration formula:

$$\text{Duration} = \frac{102.1600 - 97.8944}{2(100)(0.005)} = 4.27$$

Interpreting Duration

The duration of a security can be interpreted as the approximate percentage change in the price for a 100 basis point parallel shift in the yield curve. Thus a bond with a duration of 4.8 will change by approximately 4.8% for a 100 basis point parallel shift in the yield curve. For a 50 basis point parallel shift in the yield curve, the bond's price will change by approximately 2.4%; for a 25 basis point parallel shift in the yield curve, 1.2%, etc.

A credit union that anticipates a decline in interest rates may decide to extend (i.e., increase) the duration of the trading and available for sale portfolios.[1]

---

[1] How a portfolio's duration is calculated will be discussed below.

Suppose that the portfolio manager increases the present portfolio duration of 3 to 5. This means that for a 100 basis point change in interest rates, the portfolio will change by about 2% more than if the portfolio duration was left unchanged.

Dollar Duration

Duration is related to percentage price change. However, for two bonds with the same duration, the dollar price change will not be the same. For example, consider two bonds, W and X. Suppose that both bonds have a duration of 5, but that W is trading at par while X is trading at 90. A 100 basis point change for both bonds will change the price by approximately 5%. This means a price change of $5 (5% times $100) for W and a price change of $4.5 (5% times $90) for V.

The dollar price volatility of a bond can be measured by multiplying duration by the full dollar price and the number of basis points (in decimal form) and is called the dollar duration.[2] That is:

Dollar duration = Duration × Dollar price × Yield change (in decimal)

The dollar duration for a 100 basis point change in yield is:

Dollar duration = Duration × Dollar price × 0.01

So, for bonds W and X, the dollar duration for a 100 basis point change in yield is:

For bond W: Dollar duration = $5 \times 100 \times 0.01$ = 5.0
For bond X: Dollar duration = $5 \times 90 \times 0.01$ = 4.5

MODIFIED DURATION
VERSUS EFFECTIVE DURATION

A popular form of duration that is used by practitioners is *modified duration*. Modified duration is the approximate percentage change in a bond's price for a 100 basis point change in yield assuming that the bond's cash flow does *not* change when yields change. What this means is that in calculating the values used in the numerator of the duration formula, the cash flow used to calculate the initial value is assumed. Therefore, the change in the bond's value when the yield changes by a small number of basis points is due solely to discounting at the new yield level.

The assumption that the cash flow will not change when the yield changes makes sense for option-free bonds such as noncallable Treasury securities. This is because the payments made by the U.S. Department of the Treasury

---

[2] For a one basis point change in yield, the dollar price change will give the same result as the price value of a basis point or dollar value of an 01.

to investors does not change when the yield changes. However, the same cannot be said for callable and putable bonds and mortgage-backed securities. For these securities, a change in yield will alter the expected cash flow.

The price/yield relationship for callable bonds and mortgage pass-through securities is shown in Exhibit 4. As yields in the market decline, the likelihood that yields will decline further so that the issuer or homeowner will benefit from calling the bond increases. The exact yield level at which investors begin to view the issue likely to be called may not be known, but we do know that there is some level. In Exhibit 4, at yield levels below y*, the price/yield relationship for the callable bond departs from the price/yield relationship for the noncallable bond. If, for example, the market yield is such that a noncallable bond would be selling for 109, but since it is callable would be called at 104, investors would not pay 109. However, for the sake of illustration, if 109 was actually the price paid, the investor would only receive the call price of 104 on a bond they purchased for 109, because the bond would be called. Notice that for a range of yields below y*, there is price compression — that is, there is limited price appreciation as yields decline. The portion of the callable bond price/yield relationship below y* is said to be *negatively convex*.

Negative convexity means that the price appreciation will be less than the price depreciation for a large change in yield of a given number of basis points. For a bond that is option-free and exhibits positive convexity, the price appreciation will be greater than the price depreciation for a large change in yield. The price changes resulting from bonds exhibiting positive convexity and negative convexity can be expressed as follows:

Exhibit 4: Price/Yield Relationship for an Option-Free Bond and a Callable Bond

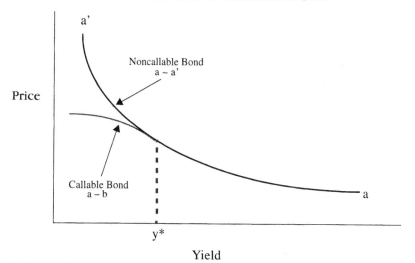

Exhibit 5: Modified Duration Versus Effective Duration

Duration
Interpretation: Generic description of the sensitivity of a bond's price (as a percentage of initial price) to yield changes

Modified Duration	*Effective Duration*
Duration measure in which it is assumed that yield changes do not change the expected cash flow	Duration in which recognition is given to the fact that yield changes may change the expected cash flow

	Absolute value of percentage price change for:	
Change in interest rates	Positive convexity	Negative convexity
−100 basis points	X%	less than Y%
+100 basis points	less than X%	Y%

The two valuation models described in Chapter 8 take into account how shifts in the yield curve will affect cash flow. Thus, when the values used in the numerator are obtained from these valuation models, the resulting duration takes into account both the discounting at different interest rates and how the cash flow can change. When duration is calculated in this manner, it is referred to as *effective duration* or *option-adjusted duration*. Exhibit 5 summarizes the distinction between modified duration and effective duration.

The difference between modified duration and effective duration for fixed-income securities with an embedded option can be quite dramatic. For example, a callable agency bond could have a modified duration of 6 but an effective duration of only 2. For certain collateralized mortgage obligations, the modified duration could be 7 and the effective duration 40! Thus, using modified duration as a measure of the price sensitivity of a security would be misleading. The more appropriate measure for any security with an embedded option is effective duration.

Macaulay Duration

It is worth comparing the modified duration formula presented above to that commonly found in the literature. It is common in the literature to find the following formula for modified duration:[3]

$$\frac{1}{(1 + \text{yield}/k)} \left[\frac{1\text{PVCF}_1 + 2\text{PVCF}_2 + 3\text{PVCF}_3 + \ldots + n\text{PVCF}_n}{k \times \text{Price}} \right]$$

where

k = number of periods, or payments, per year (e.g, k = 2 for semiannual pay bonds and k = 12 for monthly pay bonds)

---

[3] More specifically, this is the formula for modified duration for a bond on a coupon anniversary date.

n   = number of periods until maturity (i.e., number of years to maturity times k)

yield   = yield to maturity of the bond

$PVCF_t$ = present value of the cash flow in period t discounted at the yield to maturity

The expression in the bracket for the modified duration in the above formula is a measure formulated in 1938 by an economist, Frederick Macaulay.[4] This measure is popularly referred to as *Macaulay duration*. Thus, modified duration is commonly expressed as:

$$\text{Modified duration} = \frac{\text{Macaulay duration}}{(1 + \text{Yield}/k)}$$

The general formulation for duration as given earlier provides a short-cut procedure for determining a bond's modified duration. Because it is easier to calculate the modified duration using the short-cut procedure, many vendors of analytical software will use it rather than the long formula to reduce computation time. But, once again, it must be emphasized that modified duration is a flawed measure of a bond's price sensitivity to interest rate changes for a bond with an embedded option.

PORTFOLIO DURATION

A portfolio's (effective) duration can be obtained by calculating the weighted average of the duration of the bonds in the portfolio. The weight is the proportion of the portfolio that a security comprises. Mathematically, a portfolio's duration can be calculated as follows:

$$W_1 D_1 + W_2 D_2 + W_3 D_3 + \dots + W_K D_K$$

where

W_i = market value of bond i/market value of the portfolio

D_i = effective duration of bond i

K   = number of bonds in the portfolio

To illustrate this calculation, consider the following 3-bond portfolio:

Bond	Par amount owned	Price	Effective Duration
1	$40 million	$40,000,000	3.4
2	50 million	42,313,750	5.0
3	10 million	13,785,860	0.6

The market value for the portfolio is $96,099,610.

---

[4] Frederick Macaulay, *Some Theoretical Problems Suggested by the Movement of Interest Rates, Bond Yields, and Stock Prices in the U.S. Since 1856* (New York: National Bureau of Economic Research, 1938).

In this illustration, K is equal to 3 and:

$$W_1 = 40,000,000/96,099,610 = 0.416 \qquad D_1 = 3.4$$
$$W_2 = 42,313,750/96,099,610 = 0.440 \qquad D_2 = 5.0$$
$$W_3 = 13,785,860/96,099,610 = 0.144 \qquad D_3 = 0.6$$

The portfolio's duration is:

$$0.416(3.4) + 0.440(5.0) + 0.144(0.6) = 3.7$$

A portfolio duration of 3.7 means that for a 100 basis change in the yield for *all* three bonds, the market value of the portfolio will change by approximately 3.7%. But keep in mind, the yield on all three bonds must change by 100 basis points for the duration measure to be useful. This is a critical assumption and its importance cannot be overemphasized. We shall return to this point later in this chapter.

Similarly, the dollar duration of a portfolio can be obtained by calculating the weighted average of the dollar duration of the bonds in the portfolio.

DURATION OF A FLOATER

For a floating-rate security, the greater the reset frequency, the smaller the duration. When the coupon reset date is close, the duration is close to zero. All of this assumes that the spread over the reference rate that the market requires does not change and that there are no caps or floors.

If there is a cap, then the floating-rate security's duration will take on the characteristics of a fixed-rate security if the coupon rate that would be set in the absence of the cap is significantly above the cap rate. The same is true if there is a floor and the coupon rate that would be set in the absence of the floor is significantly below the floor rate.

DURATION OF AN INVERSE FLOATER

An inverse floater is a security whose coupon rate changes inversely with the change in the reference rate. It is common to create an inverse floater by splitting a fixed-rate security into a floater and inverse floater. There are inverse floaters in the structured note and CMO markets, the largest issuance being in the latter market. The fixed-rate security from which the floater and inverse floater are created is called the collateral.

The duration of an inverse floater will be a multiple of the duration of the collateral from which it is created. To see this, suppose that a 30-year fixed-rate bond with a market value of $100 million is split into a floater and an inverse floater with a market value of $80 million and $20, respectively. Assume also that the duration for the collateral (i.e., the 30-year fixed-rate bond) is 8. For a 100 basis point change in interest rates, the collateral's value will change by approximately 8% or $8 million (8% times $100 million). This means that by splitting the collateral's value, the combined change in value for a 100 basis change in interest rates for the floater and inverse floater must be $8 million. If the duration of the floater is small as just explained, this means that the entire $8 million change in value must come from the inverse floater. For this to occur, the duration of the inverse floater must be 40. That is, a duration of 40 will mean a 40% change in the value of the inverse floater for a 100 basis point change in interest rates and a change in value of $8 million (40% times $20 million).

Notice from our illustration that the duration of the inverse floater is greater than the number of years to maturity of the collateral. Portfolio managers who interpret duration in terms of years (Macaulay duration) are confused that a security can have a duration greater than the collateral from which it is created. It cannot be emphasized enough that a credit union portfolio manager using duration in terms of years could be making serious errors in analysis.

CONVEXITY MEASURE AS A SECOND ORDER APPROXIMATION OF PRICE CHANGE

Notice that the duration measure indicates that regardless of whether the yield curve is shifted up or down, the approximate percentage price change is the same. However, this does not agree with the properties of a bond's price volatility described earlier in this chapter. Specifically, Property 2 states that for small changes in yield the percentage price change will be the same for an increase or decrease in yield. Property 3 states that for large changes in yield this is not true. This suggests that duration is only a good approximation of the percentage price change for a small change in yield.

To see this, consider once again the 6% 5-year bond selling to yield 6% with a duration of 4.27. If yields increase instantaneously by 10 basis points (from 6% to 6.1%), then using duration the approximate percentage price change would be −0.43% (−4.27% divided by 10, remembering that duration is the percentage price change for a 100 basis point change in yield). Notice from the second panel of Exhibit 3 that the actual percentage price change is −0.43%. Similarly, if the yield decreases instantaneously by 10 basis points (from 6.00% to 5.90%), then the percentage change in price would be +0.43%. From the second panel of Exhibit 3, the actual percentage price change would be +0.43%. This example illustrates that for small changes in yield, duration does an excellent job of approximating the percentage price change.

Instead of a small change in yield, let's assume that yields increase by 200 basis points, from 6% to 8%. The approximate percentage change is −8.54% (−4.27%

times 2). As can be seen from the second panel of Exhibit 3, the actual percentage change in price is only −8.11%. Moreover, if the yield decreases by 200 basis points from 6% to 4%, the approximate percentage price change based on duration would be +8.54%, compared to an actual percentage price change of +8.98%. Thus, the approximation is not as good for a 200 basis point change in yield.

Duration is in fact a first approximation for a small change in yield. The approximation can be improved by using a second approximation. This approximation is referred to as a bond's *convexity*. The use of this term in the industry is unfortunate since the term convexity is also used to describe the shape or curvature of the price/yield relationship, as explained earlier in this chapter. The convexity measure of a security can be used to approximate the change in price that is not explained by duration.

Convexity Measure

The convexity measure of any bond can be approximated using the following formula:

$$\text{Convexity measure} = \frac{\text{Value if rates fall} + \text{Value if rates rise} - 2(\text{Initial value})}{2(\text{Initial value})(\text{Change in yield in decimal})^2}$$

where the notation is the same as used earlier for duration.

For our hypothetical 6% 5-year bond selling to yield 6%, we know that for a 50 basis point change in rates:

change in yield in decimal	=	0.0050
initial value	=	100.0000
value if rates fall	=	102.1600
value if rates rise	=	97.8944

Substituting these values into the convexity measure formula,

$$\text{Convexity measure} = \frac{102.1600 + 97.8944 - 2(100.0000)}{2(100.0000)(0.005)^2} = 10.88$$

Percentage Price Change Adjustment for Convexity

Given the convexity measure, the approximate percentage change adjustment due to the bond's convexity (i.e., the percentage price change not explained by duration) is:

$$\text{Convexity measure} \times (\text{Change in yield in decimal})^2$$

For example, for the 6% coupon bond maturing in 5 years, the convexity adjustment to the percentage price change if the yield increases from 6% to 8% is:

$$10.88 \times (0.02)^2 = 0.0044 = 0.44\%$$

If the yield decreases from 6% to 4%, the convexity adjustment to the approximate price change would also be 0.44%.

The approximate percentage price change based on duration and the convexity adjustment is found by simply adding the two estimates. So, for example, if yields change from 6% to 8%, the estimated percentage price change would be:

Estimated change using duration	= −8.54%
Estimated adjustment for convexity	= +0.44%
Total estimated percentage price change	= −8.10%

The actual percentage price change is −8.11%. For a decrease of 200 basis points, from 6% to 4%, the approximate percentage price change would be as follows:

Estimated change using duration	= +8.54%
Estimated adjustment for convexity	= +0.44%
Total estimated percentage price change	= +8.98%

The actual percentage price change is +8.98%. Thus, duration with the convexity adjustment does an excellent job of estimating the sensitivity of our bond's price change to large changes in yield.

Modified Convexity and Effective Convexity

The prices used to calculate the convexity measure can be obtained by either assuming that when yields change the expected cash flow does not change or it does change. In the former case, the resulting convexity is referred to as *modified convexity*. Actually, in the industry, convexity is not qualified by the adjective modified. Thus, in practice the term convexity typically means the cash flow is assumed not to change when yields change. *Effective convexity*, in contrast, assumes that the cash flow does change when yields change. This is the same distinction made for duration.

As with duration, for bonds with embedded options there could be quite a difference between the calculated modified convexity and effective convexity. In fact, for all option-free bonds, either convexity measure will have a positive value. For callable bonds and mortgage-backed securities, the calculated effective convexity can be negative when the calculated modified convexity gives a positive value.

DURATION, CONVEXITY, AND NONPARALLEL YIELD CURVE SHIFTS

Duration is an approximation of the percentage price for a parallel shift in the yield curve. This measure of interest rate risk assumes that all interest rates change by the same number of basis points. The same applies to the convexity measure.

Exhibit 6: Three Hypothetical Bonds to Illustrate the Limitations of Duration and Convexity

Bond	Coupon rate (%)	Price ($)	Yield to maturity (%)	Maturity (years)
A	6.500	100	6.500	5
B	8.000	100	8.000	20
C	7.500	100	7.500	10

Calculation of duration: Change yield up and down by 10 basis points

Bond	Value if rates rise ($)	Value if rates fall ($)	Duration	Convexity
A	99.5799	100.4222	4.21122	10.67912
B	99.0177	100.9970	9.89681	73.63737
C	99.3083	100.6979	6.94821	31.09724

Two portfolios with the same duration may perform quite differently if the yield curve does not shift in a parallel fashion. To illustrate this point, consider the three bonds shown in Exhibit 6. Bond A is the short-term bond, bond B is the long-term bond, and bond C is the intermediate term bond. Each bond is selling at par and it is assumed the next coupon payment is six months from now. The duration and convexity for each bond are calculated in the exhibit. Since the bonds are trading at par value, the duration and convexities are then the dollar duration and dollar convexity.

Suppose that the following two portfolios are constructed. The first portfolio consists of only bond C, a 10-year bond and shall be referred to as the "bullet portfolio." The second portfolio consists of 51.86% of bond A and 48.14% of bond B and this portfolio shall be referred to as the "barbell portfolio."

The dollar duration of the bullet portfolio is 6.49821. Recall that dollar duration is a measure of the dollar price sensitivity of a bond or a portfolio. The dollar duration of the barbell is the weighted average of the dollar duration of the two bonds and is computed below:

$$0.5186(4.21122) + 0.4814(9.89681) = 6.49821$$

The dollar duration of the barbell is equal to the dollar duration of the bullet. In fact, the barbell portfolio was designed to produce this result.

Duration is just a first approximation of the change in price resulting from a change in interest rates. The convexity measure provides a second approximation. The dollar convexity measure of the two portfolios is not equal. The dollar convexity measure of the bullet portfolio is 31.09724. The dollar convexity measure of the barbell is a weighted average of the dollar convexity measure of the two bonds. That is,

$$0.5186(10.67912) + 0.4814(73.63737) = 40.98658$$

Thus, the bullet has a dollar convexity measure that is less than that of the barbell portfolio.

Exhibit 7: Comparison of Yield, Dollar Duration, and Dollar Convexity of Bullet and Barbell Portfolios

Parameter	Portfolio	
	Bullet	Barbell
Yield	7.25%	7.22%
Dollar duration	6.49821	6.49821
Dollar convexity	31.09724	40.98658

The "yield" for the two portfolios is not the same. The yield for the bullet is simply the yield to maturity of bond C, 7.50%. The traditional yield calculation for the barbell portfolio, which is found by taking a weighted average of the yield to maturity of the two bonds included in the portfolio, is 7.22%. This would suggest that the "yield" of the bullet portfolio is 28 basis points greater than the barbell portfolio. Thus, both portfolios have the same dollar duration but the yield of the bullet portfolio is greater than the yield of the barbell portfolio. However, the dollar convexity of the barbell portfolio is greater than that of the bullet portfolio. The difference in the two yields is sometimes referred to as the "cost of convexity." This is summarized in Exhibit 7.

Which is the better portfolio in which to invest? As we stressed in the previous chapters, the answer depends on the investment objectives and investment horizon. Let's assume a six month investment horizon. The last column of Exhibit 8 shows the difference in the return over a 6-month investment horizon for the two portfolios, assuming that the yield curve shifts in a "parallel" fashion.[5] By parallel it is meant that the yield for the short-term bond (A), the intermediate-term bond (C), and the long-term bond (B) change by the same number of basis points, shown in the first column of the exhibit. The return reported in the last column of Exhibit 8 is:

Bullet portfolio's return − Barbell portfolio's return

Thus, a positive value in the last column means that the bullet portfolio outperformed the barbell portfolio while a negative sign means that the barbell portfolio outperformed the bullet portfolio.

Which portfolio is the better investment alternative if the yield curve shifts in a parallel fashion *and* the investment horizon is six months? The answer depends on the amount by which yields change. Notice in the last column that the if yields change by less than 100 basis points, the bullet portfolio will outperform the barbell portfolio. The reverse is true if yields change by more than 100 basis points.

[5] Note that no assumption is needed for the reinvestment rate since the three bonds shown in Exhibit 8 are assumed to be trading right after a coupon payment has been made and therefore there is no accrued interest.

Exhibit 8: Performance of Bullet and Barbell Portfolios Over a 6-Month Horizon Assuming a Parallel Yield Curve Shift

Yield change (in bp)	Price plus coupon ($)			Total return (%)		
	A	B	C	Bullet	Barbell	Difference*
−300	115.6407	141.0955	126.7343	53.47	55.79	−2.32
−250	113.4528	133.6753	122.4736	44.95	46.38	−1.43
−200	111.3157	126.8082	118.3960	36.79	37.55	−0.76
−150	109.2281	120.4477	114.4928	28.99	29.26	−0.27
−100	107.1888	114.5512	110.7559	21.51	21.47	0.05
−50	105.1965	109.0804	107.1775	14.35	14.13	0.22
−25	104.2176	106.4935	105.4453	10.89	10.63	0.26
0	103.2500	104.0000	103.7500	7.50	7.22	0.28
25	102.2935	101.5961	102.0907	4.18	3.92	0.27
50	101.3481	99.2780	100.4665	0.93	0.70	0.23
100	99.4896	94.8852	97.3203	−5.36	−5.45	0.09
150	97.6735	90.7949	94.3050	−11.39	−11.28	−0.11
200	95.8987	86.9830	91.4146	−17.17	−16.79	−0.38
250	94.1640	83.4271	88.6433	−22.71	−22.01	−0.70
300	92.4686	80.1070	85.9857	−28.03	−26.96	−1.06

*A positive sign indicates that the bullet portfolio outperformed the barbell portfolio; a negative sign indicates that the barbell portfolio outperformed the bullet portfolio.

Now let's look at what happens if the yield curve does not shift in a parallel fashion. The last columns of Exhibits 9 and 10 show the relative performance of the two portfolios for a nonparallel shift of the yield curve. Specifically, in Exhibit 9 it is assumed that if the yield on bond C (the intermediate-term bond) changes by the amount shown in the first column, bond A (the short-term bond) will change by the same amount plus 30 basis points, whereas bond B (the long-term bond) will change by the same amount shown in the first column less 30 basis points. That is, the nonparallel shift assumed is a flattening of the yield curve. For this yield curve shift, the barbell will outperform the bullet for the yield changes assumed in the first column. While not shown in the exhibit, for changes greater than 300 basis points for bond C, the opposite would be true. In Exhibit 10, the nonparallel shift assumes that for a change in bond C's yield, the yield on bond A will change by the same amount minus 30 basis points, whereas that on bond B will change by the same amount plus 30 points. That is, it assumes that the yield curve will steepen. In this case, the bullet portfolio would outperform the barbell portfolio for all but a change in yield greater than 250 basis points for bond C.

The key point here is that looking at measures such as yield (yield-to-maturity or some type of portfolio yield measure), duration or convexity tells us little about performance over some investment horizon because performance depends on the magnitude of the change in yields and how the yield curve shifts.

Exhibit 9: Performance of Bullet and Barbell Portfolios Over a 6-Month Horizon Assuming a Flattening of the Yield Curve

Yield change	Price plus coupon ($)			Total return (%)		
for C (in bp)	A	B	C	Bullet	Barbell	Difference*
−300	114.3218	145.8342	126.7343	53.47	58.98	−5.51
−250	112.1645	138.0579	122.4736	44.95	49.26	−4.31
−200	110.0573	130.8648	118.3960	36.79	40.15	−3.36
−150	107.9989	124.2057	114.4928	28.99	31.60	−2.62
−100	105.9879	118.0356	110.7559	21.51	23.58	−2.06
−50	104.0232	112.3139	107.1775	14.35	16.03	−1.67
−25	103.0578	109.6094	105.4453	10.89	12.42	−1.53
0	102.1036	107.0033	103.7500	7.50	8.92	−1.42
25	101.1603	104.4914	102.0907	4.18	5.53	−1.35
50	100.2279	102.0699	100.4665	0.93	2.23	−1.30
100	98.3949	97.4829	97.3203	−5.36	−4.09	−1.27
150	96.6037	93.2142	94.3050	−11.39	−10.06	−1.33
200	94.8531	89.2380	91.4146	−17.17	−15.70	−1.47
250	93.1421	85.5311	88.6433	−22.71	−21.04	−1.67
300	91.4697	82.0718	85.9857	−28.03	−26.11	−1.92

Assumptions: Change in yield of bond C (column 1) results in a change in the yield of bond A plus 30 basis points. Change in yield of bond C (column 1) results in a change in the yield of bond B minus 30 basis points.

*A positive sign indicates that the bullet portfolio outperformed the barbell portfolio; a negative sign indicates that the barbell portfolio outperformed the bullet portfolio.

The statement made earlier that there is a trade-off between convexity and yield does not necessarily arise in the market. This should not be surprising since as argued in Chapter 9, the yield measure is not a good indicator of the potential return. To illustrate this, consider the three hypothetical bonds shown in Exhibit 11. A barbell portfolio with the same dollar duration as the bullet portfolio was constructed. At the bottom of the exhibit is the yield, dollar duration, and dollar convexity. Notice that the average yield and the dollar convexity are greater for the barbell portfolio than the bullet portfolio. Thus, it would seem that the barbell portfolio in our illustration would perform better than the bullet portfolio over a 6-month investment horizon. This is, in fact, the case for a parallel shift in the yield, as can be seen in Exhibit 12. However, this is not the case for a nonparallel yield curve shift. Exhibit 13 shows that if the yield curve steepens as assumed in the exhibit, the bullet outperforms the barbell over the 6-month investment horizon.

Exhibit 10: Performance of Bullet and Barbell Portfolios Over a 6-Month Horizon Assuming a Steepening of the Yield Curve

Yield change	Price plus coupon ($)			Total return (%)		
for C (in bp)	A	B	C	Bullet	Barbell	Difference[*]
−300	116.9785	136.5743	126.7343	53.47	52.82	0.65
−250	114.7594	129.4918	122.4736	44.95	43.70	1.24
−200	112.5919	122.9339	118.3960	36.79	35.14	1.65
−150	110.4748	116.8567	114.4928	28.99	27.09	1.89
−100	108.4067	111.2200	110.7559	21.51	19.52	1.99
−50	106.3863	105.9874	107.1775	14.35	12.39	1.97
−25	105.3937	103.5122	105.4453	10.89	8.98	1.91
0	104.4125	101.1257	103.7500	7.50	5.66	1.84
25	103.4426	98.8243	102.0907	4.18	2.44	1.74
50	102.4839	96.6046	100.4665	0.93	−0.69	1.63
100	100.5995	92.3963	97.3203	−5.36	−6.70	1.34
150	98.7582	88.4758	94.3050	−11.39	−12.38	0.99
200	96.9587	84.8200	91.4146	−17.17	−17.77	0.60
250	95.2000	81.4080	88.6433	−22.71	−22.88	0.17
300	93.4812	78.2204	85.9857	−28.03	−27.73	−0.30

Assumption: Change in yield of bond C (column 1) results in a change in the yield of bond A minus 30 basis points. Change in yield of bond C (column 1) results in a change in the yield of bond B plus 30 basis points.

*A positive sign indicates that the bullet portfolio outperformed the barbell portfolio; a negative sign indicates that the barbell portfolio outperformed the bullet portfolio.

Exhibit 11: Three Hypothetical Bonds to Illustrate the Lack of Trade-Off Between Yield and Convexity

Bond	Coupon rate (%)	Price ($)	Yield to maturity (%)	Maturity (years)
X	7.900	100	7.900	2
Y	8.800	100	8.800	7
Z	8.200	100	8.200	4

Bullet portfolio: Bond Z
Barbell portfolio: Bonds X and Y as follows
  Bond X: 53.86%
  Bond Y: 46.14%

Parameters

Parameter	Portfolio	
	Bullet	Barbell
Yield	8.20%	8.32%
Dollar duration	3.35253	3.35253
Dollar convexity	6.90699	8.89010

Exhibit 12: Performance of Bullet and Barbell Portfolios Over a 6-Month Horizon Assuming a Parallel Yield Curve Shift

Yield change (in bp)	Price plus coupon ($)			Total return (%)		
	X	Y	Z	Bullet	Barbell	Difference*
−300	108.2382	120.4549	113.5879	27.18	27.75	−0.57
−250	107.5063	117.5671	111.9321	23.86	24.30	−0.43
−200	106.7813	114.7679	110.3069	20.61	20.93	−0.32
−150	106.0633	112.0545	108.7117	17.42	17.66	−0.23
−100	105.3522	109.4239	107.1459	14.29	14.46	−0.17
−50	104.6477	106.8733	105.6089	11.22	11.35	−0.13
−25	104.2980	105.6272	104.8510	9.70	9.82	−0.12
0	103.9500	104.4000	104.1000	8.20	8.32	−0.12
25	103.6036	103.1915	103.3559	6.71	6.83	−0.12
50	103.2589	102.0013	102.6187	5.24	5.36	−0.12
100	102.5742	99.6748	101.1644	2.33	2.47	−0.14
150	101.8960	97.4180	99.7365	−0.53	−0.34	−0.19
200	101.2242	95.2286	98.3345	−3.33	−3.08	−0.25
250	100.5587	93.1044	96.9579	−6.08	−5.76	−0.32
300	99.8993	91.0431	95.6061	−8.79	−8.37	−0.41

* A positive sign indicates that the bullet portfolio outperformed the barbell portfolio; a negative sign indicates that the barbell portfolio outperformed the bullet portfolio.

Exhibit 13: Performance of Bullet and Barbell Portfolios Over a 6-Month Horizon Assuming a Steepening of the Yield Curve

Yield change for Z (in bp)	Price plus coupon ($)			Total return (%)		
	X	Y	Z	Bullet	Barbell	Difference*
−300	108.6807	118.7114	113.5879	27.18	26.62	0.56
−250	107.9446	115.8771	111.9321	23.86	23.21	0.65
−200	107.2155	113.1298	110.3069	20.61	19.89	0.72
−150	106.4933	110.4664	108.7117	17.42	16.65	0.77
−100	105.7780	107.8842	107.1459	14.29	13.50	0.79
−50	105.0696	105.3802	105.6089	11.22	10.43	0.79
−25	104.7179	104.1568	104.8510	9.70	8.92	0.78
0	104.3678	102.9520	104.1000	8.20	7.43	0.77
25	104.0195	101.7655	103.3559	6.71	5.96	0.75
50	103.6728	100.5969	102.6187	5.24	4.51	0.73
100	102.9842	98.3125	101.1644	2.33	1.66	0.67
150	102.3022	96.0964	99.7365	−0.53	−1.12	0.60
200	101.6265	93.9464	98.3345	−3.33	−3.83	0.50
250	100.9572	91.8602	96.9579	−6.08	−6.48	0.40
300	100.2942	89.8356	95.6061	−8.79	−9.06	0.28

Assumption: Change in yield of bond Z (column 1) results in a change in the yield of bond X minus 30 basis points. Change in yield of bond Z (column 1) results in a change in the yield of bond Y plus 30 basis points.

*A positive sign indicates that the bullet portfolio outperformed the barbell portfolio; a negative sign indicates that the barbell portfolio outperformed the bullet portfolio.

KEY POINTS

1. The price/yield relationship for an option-free bond is convex.

2. A property of an option-free bond is that for a small change in yield, the percentage price change is roughly the same, whether the yield increases or decreases.

3. A property of an option-free bond is that for a large change in yield, the percentage price change is not the same for an increase in yield as it is for a decrease in yield.

4. A property of an option-free bond is that for a given change in basis points, the percentage price increase is greater than the percentage price decrease.

5. The coupon and maturity of an option-free bond affect its price volatility.

6. For a given term to maturity and initial yield, the lower the coupon rate, the greater the price volatility of a bond.

7. For a given coupon rate and initial yield, the longer the term to maturity, the greater the price volatility.

8. For a given change in yield, price volatility is less when yield levels in the market are high than when yield levels are low.

9. The percentage price change of a bond can be estimated by changing the yield by a small number of basis points and observing how the price changes.

10. Duration is only as good as the valuation model that provides the values when rates change.

11. The duration of a bond measures the approximate percentage price change for a 100 basis point change in yield, assuming a parallel shift in the yield curve.

12. The dollar duration measures the dollar price change of a bond.

13. Modified duration is the approximate percentage change in a bond's price for a 100 basis point parallel shift in the yield curve assuming that the bond's cash flow does not change when the yield curve shifts.

14. Callable bonds and mortgage pass-through securities exhibit negative convexity — the percentage price change for a rise in rates is greater than for a decline in rates by the same number of basis points.

15. Modified duration is not a useful measure of the price sensitivity for securities with embedded options.

16. Effective duration or option-adjusted duration is the approximate percentage price change of a bond for a 100 basis point parallel shift in the yield curve allowing for the cash flow to change as a result of the change in yield.

17. The difference between modified duration and effective duration for fixed-income securities with an embedded option can be quite dramatic.

18. The estimate of the price sensitivity of a bond based on duration can be improved by using a bond's convexity.

19. As with duration, the convexity of a bond can be measured assuming that the cash flow does not change when yield changes (modified convexity) or assuming that it does change when yield changes (effective convexity).

20. Assuming the spread over the reference rate that the market requires does not change and that there are no caps or floors, the duration for a floating-rate security is smaller, the greater the reset frequency.

21. The duration of an inverse floater is a multiple of the duration of the fixed-rate security from which it is created.

22. Both modified duration and effective duration assume that any change in interest rates is the result of a parallel shift in the yield curve.

23. Two portfolios can have the same duration and perform differently for a non-parallel shift in the yield curve.

Chapter 11

Total Return Analysis and Stress Testing

The objectives of this chapter are to:

1. explain what the total return measure is, how it is calculated, and why it should be used in assessing the potential performance of a portfolio or strategy;

2. explain what scenario analysis is;

3. explain how to calculate the total return for a mortgage-backed security;

4. explain how the total return for a bond portfolio should be calculated;

5. explain how option-adjusted spread analysis can be incorporated into the total return framework; and,

6. discuss the stress testing required by Part 703 for individual securities and the portfolio.

In managing the interest rate risk of a credit union portfolio, it is necessary to quantify how the price of a security held and the value of the entire portfolio changes when interest rates change. In the previous chapter we described how the duration and convexity measures can be used for this purpose. We emphasized, however, the limitations of these interest rate risk measures. In this chapter we look at an approach to assessing the price sensitivity of individual investments and the entire portfolio that overcomes the drawbacks of duration and convexity. This approach is called *total return analysis*. We will also see how this analysis is used for stress testing individual investments and the entire portfolio of a credit union as mandated by Part 703.

TOTAL RETURN ANALYSIS

A portfolio manager who purchases a bond can expect to receive a *dollar* return from one or more of the following sources: (1) the coupon interest payments made by the issuer, (2) any capital gain (or capital loss — negative dollar return) when the bond matures, is called, is put, is refunded, or is sold, and (3) reinvestment income from investing interim cash flows (coupon interest payments and principal received prior to the maturity date). Any measure of the potential return from holding a bond over some investment horizon should consider these three sources of return.

In Chapter 9, we emphasized why yield measures are of limited value with respect to assessing the potential performance over some investment horizon. If yield measures offer little insight into the potential performance of a bond or bond portfolio, what measure can be used? The proper measure is one that considers all three sources of potential dollar return over the investment horizon. It is the return (interest rate) that will make the proceeds (i.e., price plus accrued interest) invested grow to the projected total dollar return at the end of the investment horizon and is referred to as the *total return*.[1]

The total return requires that the portfolio manager specify:

- an investment horizon
- a reinvestment rate
- a selling price for the bond at the end of the investment horizon (which depends on the assumed yield to maturity for the bond at the end of the investment horizon).

More formally, the steps for computing a total return over some investment horizon are as follows:

---

[1] The total return is also referred to as the *horizon return*.

Step 1: Compute the total coupon payments plus the interest on interest based on an assumed reinvestment rate. The reinvestment rate is one-half the annual interest rate that the portfolio manager assumes can be earned on the reinvestment of coupon interest payments.[2]

Step 2: Determine the projected sale price at the end of the investment horizon. We refer to this as the *horizon price*. The horizon price will depend on the projected yield on comparable bonds at the end of the investment horizon. We refer to the yield at the end of the investment horizon as the *horizon yield*.

Step 3: Add the values computed in Steps 1 and 2. The sum is the *total future dollars* that will be received from the investment given the assumed reinvestment rate and projected horizon yield.

Step 4: To obtain the semiannual total return, use the following formula:

$$\left(\frac{\text{Total future dollars}}{\text{Full purchase price}}\right)^{1/\text{Length of horizon}} - 1$$

where the full purchase price includes accrued interest.

Step 5: For semiannual pay bonds, double the interest rate found in Step 4. The resulting interest rate is the total return expressed on a bond-equivalent basis. Instead, the total return can be expressed on an effective rate basis by using the following formula:

$$(1 + \text{Semiannual total return})^2 - 1$$

The decision as to whether to calculate the total return on a bond-equivalent basis or an effective rate basis depends on the situation. If the total return is being compared to a benchmark index that is calculated on a bond-equivalent basis, then the total return should be calculated in that way. However, if the bond is being used to satisfy liabilities that are calculated on an effective rate basis, then the total return should be calculated in that way. A graphical depiction of the total return calculation is presented in Exhibit 1.

To illustrate the computation of the total return, suppose that a portfolio manager with a 1-year investment horizon is considering purchasing a 6-year 7% coupon bond for $95.31. The next coupon payment is six months from now. The yield to maturity for this bond is 8%. The portfolio manager expects that the coupon payments can be reinvested at an annual interest rate of 6% and that at the end of the investment horizon the 5-year bond will be selling to offer a yield to maturity of 7.2% (i.e., the horizon yield is 7.2%). The total return for this bond is computed in Exhibit 2.

---

[2] A portfolio manager can choose multiple reinvestment rates for cash flows from the bond over the investment horizon.

Exhibit 1: Graphical Depiction of Total Return Calculation

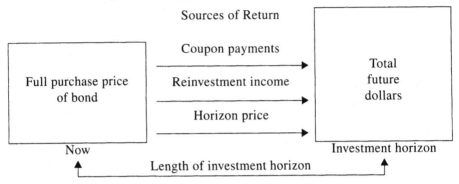

Total return is the interest rate that will make the full purchase price of the bond grow to the total future dollars

Scenario Analysis

An oft-cited objection to the total return by some credit unions is that it requires their portfolio manager to make assumptions about reinvestment rates and horizon yields, as well as to think in terms of an investment horizon. Unfortunately, some credit unions find it more comforting in meaningless measures such as yield because they do not require them to incorporate their expectations into the calculations. This position, however, is not true. As explained in the previous chapter, *the acceptance of a yield number means that an assumption or assumptions were accepted.*

Total return enables the portfolio manager and the board to analyze the performance of a portfolio based on different interest rate scenarios for reinvestment rates and horizon yields. This type of analysis, referred to as *scenario analysis*, allows a portfolio manager to see how sensitive the bond's performance is to each assumption. Therefore, the portfolio manager can get a much better idea of the possible outcomes of bonds using total return.

A portfolio manager should be more comfortable looking at the bonds' total return profile using different interest rate assumptions rather than blindly relying upon the implicit assumptions incorporated into conventional yield measures.

Total Return for a Mortgage-Backed Security

In calculating total return of mortgage-backed securities, the total future dollar will depend on (1) the projected principal repayment (scheduled plus prepayments) and (2) the interest earned on reinvestment of the projected interest payments and the projected principal repayments. To obtain the total future dollars, a prepayment rate over the investment horizon must be assumed.

Exhibit 2: Illustration of Calculation of Total Return

Assumptions:

> Bond: 7% 6-year bond selling for $95.31 (yield to maturity is 8%)
> Reinvestment rate: 6%
> Investment horizon: 1 year
> Horizon yield: 7.2%

Calculation:

Step 1: Compute the total coupon payments plus reinvestment income assuming an annual reinvestment rate of 6%, or 3% every six months. The coupon payments are $3.5 per $100 of par value every six months for 1 year or 2 periods (the length of the investment horizon). The total coupon interest is $7. The reinvestment income is found by computing the interest on $3.5 reinvested for one 6-month period at 3%, or $0.105. The total coupon payments plus reinvestment income is $7.105 ($7 plus $0.105).

Step 2: The projected sale price at the end of 1 year (i.e., the horizon price) assuming that the required yield to maturity for 5-year bonds (i.e., horizon yield) is 7.2% is $99.17.

Step 3: Adding the amounts in Steps 1 and 2 gives the total future dollars of $106.275.

Step 4: Compute the following:

$$\left(\frac{\$106.275}{\$95.31}\right)^{1/2} - 1 = (1.11505)^{0.5} - 1$$

$$= 1.05596 - 1 = 0.05596 \text{ or } 5.596\%$$

Step 5: Doubling 5.596% gives a total return of 11.19% on a bond-equivalent basis. On an effective rate basis, the horizon return is:

$$(1.05596)^2 - 1 = 1.1151 - 1$$
$$= 0.1151 = 11.51\%$$

For a monthly-pay MBS, the monthly total return is then found using the following formula:

Monthly total return =

$$\left(\frac{\text{Total future dollars}}{\text{Full purchase price}}\right)^{1/\text{Number of months in horizon}} - 1$$

The monthly total return can be annualized on a bond-equivalent yield basis as follows:

Bond-equivalent annual return =

$$2[(1 + \text{Monthly total return})^6 - 1]$$

or, by computing the effective annual return as follows:

$$\text{Effective annual return} = (1 + \text{Monthly total return})^{12} - 1$$

To illustrate the calculation of total return for a mortgage-backed security, suppose a portfolio manager is considering investing in a passthrough with a 9% passthrough (coupon) rate, 360 months remaining to maturity, and an original mortgage balance of $100,000. The price of this passthrough is $94,521. The cash flow yield assuming 100% PSA is 10.21%. The portfolio manager has a 6-month investment horizon and believes the following:

(1) for the next six months the prepayment rate will be 100% PSA,
(2) the projected cash flow can be reinvested at 0.5% per month,
(3) the passthrough will sell to yield 7.62% at the end of the investment horizon, and[3]
(4) the projected PSA prepayment rate at the end of the investment horizon will be 185% PSA.

Based on the first assumption, the projected interest, scheduled principal, and prepayments (PIPP) for the first six months is:

End of month	Projected PIPP
1	$816
2	832
3	849
4	865
5	881
6	897

---

[3] In this illustration we will use the cash flow yield to determine the price at the horizon date.

The projected PIPP plus interest from reinvesting the cash flow at 0.5% per month is shown below:

End of month	Projected PIPP	Projected PIPP plus reinvestment income
1	$816	$837
2	832	849
3	849	862
4	865	874
5	881	885
6	897	897
Total	$5,204	

At the end of the investment horizon, this passthrough would have a remaining mortgage balance of $99,181 and remaining maturity of 355 months. Assuming an horizon yield of 7.62% and a prepayment rate of 185% PSA, the projected price of this passthrough would be $106,210.

The total future dollars is then:

projected PIPP plus reinvestment income	=	$5,204
projected price	=	106,210
total future dollars	=	$111,414

The total monthly return is:

$$\left(\frac{\$111,414}{\$94,521}\right)^{1/6} - 1 = 0.02778$$

On a bond-equivalent basis, the total return is:

$$2[(1.02778)^6 - 1] = 0.3574 = 35.74\%$$

On an effective rate basis, the total return is:

$$(1.02778)^{12} - 1 = 0.3893 = 38.93\%$$

Portfolio Total Return

A more appropriate measure for assessing the potential performance of a portfolio is its total return. This is determined by first calculating the total future dollars of each bond in the portfolio under a given scenario considering horizon yields, reinvestment rates, and spreads. The sum of all the total future dollars for each bond in the portfolio is then calculated. The portfolio total return is then found as explained earlier for a given bond: It is the interest rate that will make the market value of the portfolio today grow to the portfolio's total future dollars.

By using scenario analysis, a portfolio manager, an asset/liability committee, or a board can assess the potential performance of the portfolio. Corrective action can be taken to rebalance a portfolio if a scenario that is expected to occur will be detrimental to the performance of the credit union. The portfolio yield measures often calculated provide no such warning.

OAS-Total Return

In Chapter 8, the option-adjusted spread (OAS) was described. The OAS can be incorporated into a total return analysis to determine the horizon price. This requires a valuation model. At the end of the investment horizon, it is necessary to specify how the OAS is expected to change. The horizon price can be "backed out" of a valuation model. This technique can be extended to the total return framework by making assumptions about the required variables at the horizon date.

Assumptions about the OAS value at the investment horizon reflect the expectations of the portfolio manager. It is common to assume that the OAS at the horizon date will be the same as the OAS at the time of purchase. A total return calculated using this assumption is sometimes referred to as a *constant-OAS total return*. Alternatively, some portfolio managers will make bets on how the OAS will change — either widening or tightening. The total return framework can be used to assess how sensitive the performance of a fixed-income security with an embedded option is to changes in the OAS.

STRESS TESTING

Total return analysis is a more comprehensive measure of the interest rate risk of an individual investment and portfolio. The proposed revision to Part 703 requires that the total return analysis be applied at least monthly for certain individual investments and the entire portfolio to ensure that the risk remains within the policy guidelines established by the board. The total return analysis required by the proposed revision to Part 703 is referred to as a *stress test* or *interest rate shock test*.

It is important to understand that Part 703 uses the term total return in two ways. In terms of the stress test, total return is used in the same context that we have used it in this chapter. A more descriptive name might be *potential total return*. The second use is in the context of another reporting requirement. Part 703 requires that a credit union not only look at the potential interest rate risk, but that it report on how individual investments actually performed since the date of purchase and how individual investments and the portfolio performed over the last month. The use of total return in this context means the *actual* or *historical total return*. In our discussion below regarding the stress test, when we refer to total return we mean potential total return.

The proposed revision to Part 703 requires that if certain criteria are met by a federal credit union, the total return for the entire portfolio and each investment in the portfolio be calculated assuming a *parallel* and *immediate shift* in the yield curve of plus 300 basis points and minus 300 basis points. Excluded from the individual investments that are subject to the stress test are other major portions of the balance sheet, specifically loans and shares. The total return is to be calculated on a percentage basis and a dollar basis. Since the stress test is based on an immediate shift, there is no coupon income or reinvestment income. Thus, the total return is simply the change in market or fair value.

Whether a credit union is subject to the stress test requirement depends on the types of investments in its portfolio. Specifically, the credit union must begin by focusing on securities that the NCUA has determined has greater potential risk. The securities that fall into this category are securities that have any one of the following features: (1) securities that amortize, (2) securities that have embedded options, (3) securities that have a maturity greater than three years, and (4) securities that have a floating rate related to multiple reference indexes or float inversely with a reference rate. The aggregate value of all the securities with any of these features is then compared to the credit union's capital to determine whether stress testing is required. If the aggregate value is greater than capital, the credit union is required to stress test. Credit unions which keep all of their investments in fully insured certificates of deposit and in corporate credit union shares and deposits would not be required to report this information because such investments are not marketable securities. However, if a credit union has the bulk of its investments in a corporate credit union, the investing credit union is exposed to the risk that the NCUA board may provide notice that the corporate credit union is no longer operating in compliance with Part 704. It appears as though the NCUA would be conducting the stress testing of corporate credit unions on behalf of natural person credit unions.

Documentation regarding the stress test results must be prepared at least once a month. The report must to be distributed to each member of the asset/liability committee or investment committee with a summary furnished to the board of directors. In the absence of such a committee, a federal credit union must furnish the report to each member of the board of directors.

KEY POINTS

1. The proper measure for assessing the potential return of a portfolio strategy is the total return.

2. Calculation of the total return to an investment horizon that is less than the maturity date requires specification of the reinvestment rate and the horizon yield.

3. The horizon yield is needed to obtain the horizon price of the bond at the end of the investment horizon.

4. A semiannual return can be annualized on a bond-equivalent basis or on an effective rate basis, the selection depending on the manager's investment objective.

5. For a mortgage-backed security, total return requires an assumption about prepayment rates.

6. Option-adjusted spread analysis can be incorporated into a total return analysis by specifying the OAS at the end of the investment horizon.

7. When the OAS is not assumed to change from its initial value, the total return is said to be calculated on a constant OAS basis.

8. Scenario analysis involves calculating the total return under different assumptions regarding the reinvestment rate and horizon yield.

9. The proposed revision to Part 703 requires stress testing of individual investments and the entire portfolio if certain conditions are met.

10. Stress testing, also called interest rate shock testing, is used to ensure that interest rate risk remains within the policy guidelines established by the board.

11. Stress testing involves assessing the total return (on a percentage and dollar basis) for the entire portfolio and each investment in the portfolio if there is a parallel and immediate shift in the yield curve of plus 300 basis points and minus 300 basis points.

12. Stress testing is required if the aggregate value of securities classified as having greater potential risk exceeds the credit union's capital.

Chapter 12

Overview of Investment Strategies

The objectives of this chapter are to:

1. explain the distinction between active and passive investment strategies;

2. discuss two passive investment strategies — buy-and-hold and indexing;

3. explain what an interest rate expectations strategy is;

4. describe several yield curve strategies; and,

5. demonstrate why it is necessary to use the dollar duration when implementing a yield spread strategy.

Up to this point, we have described the various fixed-income securities in which a credit union may invest, examined how fixed-income securities should be valued, and explained how to measure interest-rate risk. In this chapter, we turn our attention to various portfolio strategies.

ACTIVE VERSUS PASSIVE PORTFOLIO STRATEGIES

Bond portfolio strategies can be classified as either *active portfolio strategies* or *passive strategies*. Essential to all active strategies is specification of expectations about the factors that influence the performance of bonds — changes in the level of interest rates, shifts in the yield curve, changes in spreads between bond sectors, for example. Passive portfolio strategies involve no expectational input. The strategy selected by the board of a credit union should be consistent with the objectives and policy guidelines of the credit union and its risk tolerance.

PASSIVE PORTFOLIO STRATEGIES

There are two types of passive portfolio strategies: buy-and-hold and indexing.

Buy-and-Hold Strategy

As the name indicates, in a *buy-and-hold strategy* the portfolio manager simply buys bonds and holds them to the maturity or call date. To determine the potential outcome of a buy-and-hold strategy, it is necessary to assess the total return over the time the bond is held.

A common misconception about the buy and hold strategy is that a total return need not be calculated. This is incorrect. Total return is a *tool* that should be used to assess the potential outcome of a position or strategy. It is *not* a strategy. The mistake made is that bonds are purchased on the basis of yield and held to maturity — i.e., a buy-and-hold strategy. However — and we emphasize this again — *the yield does not tell us what the return will be even if the bond is held to the maturity or assumed call date.*

Indexing

An *indexing strategy* involves designing a portfolio so that its performance will match the performance of some bond index. In indexing, performance is measured in terms of total return achieved over some investment horizon. One reason for the popularity of indexing as a bond portfolio strategy is that empirical evidence suggests that historically, the overall performance of active bond managers has been poor.

The problem with a credit union pursuing this strategy is that while indexing matches the performance of some bond index, the performance of that index does not mean that the credit union will accomplish its return objective. The bond index's return is not necessarily related to the credit union's return objective.

ACTIVE PORTFOLIO STRATEGIES

There are variety of active portfolio strategies. Below we discuss each. The potential outcome and associated risks of a strategy should be assessed using the total return framework.

Interest Rate Expectations Strategies

A portfolio manager who believes that he or she can accurately forecast the future level of interest rates will alter the portfolio's sensitivity to interest rate changes. As duration is a measure of price sensitivity to interest rate changes, this involves increasing a portfolio's duration if interest rates are expected to fall; and reducing duration if interest rates are expected to rise. The degree to which the duration is permitted to deviate from the duration adopted by the credit union will depend on the credit union's risk tolerance.

A portfolio's duration may be altered by swapping (or exchanging) bonds in the portfolio for new bonds that will achieve the target portfolio duration. Such swaps are commonly referred to as *rate anticipation swaps*. The key to this active strategy is, of course, an ability to forecast the direction of future interest rates. The academic literature, however, does not support the view that interest rates can be forecasted so that risk-adjusted excess returns can be consistently realized. It is doubtful whether betting on future interest rates will provide a consistently superior return. A manager of a credit union portfolio who can predict the movement of interest rates consistently is foolish to work for any credit union. Indeed, that manager would be making a mistake to work for any financial institution. Given the instruments in the marketplace available for leveraging, a person with the gift of perfectly predicting interest rate movements could in a short period become the wealthiest individual in the world.

What too often occurs is that a manager makes a few right calls on the direction of interest rates and the credit union is rewarded handsomely. Board's then view this manager as an interest rate guru and do not question when the manager makes riskier interest rate bets. Eventually, the bet goes wrong and the credit union's economic well being is substantially impaired.

There are other active strategies that rely on forecasts of future interest rate levels. Future interest rates, for instance, affect the value of options embedded in callable bonds and the value of prepayment options embedded in mortgage-backed securities. Callable bonds with coupon rates above the expected future interest rate will underperform relative to noncallable bonds or low-coupon bonds. This is because of the negative convexity feature of callable bonds described in Chapter 10. For the wide range of mortgage-backed securities, the effect of interest rates on prepayments cause some to benefit from higher future interest rates and others to benefit from lower future interest rates. For certain structured notes, there are interest rate bets embedded in the instrument.

Yield Curve Strategies

The yield curve for U.S. Treasury securities shows the relationship between their maturities and yields. The shape of the yield curve changes over time. *Yield curve strategies* involve positioning a portfolio to capitalize on expected changes in the shape of the Treasury yield curve. Here we will describe the different ways in which the Treasury yield curve has shifted and the different types of yield curve strategies. In our discussion of the limitations of duration in Chapter 10, we demonstrated how the total return framework can be used to assess the potential outcome of yield curve strategies.

Types of Shifts in the Yield Curve and Impact on Historical Returns A shift in the yield curve refers to the relative change in the yield for each Treasury maturity. A *parallel shift in the yield curve* refers to a shift in which the change in the yield on all maturities is the same. A *nonparallel shift in the yield curve* means that the yield for all maturities does not change by the same number of basis points.

Historically, two types of nonparallel yield curve shifts have been observed: a twist in the slope of the yield curve and a change in the humpedness of the yield curve. All of these shifts are graphically portrayed in Exhibit 1. A twist in the slope of the yield curve refers to a flattening or steepening of the yield curve. In practice, the slope of the yield curve is measured by the spread between some long-term Treasury yield and some short-term Treasury yield. For example, most practitioners refer to the slope as the difference between the 30-year Treasury yield and the 2-year Treasury yield. Others refer to it as the spread between the 30-year Treasury yield and the 3-month bill rate. Regardless of how it is defined, a *flattening of the yield curve* means that the yield spread between the yield on a long-term and short-term Treasury has decreased; a *steepening of the yield curve* means that the yield spread between a long-term and short-term Treasury has increased. The other type of nonparallel shift, a change in the humpedness of the yield curve, is referred to as a *butterfly shift*.

Frank Jones analyzed the types of yield curve shifts that occurred between 1979 and 1990.[1] He found that the three types of yield curve shifts are not independent, with the two most common types of yield curve shifts being (1) a downward shift in the yield curve combined with a steepening of the yield curve and (2) an upward shift in the yield curve combined with a flattening of the yield curve. These two types of shifts in the yield curve are depicted in Exhibit 2. For example, his statistical analysis indicated that an upward parallel shift in the Treasury yield curve and a flattening of the yield curve have a correlation of 0.41. This suggests that an upward shift of the yield curve by 10 basis points is consistent with a 2.5 basis point flattening of the yield curve. Moreover, he finds that an upward shift and flattening of the yield curve is correlated with a positive butterfly (less humpedness), while a downward shift and steepening of the yield curve is correlated with a negative butterfly (more humpedness).

---

[1] Frank J. Jones, "Yield Curve Strategies," *Journal of Fixed Income* (September 1991), pp. 43-51.

Exhibit 1: Types of Yield Curve Shifts

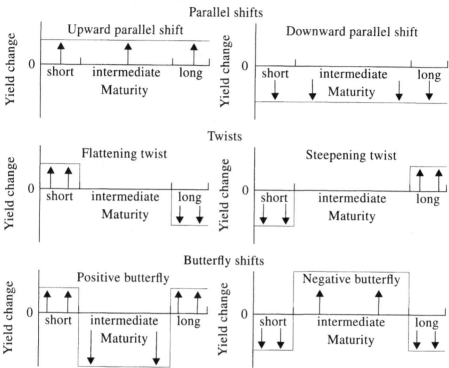

Jones also provides empirical evidence of the importance of changes in the yield curve in determining returns of Treasury securities for various maturity sectors from 1979 to 1990. He finds that parallel shifts and twists in the yield curve are responsible for 91.6% of Treasury returns, while 3.4% of the return is attributable to butterfly shifts and the balance, 5%, to unexplained factor shifts.[2]

The implication is that yield curve strategies require a forecast of the direction of the shift and a forecast of the type of twist.

Strategies In portfolio strategies that seek to capitalize on expectations based on short-term movements in yields, the dominant source of return is the impact on the price of the bonds in the portfolio. This means that the maturity of the bonds in the portfolio will have an important impact on the portfolio's return. For example, a total return over a 1-year investment horizon for a portfolio consisting of bonds all maturing in one year will not be sensitive to changes in how the yield curve shifts one year from now. In contrast, the total return over a 1-year invest-

---

[2] These findings are consistent with those reported in the previous chapter by Robert Litterman and Jose Scheinkman, "Common Factors Affecting Bond Returns," *Journal of Fixed Income* (June 1991), pp. 54-61.

ment horizon for a portfolio consisting of bonds all maturing in 10 years will be sensitive to how the yield curve shifts, because one year from now the value of the portfolio will depend on the yield offered on 9-year bonds.

A portfolio consisting of equal proportions of bonds maturing in one year and bonds maturing in 10 years will have quite a different total return over a 1-year investment horizon than the two portfolios we previously described when the yield curve shifts. The price of the 1-year bonds in the portfolio will not be sensitive to how the 1-year yield has changed but the price of the 10-year bonds will be highly sensitive to how long-term yields have changed.

The key point is that for short-term investment horizons, the spacing of the maturity of bonds in the portfolio will have a significant impact on the total return. Consequently, yield curve strategies involve positioning a portfolio with respect to the maturities of the bonds across the maturity spectrum included in the portfolio. There are three yield curve strategies: (1) bullet strategies, (2) barbell strategies, and (3) ladder strategies. Each of these strategies is depicted in Exhibit 3.

Exhibit 2: Combinations of Yield Curve Shifts
Upward Shift/Flattening/Positive Butterfly

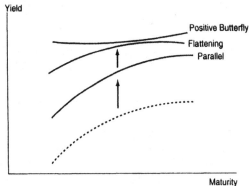

Downward Shift/Steepening/Negative Butterfly

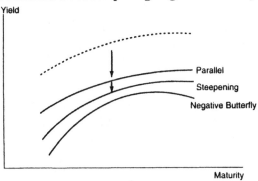

Exhibit 3: Yield Curve Strategies: Bullet, Barbell, and Ladder

Bullet Strategy
Spikes indicate maturing principal
Comment: Bullet concentrated around year 4

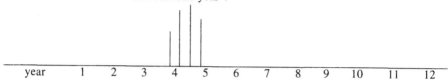

Barbell Strategy
Spikes indicate maturing principal
Comment: Barbell below and above 4 years

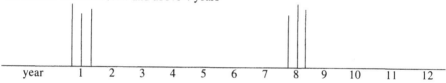

Ladder Strategy
Spikes indicate maturing principal
Comment: Laddered up to year 8

In a *bullet strategy*, the portfolio is constructed so that the maturity of the bonds in the portfolio are highly concentrated at one point on the yield curve. In a *barbell strategy*, the maturity of the bonds included in the portfolio are concentrated at two extreme maturities. Actually, in practice when portfolio managers refer to a barbell strategy, it is relative to a bullet strategy. For example, a bullet strategy might be to create a portfolio with maturities concentrated around 4 years while a corresponding barbell strategy might be a portfolio with 1-year and 8-year maturities. In a *ladder strategy* the portfolio is constructed to have approximately equal amounts of each maturity. So, for example, a portfolio might have equal amounts of bonds with 1-year to maturity, 2-years to maturity, etc.

Each of these strategies will result in different performance when the yield curve shifts. The actual performance will depend on both the type of shift and the magnitude of the shift. Thus, no general statements can be made about the optimal yield curve strategy. This was demonstrated in Chapter 10.

Yield Spread Strategies

The bond market is classified into sectors in several ways: by type of issuer (Treasury, agencies, corporates, and mortgage-backeds), quality or credit (risk-free Treasuries, triple-A, double-A, etc.), coupon (high-coupon/premium bonds, current-coupon/par bonds, and low-coupon/discount bonds), and maturity (short-, intermediate-, and long-term). Yield spreads between maturity sectors involve changes in the yield curve as we have discussed in the previous section.

Yield spread strategies involve positioning a portfolio to capitalize on expected changes in yield spreads between sectors of the bond market in which the credit union is permitted to invest. Swapping (or exchanging) one bond for another when the portfolio manager believes that the prevailing yield spread between the two bonds in the market is out of line with their historical yield spread, and that the yield spread will realign by the end of the investment horizon, are called *intermarket spread swaps*.

The Importance of Dollar Duration Weighting of Yield Spread Strategies

What is critical in assessing yield spread strategies is to compare positions that have the same dollar duration. To understand why, consider two bonds, X and Y. Suppose that the price of bond X is 80 and has a duration of 5 while bond Y has a price of 90 and has a duration of 4. Since duration is the approximate percentage change per 100 basis point change in yield, a 100 basis points change in yield for bond X would change its price by about 5%. Based on a price of 80, its price will change by about $4 per $80 of market value. Thus, its dollar duration for a 100 basis point change in yield is $4 per $80 of market value. Similarly, for bond Y, its dollar duration for a 100 basis point change in yield per $90 of market value can be determined. In this case it is $3.6. So, if bonds X and Y are being considered as alternative investments in some strategy other than one based on anticipating interest rate movements, the amount of each bond in the strategy should be such that they will both have the same dollar duration.

To illustrate this, suppose that a portfolio manager owns $10 million of par value of bond X which has a market value of $8 million. The dollar duration of bond X per 100 basis point change in yield for the $8 million market value is $400,000. Suppose further that this portfolio manager is considering exchanging bond X that it owns in its portfolio for bond Y. If the portfolio manager wants to have the same interest rate exposure (i.e., dollar duration) for bond Y that she currently has for bond X, she will buy a market value amount of bond Y with the same dollar duration. If the portfolio manager purchased $10 million of *par value* of bond Y and therefore $9 million of *market value* of bond Y, the dollar price change per 100 basis change in yield would be only $360,000. If, instead, the portfolio manager purchased $10 million of *market value* of bond Y, the dollar duration per 100 basis point change in yield would be $400,000. Since bond Y is trading at 90, $11.11 million of par value of bond Y must be purchased to keep the dollar duration of the position from bond Y the same as for bond X.

Mathematically, this problem can be expressed as follows:
Let:

$\$D_X$ = dollar duration per 100 basis point change in yield for bond X for the market value of bond X held

MD_Y = duration for bond Y

MV_Y = market value of bond Y needed to obtain the same dollar duration as bond X

Then, the following equation sets the dollar duration for bond X equal to the dollar duration for bond Y:

$$\$D_X = (MD_Y/100)MV_Y$$

Solving for MV_Y,

$$MV_Y = \$D_X/(MD_Y/100)$$

Dividing by the price per $1 of par value of bond Y gives the par value of Y that has an approximately equivalent dollar duration as bond X.

In our illustration, $\$D_X$ is $400,000 and MD_Y is 4, then

$$MV_Y = \$400,000/(4/100) = \$10,000,000$$

Since the market value of bond Y is 90 per $100 of par value, the price per $1 of par value is 0.9. Dividing $10 million by 0.9 indicates that the par value of bond Y that should be purchased is $11.11 million.

Failure to adjust a portfolio repositioning based on some expected change in yield spread so as to hold the dollar duration the same means that the outcome of the portfolio will be affected by not only the expected change in the yield spread, but also a change in the yield level. Thus, a manager would be making a conscious yield spread bet and possibly an undesired bet on the level of interest rates.

Credit Spreads Credit or quality spreads change because of expected changes in economic prospects. Credit spreads between Treasury and non-Treasury issues widen in a declining or contracting economy and narrow during economic expansion. The economic rationale is that in a declining or contracting economy, corporations experience a decline in revenue and reduced cash flow, making it difficult for corporate issuers to service their contractual debt obligations. To induce investors to hold non-Treasury securities of lower quality issuers, the yield spread relative to Treasury securities must widen. The converse is that during economic expansion and brisk economic activity, revenue and cash flow pick up, increasing the likelihood that corporate issuers will have the capacity to service their contractual debt obligations. Yield spreads between Treasury and federal agency securities will vary depending on investor expectations about the prospects that an implicit government guarantee will be honored.

Spreads Between Callable and Noncallable Securities Spreads attributable to differences in callable and noncallable bonds and differences in coupons of callable bonds will change as a result of expected changes in (1) the direction of the change in interest rates and (2) interest rate volatility. An expected drop in the level of interest rates will widen the yield spread between callable bonds and noncallable bonds as the prospects that the issuer will exercise the call option increase. The reverse is also true: the yield spread narrows if interest rates are expected to rise. An increase in interest rate volatility increases the value of the embedded call option, and thereby increases the yield spread between callable bonds and noncallable bonds. Expectations about the direction of the change in interest rates and interest rate volatility will affect the yield spread between Treasury and mortgage passthrough securities and the yield spread between low-coupon and high-coupon passthroughs.

OAS Strategies As explained in Chapter 8, the practice today is to measure the yield spread on bonds with embedded options in terms of their option-adjusted spread (OAS). A portfolio manager can position a portfolio to take advantage of expectations as to how the OAS will change over an investment horizon. As has been emphasized, however, nominal yield spreads are not a measure of relative value or potential return performance. The same is true for the OAS. A strategy that is too often suggested is that a portfolio manager should seek to maximize OAS. However, there is no reason to suspect a priori that a relative ranking of securities on the basis of OAS will correlate with actual total return rankings.

KEY POINTS

1. A buy-and-hold strategy is a passive strategy whose potential performance should be assessed using the total return framework.

2. A bond indexing strategy involves structuring a portfolio so that its total return will match that of some bond index.

3. Since an indexing strategy matches the performance of some bond index, it does not necessarily mean the credit union's return requirements will be satisfied.

4. An interest rate expectations strategy involves positioning the duration of a portfolio based on the whether rates are expected to increase or decrease.

5. It is extremely difficult to forecast the direction of interest rates consistently.

6. Yield curve strategies involve positioning a portfolio to capitalize on expected changes in the shape of the Treasury yield curve.

7. Historically, two types of nonparallel yield curve shifts have been observed: a twist in the slope of the yield curve and a change in the humpedness of the yield curve.

8. There are three yield curve strategies: a bullet strategy, a barbell strategy, and a ladder strategy.

9. Yield spread strategies involve positioning a portfolio to capitalize on expected changes in yield spreads between sectors of the bond market.

10. In repositioning a portfolio to capitalize on expected changes in yield spread, it is important to keep the dollar duration of the portfolio constant.

11. Spreads attributable to differences in callable and noncallable bonds and differences in coupons of callable bonds will change as a result of expected changes in the direction of interest rates and interest rate volatility.

12. OAS-based strategies seek to capitalize on anticipated changes in OAS over the investment horizon.

Appendix:

Time Value of Money

The notion that money has a time value is one of the most basic concepts in investment analysis. Money has a time value because of the opportunities for investing funds at some interest rate. In this appendix we review the two fundamental concepts involved in understanding the time value of money: future value and present value. Financial calculators have a feature that permits the calculation of these values.

FUTURE VALUE

Suppose a credit union invested $50,000 in a certificate of deposit (CD) that pays interest of 5% a year. At the end of one year, the CD will have a value of $52,500, consisting of $50,000 of the original principal and $2,500 of interest. Suppose that the credit union decides to reinvest the $52,500 for another year, and that the issuing bank continues paying 5% a year. The value of the CD at the end of the second year will be $55,125, determined as follows:

Principal at beginning of year 2	$52,500
Interest for year 2 ($52,500 × 0.05)	2,625
Value of CD	$55,125

The interest of $2,625 in year 2 is equal to the sum of (1) 5% interest on the original investment of $50,000 or $2,500 and (2) interest earned on the $2,500 interest earned in the first year or $125.

In general, to find the future value (FV) of an investment of P dollars for N years earning an interest rate of i (in decimal form) each year, the following formula is used:

$$FV = P(1 + i)^N$$

For example, if (1) FV is $50,000, (2) i is 0.05, and (3) N is 2, as in our previous illustration, then the future value is:

$$FV = \$50,000 \,(1.05)^2$$
$$= \$50,000 \,(1.1025) = \$55,125$$

This agrees with our earlier calculation for the future value of a 2-year CD paying interest annually at 5%.

In our illustration, we have computed the future value for whole years. The future value formula given above can be used for fractional years. For example, suppose that $50,000 is invested in a term CD with a maturity of 30 months and an annual interest rate of 5%. Since 30 months is 2.5 years, N is equal to 2.5 and the future value is then:

$$FV = \$50,000 \, (1.05)^{2.5}$$
$$= \$50,000 \, (1.129726) = \$56,486.32$$

An investment may pay interest more than one time per year. For example, interest may be semiannually, quarterly, monthly, weekly, or daily. The future value formula handles interest payments that are made more than once per year by adjusting the annual interest rate and the exponent. The annual interest rate is adjusted by dividing by the number of times that interest is paid per year. The exponent, which represents the number of years, is adjusted by multiplying the number of years by the number of times that interest is paid per year.

For example, suppose that in our illustration of the 2-year term CD that interest is paid semiannually, rather than annually. Then, the interest rate is found by dividing 5% by 2 to get 2.5%. The number of years is adjusted to 4 (2 years times 2 payments per year). The future value is then:

$$FV = \$50,000 \, (1.025)^{4}$$
$$= \$50,000 \, (1.1038125) = \$55,190.64$$

Notice that if interest is only paid once per year, the future value of the 2-year CD would be $55,125 instead of $55,190.64. The higher future value when interest is paid semiannually reflects the more frequent opportunity for reinvesting interest earned.

In general, if different interest rates are paid or expected to be paid over time, the future value can be found as follows:

$$FV = P \, (1 + i_1) \, (1 + i_2) \, (1 + i_3) \, ... \, (1 + i_N)$$

where the interest rate i for each year or period is denoted by a subscript. For example, assuming annual interest payments for a $50,000 investment in a 1-year CD today and rolled over annually for the next two years, the future value will depend on the 1-year CD rate each time the funds are rolled over. Assuming that the 1-year CD rate today is 5% and that it is expected that the 1-year CD rate one year from now will be 6% and the 1-year CD rate two years from now will be 6.5%, then the future value is:

$$FV = \$50,000 \, (1.05) \, (1.06) \, (1.065) = \$59,267.25$$

There are two applications of the future value concept. First, the future value is used to determine the amount of a future liability. Second, the future value is used to determine the amount by which an investment today will grow to. As stressed in Chapter 9, there are limitations when using yield measures. Instead, a credit union manager should recast investment outcomes in terms of future dollars.

PRESENT VALUE

Now that we understand future value, let's work the process in reverse. That is, given the future value of an investment, we want to determine the amount of money that must be invested today in order to realize that future value. The amount of money that must be invested today is called the *present value* (also called the *discounted value*). As explained in Chapter 9, in order to calculate the yield on an investment, present value calculations are required. Moreover, as explained in Chapter 10, to determine the value of an investment, it is necessary to determine the present value of the expected cash flows.

The present value (denoted by PV) of some future value (denoted by FV) to be received N years from now if an interest rate i can be earned on any sum invested is:

$$PV = \frac{FV}{(1+i)N}$$

The interest rate (i) used to obtain the present value is called the *discount rate*.

To illustrate the present value formula, suppose that $100,000 is to be received three years from now. The present value assuming an interest rate or discount rate of 6% can be earned on any amount invested today, is:

PV = $100,000
N = 3
i = 0.06

$$PV = \frac{\$100,000}{(1.06)^3} = \frac{\$100,000}{1.191016} = \$83,961.93$$

This means that if $83,961.93 is invested today at 6% interest for three years, the future value will be $100,000.

There are two important properties of the present value. First, the higher the discount rate used, the lower the present value is. In our previous illustration, if the discount rate used is 8% rather than 6%, then the future value would be $79,383.22 rather than $83,961.93. The lower the discount rate used, the higher the present value is. Thus, the present value changes in the opposite direction to the change in the discount rate. Since the value of an investment is equal to the present value of its cash flows, this explains why the price of a bond changes in the opposite direction to the change in the market interest rate.

The second property is that for a given discount rate, the further into the future a future value will be received, the lower its present value. For example, suppose that the future value of $100,000 is to be received five years from now rather than three years from now. Assuming a discount rate of 6%, then the present value is $74,725.82.

When analyzing an investment, the future values are simply the projected cash flows of the investment. The present value of a series of future values is simply the sum of the present value of each future value. For example, suppose that an investment with the following projected cash flows is purchased:

Year	Cash Flow (Future Value)
1	$20,000
2	25,000
3	30,000

Suppose further that the discount rate at which each cash flow should be discounted is 6.25%. The present value for each cash flow is found as follows:

Year 1:

$$PV = \frac{\$20,000}{(1.0625)^1} = \$18,823.53$$

Year 2:

$$PV = \frac{\$25,000}{(1.0625)^2} = \$22,145.33$$

Year 3:

$$PV = \frac{\$30,000}{(1.0625)^3} = \$25,011.19$$

The present value is then the sum of $18,823.53, $22,145.33, and $25,011.19. The sum is $65,980,05. This present value means that if $65,980.05 is invested today at 6.25% interest, $20,000 can be withdrawn one year from now, $25,000 can be withdrawn two years from now, and $30,000 can be withdrawn three years from now. At the end of three years, there will be no funds available after the last withdrawal. Equivalently, the present value of $65,980.05 when invested at 6.25% will provide the same cash flows as the investment.

In our illustration, we used the same discount rate to calculate the present value of each cash flow. As explained in Chapter 10, there are theoretical reasons for using a different discount rate for each cash flow. For example, suppose that the corresponding discount rate for each cash flow is as shown below:

Year	Cash Flow (Future Value)	Discount Rate
1	$20,000	6.25%
2	25,000	7.15%
3	30,000	7.48%

The present value for the $20,000 cash flow would be the same as above, $18,823.53, since a discount rate of 6.25% is used. For years 2 and 3, the present value of the cash flow is calculated below:

Year 2:

$$PV = \frac{\$25,000}{(1.0715)^2} = \$21,774.87$$

Year 3:

$$PV = \frac{\$30,000}{(1.0748)^3} = \$24,162.30$$

The present of the cash flow is then $64,760.70 ($18,823.53 + $21,774.87 + $24,162.30).

Index

PaineWebber
Credit Union Services Group
The Annual Investment School for Credit Unions

*We believe that education will better
prepare you to make investment decisions
that can positively impact your
credit union's investment portfolio.*

*We also believe that working with our Group
on the management of your portfolio
can result in a strategic alliance
that benefits the financial performance
of your credit union.*

PaineWebber Credit Union Services Group has only one business–credit unions. Created in 1986, our group has been committed to excellent service to credit unions providing professional leadership in the fields of Investment Services and Asset-Liability Management.

One key reason for our longevity is education. We believe in providing you, the credit union, with the knowledge and tools to help you make better investment decisions. That's why we created **The Annual Investment School for Credit Unions**, ongoing educational forums covering topics such as:

- Investment products
- Asset and liability strategies–credit union specific
- Legal and regulatory concerns
- New N.C.U.A. rulings
- Technologically advanced tools, software packages

**For more information on
our Credit Unions Services Group, or
our Investment School for Credit Unions,
call Regina Wickard at (800) 782-2306.**

PaineWebber
Invest With More Intelligence.™

1500 Abbott Road, Suite 200, East Lansing, MI 48823

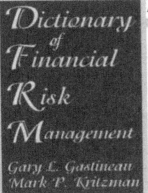

BOOK ORDER FORM

Name: _____

Company: _____

Address: _____

City: _____ State: _____ Zip: _____

Phone: _____ FAX: _____

Books Published by Frank J. Fabozzi Associates:

Book	Price:	Quantity:	Sub-Total:
Bond Portfolio Management, Fabozzi, 1996	$65		
Valuation of Fixed Income Securities and Derivatives (2nd Ed.) Fabozzi, 1995	$50		
Measuring and Controlling Interest Rate Risk, Fabozzi, 1996	$55		
Corporate Bonds: Structures & Analysis Wilson and Fabozzi, 1996	$65		
Collateralized Mortgage Obligations: Structures & Analysis (2nd Ed) Fabozzi, Ramsey, and Ramirez, 1994	$50		
Asset-Backed Securities, Bhattacharya and Fabozzi (Eds.), 1996	$75		
The Handbook of Commercial Mortgage-Backed Securities Fabozzi and Jacob (Eds), 1996	$95		
Valuation of Interest-Sensitive Financial Instruments Babbel and Merrill, 1996	$55		
Dictionary of Financial Risk Management Gastineau and Kritzman, 1996	$45		
CMO Portfolio Management, Fabozzi (Ed.), 1994	$50		
Modeling the Market: New Theories & Techniques Focardi and Jonas, 1996	$55		
Fixed Income Securities, Fabozzi, 1997	$58		
Advances In Fixed Income Valuation Modeling & Risk Management Fabozzi (Ed.), 1997	$85		
Securities Lending and Repurchase Agreements Fabozzi (Ed.), 1997	$85		
The Handbook of Equity Style Management: Second Edition Coggin, Fabozzi and Arnott (Eds.), 1997	$63		
Basics of Mortgage-Backed Securities, Hu, 1997	$39		

SHIPPING: ($4.00 for first book, $1.00 each additional)*

*International or bulk orders please call for shipping estimate (215) 598-8930

TOTAL: [   ]

Make check payable to Frank J. Fabozzi. *Sorry, no credit card sales.*

To order, mail order form along with check to:

Frank J. Fabozzi, 858 Tower View Circle New Hope, PA 18938

FORTHCOMING BOOKS:

FOUNDATIONS OF ECONOMIC VALUE-ADDED
James Grant
TREASURY SECURITIES AND DERIVATIVES
Fabozzi
PENSION FUND INVESTMENT MANAGEMENT: SECOND EDITION
Fabozzi (Ed.)
MANAGING FIXED INCOME PORTFOLIOS
Fabozzi (Ed.)
THE HANDBOOK OF NONAGENCY MORTGAGE-BACKED SECURITIES
Fabozzi, Ramsey, Ramirez, and Marz (Eds.)

FOR INFORMATION ABOUT THESE BOOKS, CONTACT FRANK J. FABOZZI.

FOR INFORMATION ABOUT FIXED INCOME SECURITIES AND PORTFOLIO MANAGEMENT TUTORIALS, CONTACT FRANK J. FABOZZI.